The Keynesian Tradition

The Keynesian Tradition

Edited by
Robert Leeson

First published 2008 by
PALGRAVE MACMILLAN
Houndmills, Basingstoke, Hampshire RG21 6XS and
175 Fifth Avenue, New York, N.Y. 10010
Companies and representatives throughout the world

PALGRAVE MACMILLAN is the global academic imprint of the Palgrave
Macmillan division of St. Martin's Press, LLC and of Palgrave Macmillan Ltd.
Macmillan® is a registered trademark in the United States, United Kingdom
and other countries. Palgrave is a registered trademark in the European
Union and other countries.

ISBN-13: 978-1-4039-4960-8   hardback
ISBN-10: 1-4039-4960-3   hardback

This book is printed on paper suitable for recycling and made from fully
managed and sustained forest sources. Logging, pulping and manufacturing
processes are expected to conform to the environmental regulations of the
country of origin.

A catalogue record for this book is available from the British Library.

A catalogue record for this book is available from the Library of Congress.

10   9   8   7   6   5   4   3   2   1
17   16   15   14   13   12   11   10   09   08

Printed and bound in Great Britain by CPI Antony Rowe Chippenham and
Eastbourne

Contents

List of Figures and Tables

Figures

Tables

List of Contributors

Daniele Besomi is an independent researcher in Switzerland.

J.E. King is Professor of Economics in the Department of Economics and Finance at La Trobe University, Australia.

Maria Cristina Marcuzzo is Professor of Economics in the Dipartimento di Scienze Economiche at the Università di Roma La Sapienza, Italy.

Nerio Naldi is Associate Professor of Economics in the Dipartimento di Scienze Economiche at the Università di Roma La Sapienza, Italy.

Annalisa Rosselli is Professor of Economics in the Dipartimento di Economia e Istituzioni at the Università di Roma Tor Vergata, Italy.

Goulven Rubin is Lecturer in Economics at LED-PHARE, Département d'économie et de gestion, Université de Paris 8 Saint-Denis, France.

Eleonora Sanfilippo is Research Fellow in the History of Economic Thought in the Dipartimento di Scienze Economiche at the Università di Roma La Sapienza, Italy.

Warren Young is Associate Professor of Economics in the Department of Economics at Bar Ilan University, Israel.

1
Introduction

Robert Leeson

These chapters highlight an important but neglected point: economics often provides profound insights into social interaction, but economists rarely delve into the subterranean world in which their culture, tools and prejudices are forged. Market forces produce results that surprise and confound social moralists; the hands by which economists correspond and argue have, hitherto, remained largely invisible. These chapters use published and archival evidence to illuminate the internal dynamics of the knowledge production (and destruction) processes of the economics industry.

The development of modern macroeconomics has been a fractured and fractious affair. It began in the early 1930s with a deliberately constructed cleavage between John Maynard Keynes (plus his radical disciples, Joan Robinson and Richard Kahn) and those denigrated by Keynes as 'Classical' economists. Later, a further cleavage developed between the radical Post-Keynesians and the more conservative advocates of the Keynesian Neoclassical Synthesis. As these two groups (the Left Keynesians, centered in Cambridge, England, the Right Keynesians, centered in Cambridge, Massachusetts) struggled over Keynes' mantle and over theories of capital, growth and distribution, free market economists at the University of Chicago pushed economics in an anti-Keynesian direction.

In the decade before the launch of the Keynesian revolution, Keynes was transformed from an orthodox to a quasi-radical economist. The trajectory of this transformation was influenced, in part, by those around him and in particular by those who sought to nudge him along this path. Keynes had become internationally famous as a polemicist following the publication of *The Economic Consequences of the Peace* (1919); his revulsion against the 'orthodox' reaction to some of the dislocations of the inter-war

1

period laid the basis for further polemical fame (*The Economic Consequences of Mr. Churchill*, 1926).

Elsewhere in Europe (most notably Italy), the dislocations of the time had more profound implications for social and economic stability. Two contemporary Italian economists exerted a profound influence over the direction of economics. Vilfredo Pareto was a leader of the second generation of the neoclassical revolution; his approach to general equilibrium theory exerted a wide influence from the 1930s onwards. Two (Right) popularizers of the Keynesian revolution, John Hicks and Paul Samuelson, embraced this neo-Walrasian paradigm.

In 1927, Keynes invited another Italian economist, Piero Sraffa, to visit Cambridge. Sraffa's *Production of Commodities by Means of Commodities* (1960) later demonstrated – to the satisfaction of many Left Keynesians – fatal flaws in the mainstream neoclassical theory of value. Sraffa's resurrection of Ricardo's theory of value sought to provide economics with an alternative foundation to that provided by neoclassical economists, thus contributing to another Keynesian civil war: the Cambridge capital controversy. Nerio Naldi (Chapter 2) explores the origins of Sraffa's neo-Ricardian reconstruction of economics.

As the Keynesian revolution advanced, so some of the relationships within the Cambridge Faculty of Economics soured. Eleonora Sanfilippo (Chapter 3) documents the process by which one of these relationships – between Keynes and Dennis Robertson – continued (and was, in a sense, repaired) as both struggled at the British Treasury with war-time issues.

Keynes' first biographer, Roy Harrod, lent his name to one of the foundation stones of modern growth theory: the Harrod-Domar growth model. Daniele Besomi (Chapter 4) argues that Harrod believed that his analysis was more concerned with the business cycle than with growth. Besomi then describes the process by which Harrod distanced himself from his interpreters, especially Joan Robinson who 'hasn't the faintest idea what my growth theory is about' (Harrod to Sidney Weintraub).

The Chicago-trained Don Patinkin codified the Keynesian Neoclassical Synthesis and interpreted Keynesian economics, not as the economics of unemployment equilibrium, but as a disequilibrium phenomenon. Goulven Rubin (Chapter 5) explores the evolution of these ideas, from Patinkin's PhD (1947), through his *Money, Interest and Prices* (1956) to Robert Clower's 'The Keynesian Counter-Revolution: A Theoretical Appraisal' (1965).

Keynes was initially interpreted and popularized by a first generation (including Nobel laureates John Hicks, Paul Samuelson, Franco Modigliani and Lawrence Klein) and then in the 1960s re-interpreted by a second generation (in particular, Clower and Axel Leijunhuvud). Warren Young (Chapter 6) investigates the (often unacknowledged) connections between these intergenerational interpreters.

In the 1960s, the Post-Keynesians began to refer, in print, to the propagators of the Keynesian Neoclassical Synthesis and their IS-LM model as a 'bastard' progeny. John Kenneth Galbraith and Sidney Weintraub were prominent North American Post-Keynesians: John King (Chapter 7) uses the Weintraub archives to examine the interpersonal dynamics of this collective – but far from harmonious – assault on orthodoxy.

Among British Keynesians, John Robinson, Richard Kahn and Nicholas Kaldor were the dominant figures. Maria Cristina Marcuzzo and Annalisa Rosselli (Chapter 8) use the archives to shed light on the 'tensions and powerful interpersonal dynamics, love, esteem, hatred and jealousy' which attended the deliberations of those who claimed to be Keynes' true heirs.

Marcuzzo and Rosselli also cite a letter from Piero Sraffa to Charles P. Blitch: 'In economic theory, the conclusions are sometimes less interesting than the route by which they are reached'. These chapters provide many illustrations of that theme.

References

Keynes, J.M. (1919) *The Economic Consequences of the Peace,* London: Macmillan and Co., Limited.
—— (1925) *The Economic Consequences of Mr. Churchill*, London: Hogarth Press.
Patinkin, D. (1956) *Money, Interest and Prices*, Evanston, Illinois: Row, Peterson and Company.
Sraffa, P. (1960) *Production of Commodities by Means of Commodities*, Cambridge University Press.

2
Archival Research and the Reconstruction of Piero Sraffa's Intellectual Biography: An Interim Report

Nerio Naldi¹

On setting out to assess the contribution of archival research to the reconstruction of Piero Sraffa's intellectual biography, the obvious choice was to take as starting point the works published before 1994, the year when the Sraffa Papers were opened to the general public of scholars. All in all, we may say that those works offered a remarkably eloquent outline of Piero Sraffa's biography, yet they clearly left much room for improvement. First of all, in several respects they were lacking in precision. Secondly, important questions relating to Piero Sraffa's intellectual biography could not be studied without the support of documents he had kept among his papers, the significant aspects here being the content, style, and extent of his research-work, whether or not it led to the publication of books or articles. Thirdly, the importance of some areas of the development of Piero Sraffa's intellectual biography has emerged only after the Sraffa Papers became available to be studied; an instance is provided by the months he spent in London in summer 1927 when he prepared a draft of the lectures he was to deliver in Cambridge from the following October: nothing of that period and of that draft was known before the Sraffa Papers could be studied.

As it would be extremely difficult to follow all the new details regarding Sraffa's biography that have emerged through archival research, I will not attempt detailed comparison between the old and new studies on the subject. Rather I intend to select some areas which, on the one hand, already appeared crucial to the authors of early biographical essays and where, on the other hand, archival research, whether based on the Sraffa Papers or on the study of other sources, has provided significant additions to our knowledge. These considerations will be restricted to the first three decades of Sraffa's life, that is to say, up to the mid-1930s. Obviously, this choice implies that important fields will not be touched on, and in particular the work done by Sraffa in the 1940s and 1950s finalized to the completion of the edition of Ricardo's works (and in particular to the Introductions to the different volumes which form that edition – see, for instance, Gehrke and Kurz, 2002; Gehrke, 2003; Rosselli, 2001) and of his 1960 book *Production of Commodities by Means of Commodities* (see for instance de Vivo, 2000, 2003; Kurz and Salvadori, 2001, 2004, 2005a, 2005b). With regard to these areas of research there are just two points we wish to stress. First of all, as has been noted, study of the Sraffa Papers has shown that Sraffa concentrated alternately on one or the other of the two major fields of his activity, so that it may be stated that his research on what was to become *Production of Commodities* developed from 1927 to 1931, and then from 1941 to 1945, and from 1955 to 1958, while his research on the Royal Economic Society edition of the writings of David Ricardo (which was assigned to Sraffa in February 1930) mainly developed in the complementary time intervals: from 1931 to 1941, and from 1946 to 1955, with a sequel connected to the preparation of the *Index*, published in 1973 (Gehrke, 2005; de Vivo, 2000, 2003; Pasinetti, 2001). Secondly, it appears that while the notes relating to the preparation of *Production of Commodities* kept by Sraffa among his papers amount to a huge volume of material, the notes relating to the preparation of the Introductions to the edition of Ricardo – that is to say, broadly speaking, to the development of Sraffa's reading of Ricardo's texts – are extremely scanty: it seems that Sraffa kept virtually nothing of the several drafts that he had certainly prepared (as from 1948 also with the collaboration of Maurice Dobb – see Pollit, 1988; Gehrke, 2003). This is a striking asymmetry, but so far no document has emerged that might suggest how it came about.

The specific points which we propose to discuss in this paper in order to illustrate how archival research has improved our understanding of Sraffa's intellectual biography are the following. First of all, we will mention, albeit very briefly, the extremely interesting and important fields of family history, childhood and youth (Section I). Secondly, we will summarize the available information on how and when Sraffa became interested in economic themes and in economics and economic theory in particular (Section II). Thirdly, we will summarize the information that has been collected on Sraffa's political position at the onset of fascist rule in Italy (Section III). Fourthly, we will recall the results reached with regard to the question of the origin of the research project that finally evolved in to the publication of *Production of Commodities* (Section IV). Finally, we will concentrate attention on reconstructing a period (approximately the years from 1931 to 1935) when Sraffa seems to have been quite uncertain as to how he should lead his own life in the near future (Section V).

Before starting our discussion it is also important to stress that, although we will attempt no overall assessment of the literature on Piero Sraffa produced after the Sraffa Papers were opened, we have greatly benefitted from that literature and from workshops and conferences on Sraffa's work and his papers organized in particular since 1998, when the centenary of his birth was celebrated. Many of these contributions may be found in special issues of *European Journal of the History of Economic Thought* (1998, 2005), *Il Pensiero Economico Italiano* (1998) and *Review of Political Economy* (1998, 2005), and in volumes edited by Accademia dei Lincei (2004), Ciccone, Gehrke and Mongiovi (2007), Cozzi and Marchionatti (2001) and Pivetti (2000).

I.   Family, childhood and youth

With regard to reconstruction of the history of Piero Sraffa's family and his childhood and youth, the Sraffa Papers, the archives of the Jewish communities to which Sraffa's ancestors belonged and the archives of the schools attended by Piero Sraffa offer a great deal of interesting information to draw upon. Here I will simply point out that the family of Piero Sraffa's mother (Irma Tivoli (1873–1949) was born in Turin in 1873) was not from Turin, as often stated, but from Trieste and that that cultural thread probably had a certain importance also in Piero's family through the influence of his grandparents, both born in Trieste, Federico Tivoli (1832–1901) and Sofia Goldmann (1851–1939), and in particular of the latter and of her brother Cesare Goldmann (1858–1937), an important businessman who, after the death of Sofia's husband, took an active interest in the families of her six daughters.

Just as Turin did not entirely account for the roots of the family of Piero Sraffa's mother, nor did Pisa in the case of the family of Piero Sraffa's father. Angelo Sraffa (1865–1937) was born in Pisa, but his ancestors had lived in Livorno since at least the mid-eighteenth century, moving to Pisa in the early 19th century: the first of these ancestors that we have been able to trace in the archives of the Jewish community of Livorno (*Angiolo Sdraffa*, son of Giuseppe Sdraffa and of Rachele Procaccio) seems to have worked first as a porter and later as a *legatore* (book-binder).

It is also important to note that among Piero Sraffa's uncles we find important industrialists (two members of the Pontecorvo family of Pisa: when their textile firm collapsed, after the First World War, several relatives of Piero Sraffa suffered losses from its plunging shares); the president of a high court of law (Mariano D'Amelio, president of the *Corte di Cassazione*); and a banker (Enrico Consolo, head of the London branch of the *Banca Commerciale Italiana*). Finally, we may add that among Piero Sraffa's relatives we could count both fascists (notably Cesare Goldmann and Amalia Goldmann (1856–1932), painter and civil servant, younger sister of Sofia Goldmann) and anti-fascists (notably Piero Sraffa's father).

It is also worth noting that Piero Sraffa's school curriculum was marked by an early setback: in his second year at primary school, in Parma, he failed his arithmetic exam and had to repeat the year. Up to that time he had been a pupil in a privately run school and he had had to sit a yearly examin-ation in a school belonging to the educational system run by the public authorities; from then on he always attended state schools and never had to repeat a year again, although it sometimes happened that he did not pass all the exams in June and had to take further examinations in October (in Gymnastics in 1911–12 and in 1912–13, probably because of his conduct in class rather than because of poor performance; and in Mathematics in 1913–14).[2]

If we take the year 1920, when he graduated at the Faculty of Law of the University of Turin, as the end of Piero Sraffa's *youth*, we may note that the documents kept among the Sraffa Papers relating to this early phase of his life and to his family are, in general, extremely scarce. A great many documents must surely have been produced in the period by the Sraffa family and by Piero himself, but they seem to have been lost, even though no mention of any episode that explains such a loss has so far been found among the Sraffa Papers.[3]

II.   The origin of Piero Sraffa's interest in socialism and in economics

In order to discuss the origin and early development of Sraffa's interest in economic matters and in economic science in general and economic theory in particular we may start by stressing two general points.

First, these interests may have been nurtured in several ways by Piero Sraffa's family background itself: on the one hand, several members of this family had a personal interest in the activity of Italian firms and, in consequence, in the facts of the Italian economy in general, while, on the other hand, Piero Sraffa's father was, in his profession (he was a professor of Commercial Law, a successful lawyer, and for many years Rector of the *Università Commerciale Luigi Bocconi*), clearly sensitive to the importance of economic questions.[4] Indeed, according to the account Piero Sraffa related to Pierangelo Garegnani, he also used to discuss *cases* of firms' behaviour with his son, as a sort of exercise, when the latter was still a young boy – a habit which, in light of the approach to commercial law generally attributed to Angelo Sraffa, may have contributed to develop Piero Sraffa's interests in historical and economic themes.

Second, it seems very likely that Piero Sraffa's interest in economic themes developed along with his interest in social questions and in socialism, so it seems apposite to consider the two together. In this context, we may say that archival and bibliographical research has provided interesting additions to what had been written by Alessandro Roncaglia and Luigi Pasinetti (Roncaglia, 1981: 171; Pasinetti, 1983: 318–9) on the basis of personal conversations with Sraffa: that is, that the years Sraffa spent as a student in secondary schools were particularly important to his formation and his approach to economic themes and to socialism, and that in the case of the latter one of his teachers – Domenico Re – had a special influence. This information has been verified through research in archives and libraries and we now know that Domenico Re was Piero Sraffa's professor of Latin and Greek at the *Ginnasio Giuseppe Parini* in Milan in the years 1911–13, so we have some reasons to date to those years Piero Sraffa's first approach to socialism.[5] But in those years a young Italian interested in politics and in social questions could learn a lot from observation of the current situation, especially if, like Piero Sraffa, he lived in Milan or Turin.[6] After the economic slump of 1907, social conflict and strikes regained momentum in 1911, leading to acute crises: for instance, on 6 January 1913 the police opened fire on three street demonstrations and killed eight people. The same period saw heated debate on the Italian military intervention in Libya, which raised nationalist enthusiasms and caused a sharp rift within the socialist party, some members being expelled while Benito Mussolini emerged as a leading figure, appointed editor of the party's newspaper in 1912. Furthermore, in Milan the political climate was strongly influenced by non-conservative local councils and by growing support for the Socialist Party, which won the local elections in 1914 and was for the first time able to appoint the mayor of the city.

Nevertheless, it was probably in Turin, between 1913 and 1916, with his schoolmates of the *Liceo Massimo D'Azeglio*, that Piero Sraffa took a deeper approach to economic themes and Marxist issues in particular. On this point we may refer to three testimonies. First of all, according to the account he gave Sergio Steve, in 1914 Piero Sraffa *campaigned in favour of Gaetano Salvemini against Giuseppe Bevione*. This information is not entirely correct. On 14 June 1914, shortly after the strikes of the so-called *red week* and the defeat of the Italian Socialist Party in the local elections in Turin, a by-election for the national Parliament was called. In this context, on 27 June, the historian Gaetano Salvemini came to

Turin to deliver a speech in Piazza Statuto and support the socialist candidate – the industrial worker Mario Bonetto. On this occasion Salvemini was led to the dais by Umberto Cosmo, who had been Piero Sraffa's Italian teacher in 1913–14 (his first year at the Liceo D'Azeglio).[7] Most likely it was to this episode that Piero Sraffa referred to when he said he had *campaigned in favour of Gaetano Salvemini*. Secondly, Paolo Vita-Finzi, schoolmate of Piero Sraffa from 1913 to 1916 and lifelong friend, recalled the long discussions with Sraffa and other schoolmates and friends in Turin, implying that many of them were oriented towards Marxist positions (never shared by Paolo Vita-Finzi) and came to support Soviet Russia (Vita-Finzi, 1989: 27, 318, 324–5). Thirdly, Geoffrey Harcourt (who informed the present author that the source of this news was Krishna Bharadwaj and that he was fairly certain that the events she related to him took place when Sraffa was not yet at the university but still at school) wrote: 'Many of [Sraffa's] student friends were Marxists but his teachers would not allow Marx or Marxist issues to be discussed explicitly in class. However, as a student, Sraffa read Ricardo's *Principles* and discovered that much of what Ricardo had to say bore a close resemblance to what he had been reading in Marx's work. As Ricardo was eminently respectable and so acceptable to their teachers, Sraffa and his fellow students took to discussing Marxist issues under the guise of a study of Ricardo' (Harcourt, 1983: 118).

Unfortunately, Piero Sraffa's books kept in his library in Cambridge, with the exception of a 1904 edition of Edmondo De Amicis' *Cuore* (Sraffa 2189) bound in leather with Piero Sraffa's name on the back, provide no direct information on his early reading or his social, political and economic interests. But in letters sent to his son in 1912[8] Angelo Sraffa mentioned a book on the Aegean Sea (in those years Italy had gained control of some islands in that area) and answered a question Piero had asked him about Garibaldi's military campaign in 1870 in support of the French Republic which had been attacked by Prussia. This information supports the hypothesis that the young Piero Sraffa was particularly interested in politics and history. Furthermore, in a letter he sent to the Italian publisher Giulio Einaudi in 1949[9] Sraffa stated that *trenta e più anni fa* he had read *Il tramonto della schiavitù nel mondo antico* (a book by Ettore Ciccotti published in 1899) and that he had been much impressed by it. The fact that Sraffa recalled this book may be interesting because Ettore Ciccotti had been a prominent academic figure involved in the activity of the Italian Socialist Party: he had opposed the war in Libya in 1911 and had written on economic history and Marxian political philosophy.[10]

Another interesting source on the intellectual interests of Piero Sraffa and his friends at the Liceo D'Azeglio which illuminates Sraffa's early historical, political and economic interests may be found in two books that belonged to Paolo Vita-Finzi (now kept in Florence, at the Fondazione Spadolini) which, from the annotations they contain, we may presume had been acquired by Paolo Vita-Finzi between 1913 and 1916, that is to say, when he was a lyceum student: N. Machiavelli's *Il Principe* (published in 1913) was inscribed by Vita-Finzi '1914', and, most interestingly, J.S. Mill's *Principles of Political Economy* (French edition of 1854 in two volumes) bears the inscription 'Paolo Vita-Finzi Torino 1916'[.[11]

Finally, it is interesting to note that the library of the Liceo D'Azeglio still holds the Italian editions of some important texts on economics which were most probably already there in 1913–16: a fact which supports the idea that in that school Sraffa had the opportunity to cultivate his interest in economics.[12]

These approaches to economic and social themes were certainly important to Sraffa if, as Gaia Servadio (1993: 71) tells us, he decided to matriculate in Turin at the Faculty of Law because in Italy at that time no Faculty of Economics existed and that Faculty of Law could have been the best place to study economics.[13] But if these, broadly speaking, may be the roots of Piero Sraffa's interest in economic themes, it is also worth touching upon another point which relates to the early phases of his approach to economics proper, namely the role played by the Italian economist Attilio Cabiati in guiding some of Piero Sraffa's early steps in economic science when he was a university student.

The correspondence between Cabiati and Luigi Einaudi (AFLE) shows that it was not the latter, as suggested by official records of the University of Turin, but the former, then professor in Genoa, who actually directed and followed the progress of Sraffa's work for his *tesi di laurea* in 1919–20[14] and the preparation of his first journey to England, in 1921, where he was to attend courses at the London School of Economics. The evidence here can be seen in two documents kept in Turin in the Archive of the Fondazione Luigi Einaudi (AFLE, Papers of Luigi Einaudi): a letter from Cabiati to Einaudi dated 17 May 1920 ('ho suggerito a Sraffa figlio di studiare, come tesi di laurea (che darà a novembre), il problema della rivalutazione della moneta e se converrà all'Europa Continentale di ritornare all'oro, come numerario. Al giovane – che è intelligente – il tema piace molto, ma è seccato all'idea di trattarlo con Loria: non avresti niente in contrario se lo discutesse con te? E si deve fare qualcosa per giungere a questo fine? Sraffa junior ora è a Torino: se volessi fargli sapere qualcosa, scrivimi chè te lo manderò!')[15] and a letter from Cabiati to Einaudi dated 5 April 1921 ("Il figlio di Sraffa, dr. Piero, va a Londra e sarebbe lieto di un biglietto di presentazione presso qualcuno dei grandi economisti. Se puoi fargliene uno, te ne sarà gratissimo anche il padre').[16] To this evidence, however, we may add that a letter Angelo Sraffa sent to Attilio Cabiati on 22 May 1919 (AFLE, Papers of Attilio Cabiati) makes it clear that Piero Sraffa's father had explicitly asked Cabiati to follow Piero in his approach to economics. The sentence where Angelo Sraffa formulated his request is particularly interesting: 'Spero che per la tua venuta sarà qui di nuovo mio figlio, che pongo sotto la tua alta paretiana protezione'.[17] In our opinion, the reference to the *high Paretian protection* which Cabiati should have exerted over Piero Sraffa may be seen as implicitly alluding to the fact that Piero's own approach to economics, in 1919, when the *biennio rosso* of 1919–20 was at its onset in Turin with a number of factories taken under armed control by workers was heavily influenced by a radicalization of his political views in favour of a bolshevist revolution.[18]

III.   Piero Sraffa and the Italian socialist parties (1922–4)

As already stated, we will not attempt to complement earlier essays on Piero Sraffa's intellectual biography by pointing out and correcting any imprecision which now, with *archival hindsight,* can be noticed. Nevertheless, it is worth noting how the possibility of correcting instances of imprecision in earlier texts based on the study of the Sraffa Papers has fostered processes of cumulative acquisition of information leading to new results. Here I will only mention one example of this kind of process.

Several authors referred to the fact that in 1922 Sraffa worked as a civil servant in Milan, heading a newly established office in charge of preparing labour statistics. Some authors referred to this office as depending on the Municipality of Milan (*Comune*), others as depending on the Province of Milan (*Provincia*) (see Roncaglia, 1981: 174; Potier, 1987: 19; Eatwell and Panico, 1987: 446). Archival research has shown that the office (*Ufficio provinciale del lavoro*) was actually part of the Province of Milan, that it had not been newly created, and that its activity, although Sraffa actually prepared a draft programme arguing that it would have been appropriate to focus it on the collection of statistical data (Sraffa Papers B4/1/1-14), was not essentially restricted to statistics.[19] In this case a better understanding and dating of the episode has been attained in the first place with the study of documents kept among the Sraffa Papers, followed by research in the archives of the Province of Milan[20] and Piero Sraffa's correspondence with Luigi Einaudi and Giuseppe Prato kept in the archive of the Fondazione Luigi Einaudi (AFLE). But archival research has also led to a better understanding of the significance of this episode within Sraffa's biography: by relating it to the period he spent in London in 1921–2, when he did research work at the Labour Research Department and wrote three articles on British and American working class and labour movements (Sraffa, 1921a, 1921b, 1921c), and formulating a conjecture on the reasons which prompted Sraffa's decision to resign from this post.[21] Furthermore, better knowledge of this episode has cast additional light on the connections between Sraffa – who described himself as *an undisciplined communist* (Sraffa, 1924) – and members of *Turati's non-revolutionary socialist party*.[22]

The period during which Sraffa occupied the post of *Direttore* of the *Ufficio provinciale del lavoro* opened and closed with two significant events which illuminate Sraffa's political stance. At the beginning of the period we see Sraffa, after assessment by a partly technical committee, appointed to the post in April 1922 with a vote of the socialist majority of the *Consiglio Provinciale*. Research on the Sraffa Papers has also shown that one of the most prominent figures in that assembly – Nino Levi – was, or was to become, one of Piero Sraffa's closest friends.[23] At the end of the period, we see Piero Sraffa resigning from his post in December 1922, immediately after Nino Levi had resigned from his position of head of the *Deputazione Provinciale* (the executive committee of the *Consiglio Provinciale*) and the whole socialist group had resigned from the *Consiglio*.[24] We do not know whether Sraffa approved of this decision, which took place in a period of extremely strong pressure and assaults by fascist groups which had led to the *Marcia su Roma* in late October, and to the first government headed by Mussolini, but his own resignation clearly shows that he saw his activity as closely linked to the socialist majority and not of a merely technical nature.

Allusions to Sraffa's relationship with *non-revolutionary socialists* can also be found in the correspondence of Carlo Rosselli with his mother and in the correspondence between Filippo Turati and Anna Kuliscioff. From December 1923 Carlo Rosselli often mentioned Nino Levi, Fausto Pagliari and Alessandro Schiavi (all *non-revolutionary socialists*) together with Piero Sraffa, as a group of friends who often met and had long discussions (Ciuffoletti, 1979). On the other hand, Filippo Turati and Anna Kuliscioff, in June 1924, mentioned a project of the same group, namely to set up a centre for economic and social research modelled on British Fabian organizations (Turati and Kuliscioff, 1977: 280, 284). Information about these relationships is interesting because *Turati's party* and the communist party were at the opposite ends of the political spectrum of the socialist movement. Furthermore, we may conjecture that they also reflect a special phase in the evolution of Sraffa's own political views: a phase in which, after the defeat, in Italy, of the revolutionary movements of 1919–21 and facing the fascist success of 1922, Sraffa felt he had to engage in activities, both practical (at the *Ufficio del Lavoro*) and intellectual (in his relationship with Levi, Rosselli, Schiavi and Pagliari), not necessarily revolutionary but aimed at supporting the labour movement in its defence against fascist attacks, and at supporting the anti-fascist front in its attempt to restore ordinary conditions of society (that is, to close fascist rule as a parenthesis).[25] Several elements point towards this interpretation of Sraffa's own position: a letter he sent to Gramsci in 1923–4;[26] Gramsci's comment on this letter, which he sent to other communist leaders;[27] and a remark in a letter to Keynes in November 1924 where Piero Sraffa expressed his approval of a *social policy* – certainly not *revolutionary* – which most likely amounted to an attempt to reduce unemployment in Britain.[28]

Most certainly, however, Sraffa had not abandoned his ideal of socialist revolution and radical transformation of society. In fact, in his letter to Gramsci mentioned above he also wrote:

> I do not think my position is irreconcilable with being a Communist, even an undisciplined one: the 'parties of the left' will carry out the function I attribute to them, I believe, very rapidly, and it would definitely not be to the Communist Party's advantage to compromise itself with them, even because this would not in any way contribute to such a campaign. But I also feel that it is a mistake to openly oppose them and to insist too much (as *L'Unità* has been doing, for example) in deriding bourgeois 'freedom': for better or worse it is that which the workers most strongly feel they need today and it is a prerequisite to any further conquest. Just like during the war when neutrality certainly was not a socialist policy; but it was surely the best of all policies possible for the Socialist Party, because it meant most to the masses.
>
> (Sraffa, 1924).

In this respect, we believe that Leo Valiani was not too far from the truth when he described this situation, stressing that Sraffa had joined a group aiming at outlining a new socialist program and strategy for the Italian situation and that when fascism crushed the hopes of those who had been expecting its fall in 1924–25, he moved again, although always remaining sceptical of sectarianism, towards the communist viewpoint that a revolutionary change was the only way out of fascism (Valiani, 1984).[29] What Valiani apparently failed to stress was that, in any case, Sraffa seems to have considered the attempt to restore *bourgeois freedom* as a phase in the path towards a revolutionary development. On the other hand, Valiani's idea that Sraffa's attitude towards sectarianism was, at least, one of perplexity, is consistent with what we know of the position he assumed with Angelo Tasca after the latter was expelled from the Italian communist party: Sraffa did not break off the friendly relationship they had enjoyed and helped him to find earning opportunities with British newspapers (letter from Angelo Tasca to Piero Sraffa, 15 October 1929, FGGF; letter from Cecil Sprigge to Angelo Tasca, 30 May 1930, FGGF). Particularly interesting is a letter where Sraffa states that he can criticize neither Tasca nor his opponents (Sraffa wrote he felt a *methodological* difficulty preventing him from expressing a personal view: 'se riuscissi a precisare i miei dubbi, questi sarebbero, non sul sì o sul no con cui si risponde alla domanda, ma sulla natura stessa della domanda' – letter from Piero Sraffa to Angelo Tasca, 28 July 1929, FGGF),[30] and a subsequent letter where Tasca shows that he feels he is in a position to speak very frankly to Sraffa (Angelo Tasca to Piero Sraffa, 15 October 1929, FGGF).

IV.   The origin of *Production of commodities*

In this section we would like to consider some of the results achieved with archival research in understanding the origin of Sraffa's 1960 book *Production of Commodities by Means of Commodities*.

The first result reached in this context was probably that of locating with relative precision, both chronologically and conceptually, the turning point that marked the beginning of Sraffa's research on what was to become the analytical structure now familiar to scholars from that book. That turning point has been located to November 1927 thanks to documents kept among the Sraffa Papers, to a letter written by Keynes to his wife on 28 November 1927, and to annotations in Sraffa's diary under the date of 26 November 1927. In those days Keynes described Sraffa as extremely excited by his own new ideas;[31] Sraffa received Keynes's approval of the new approach he was forging; and we may reasonably suppose that the core of those new ideas rested on at least two sets of equations describing the processes of commodity production, circulation and price formation. The simpler set of equations (dubbed by Sraffa *first equations*) described an economic system whose net product was nil and was merely reintegrating its own material conditions of subsistence, while the other set of equations (*second equations*) described a system producing a positive net product (or surplus) (Naldi, 1998a: 507, 513; Naldi, 2004, 2005; de Vivo, 2000, 2003, Garegnani, 2004, 2005).[32]

Brief discussions of how the *equations* came to occupy such a prominent position in Sraffa's reflection and of some aspects of their early development will be put forward in the following two parts of this Section.

Preliminary to these discussions, however, it is worth noting that, as is well known, in late 1927 Sraffa conceived a project that extended far beyond presenting a set of price-equations: he was planning to write a book encompassing a critique of received economic theory and a *rehabilitation* of Classical and Marxian political economy via the presentation of a new theoretical analysis:

Impostazione del libro
L'unico sistema è di far la storia a ritroso, e cioè: stato attuale dell'-economia; come vi si è giunti, mostrando le differenze e la superiorità delle vecchie teorie. Poi, esporre la teoria. Se si va in ordine cronol., Petty, Fisiocr, Ric, Marx, Jevons, Marsh, bisogna farlo precedere da uno statement della mia teoria per sipegare dove si 'drive at': il che significa esporre prima *tutta* la teoria. E allora c'è il pericolo di finire come Marx, che ha pubbl. prima il Cap, e poi non è riuscito a finire l'Histoire des Doct. E il peggio si è che non è riuscito a farsi capire, senza la spiegazione storica. Il mio scopo è: I esporre la storia, che è veramente l'essenziale; II farmi capire: per il che si richiede che io vada dal noto all'ignoto, da Marshall a Marx, dalla disutilità al costo materiale
(D3/12/11/35; quoted in de Vivo, 2000: 274–5).[33]

Principio
I shall begin by giving a short 'estratto' of what I believe is the essence of the classical theories of value, i.e. of those which include W. Petty, Cantillon, Physiocrats, A. Smith, Ricardo and Marx. This is not the theory of any one of them, but an extract of what I think is common to them. I state it of course, not in their own words, but in modern terminology, and it will be useful when we proceed to examine their theories to understand their portata from the point of view of our present inquiry. It will be a sort of 'frame', a machine, into which to fit their own statements in a homogeneous pattern, so as to be able to find what is common in them, and what is the difference with the later theories.

Then I shall go over these theories very cursorily, dealing with them, not at all exaustively, but examining only those points which are relevant to my present purpose. So, of the Physiocrats, I shall not talk of . . . the physiocratie, but only of one of its basic points.
(Sraffa Papers D3/12/4/12; quoted in Pasinetti, 2001: 154; the document is undated but was probably written in late November 1927).

But some notes written by Sraffa in the very days when he met Keynes suggest that he was focusing his attention on an even wider field, and show that Sraffa was aware of the philosophical, historical and political dimensions of his research. In this respect, two notes seem particularly interesting:

Metaphysics

I foresee that the ultimate result will be a restatement of Marx, by substituting to his hegelian metaphysics and terminology our own modern metaphysics and terminology: by metaphysics here I mean, I suppose, the emotions that are associated with our terminology and frames (schemi mentali) – that is, what is absolutely necessary to make the theory living (lebendig), capable of assimilation and at all intelligible. If this is true, it is an exceptional example of how far a difference in metaphysics can make to us absolutely unintelligible an otherwise perfectly sound theory. This would be simply a translation of Marx into English, from the forms of Hegelian metaphysics to the forms of Hume's metaphysics (Keynes to-day, 26 XI. 27, has clearly outlined the divorce between English and Continental thought: the first descending from Descartes and Hobbes, the two original geniuses, to Locke, Hutcheson and ultimately Hume; the second from Spinosa (did he say that of S.?) from Kant to Hegel: they always remained foreign to one another).

If this is true it also shows (or is it an exceptional case? in physics it doesnt seem to be indifferent) how little our metaphysics affects the truth of our conclusions, and how the same truths can be expressed in two widely divergent forms. Our metaphysics is in fact embodied in our technique; the danger lies in this, that when we have succeeded in thoroughly mastering a technique, we are very liable to be mastered *by* her.

(Sraffa Papers D3/12/4/15; quoted in de Vivo, 2000: 273–4).[34]

28.XI.27
Phases of capitalism
Age of increase of population:
up to industrial revolution + French Revolution, Mercantilism (practice or theory?) absolute monarchy Ends in Malthus, Wallace (Lloyd: power = population × circulation)
Age of increase of circulating capital:
up to 1820–30 (railways, Chartism) Classical P.E. Physiocrats beginning of democracy
The series of the forms of capital must be made continuous
Age of increase of intermediate capital
up to 1870. Free trade, democracy Risorgimento

Age of increase of fixed capital
up to 1914 Protection "to infant industries"
Age of . . .
imperialism, ultima tappa. Capitalism has lost all his reasons of life, having exhausted his tasks. It simply defends itself
Age of increase of land
inventions (Ricardian improvements)

(Sraffa Papers D3/12/11/50).

After this premise, we revert to the points that – following other scholars – we have chosen to focus upon: the origin and early development of Sraffa's *equations*.

In fact, locating the starting point of the approach which was to lead to the publication of *Production of Commodities* immediately raised some questions concerning the intellectual path followed by Sraffa up to that point and from that point onward (questions which can be seen as evolving from the questions that were being asked before the Sraffa Papers were opened to the public, when Sraffa's published works were the only available source on the development of his thought and such a development was essentially conceived in terms of the relationship between his 1925–6 articles on Marshallian theory and his 1960 book).

The origin of Sraffa's *equations*

Moving backwards, so to speak, from late November 1927 we find that the most detailed answer to the question of the origin of Sraffa's *equations* was provided by Garegnani, who focused on what he calls Sraffa's *pre-lectures* – a set of manuscript notes dating to the period that Sraffa spent in London in July–September 1927 (Sraffa Papers D3/12/3). Sraffa's intention in writing those notes was most probably to prepare a text that he could use, or read, to lecture on *Advanced Theory of Value* from the coming October 1927. Drawing it up, however, turned out to be more difficult than he had expected (to the extent that, as we shall see, Sraffa seems to have considered this manuscript as *notes* but not as *lecture notes*)[35] and the text often returns to the same points, suggesting that Sraffa was looking for the best way to develop his plan (never explicitly stated in detail) in both theoretical and didactic terms. In fact, we know from various documents that, as the beginning of Michaelmas Term drew closer, Sraffa felt he could not start lecturing in October, as originally planned, and asked for a delay, first of some months, then of a full academic year, as was eventually the case (Sraffa Papers B9/1/11, 12, 14, 16; C239/2; Marcuzzo, 2004, 2005; Naldi, 1998a, 2004, 2005).

In his study of the text of the *pre-lectures*, Garegnani – the first author to discuss the document (Garegnani, 2004, 2005) – argued that in the summer of 1927 Sraffa was coming to the realization that the Classical economists' approach to the theory of value could not be described as a primitive formulation of Marshall's supply and demand approach (his *scissors*),[36] and that, on the contrary, it pivoted on an alternative depiction of the economic system and a different metaphysics.

According to Garegnani's reconstruction, in his 1925 and 1926 articles Sraffa – although strongly critical of Marshall's supply curves – had accepted the demand and supply apparatus as a fundamental toolbox and had accepted the idea that the Classical authors, too, were to be interpreted by means of those basic tools, concurring with Marshall in the idea that the Classics had not developed the demand side because of the assumption of constant costs of production:

> In this early critical position of his, Sraffa accepts the determination of price by the equilibrium between Marshallian supply and demand functions and therefore, essentially, the whole apparatus of demand and supply of the marginal theories – even if he then denies the possibility of consistently considering the influence of demand on the price of the individual commodity and, more generally, wishes to expunge the subjective element of 'utility' and 'disutility' from that apparatus. [Moreover] by accepting the Marshallian interpretation of the 'old and now obsolete theory' of Ricardo and the Classical economists in terms of 'constant returns', Sraffa implicitly attributes the same demand and supply apparatus to those authors.
>
> (Garegnani, 2005: 456)

To this starting point, in the pre-lectures Sraffa added a broad contextualization of Classical and Marginalist theories as being both marked by the idea that there had to be one single ultimate cause of value (cost in the case of Ricardo, utility for Jevons, Menger and Walras). Marshall's equilibrium approach wiped out such a primitive notion focusing attention on the 'mechanism through which the actual price of such things as boots or candles was fixed' (Sraffa Papers D3/12/3/9; Garegnani, 2005: 456–7).[37]

The reconstruction put forward by Garegnani stresses that the position reached by Sraffa in his 1925–6 articles was based on the idea that the theory of distribution could be kept separate from the theory of prices and that Marshall's method of partial, or particular, equilibria could provide a satisfactory basis for the analysis of price determination (Garegnani, 2005: 457–8). But, according to Garegnani, preparing the *pre-lectures* Sraffa, having no choice but to recognize the limitations of the *particular* equilibria method and turning his attention to general equilibrium, saw that an ultimate standard of value was nevertheless required (Sraffa Papers D3/12/3/38-9, see also D3/12/3/42-3; Garegnani, 2005: 463). Garegnani interprets this conclusion in the sense that Sraffa saw no satisfactory solution to the difficulties or limitations of partial equilibrium method in general equilibrium, while some *ultimate standard of value* – although, he believed, it had yet to be brought to light – could provide such a solution (Sraffa Papers D3/12/3/38-9; Garegnani, 2005: 463–4). In fact, Sraffa pursued a direct search for an ultimate standard, but, aware as he was of the limited possibilities at hand, it is not clear if he pursued it only for didactic ends or in the expectation of finding a real solution to the problem. In any case, following the Classics he considered labour, but he did not take labour as the *ultimate* basis of production; he further reduced it to the amount of consumption goods necessary to the subsistence of the workers and considered that if one of these commodities could be said to be absolutely necessary, then by means of this commodity the 'difficulty of reducing to a common measure the various things entering into real cost would solve by itself' (Sraffa Papers D3/12/3/44; Garegnani, 2005: 465). But, even granting that such an absolutely necessary commodity does not exist, Sraffa felt he could defend this approach, suggesting that the amount of necessaries to the subsistence of the worker, although imperfect, is a better measure of cost than disutility or wages: 'I contend, however, that the amount of necessaries varies much less between different workers, than vary a) their disutilities, b) their wages' (Sraffa Papers D3/12/3/46).

According to Garegnani, having got so far, Sraffa made no substantial steps forward in the *pre-lectures*. However, he did achieve an important result shortly afterwards – most probably in late November – in an attempt to reduce various inputs of a production process to the *absolutely necessary commodity* whose existence he had postulated. Through this attempt it became clear to him that exchange ratios, or *ratios of absolute values*, could be determined that would reflect *purely numerical relations between things* (Sraffa Papers D3/12/5; Garegnani, 2005: 465–6)[38] and, together with the *price equations* or *production equations* from which they were derived, would provide 'a way of representing "physical real costs" – what is *physically necessary* for the commodity's production – more direct than the "necessary commodity"' (Garegnani, 2005: 467).

Sraffa faced a struggle to express even for his own understanding the basic result he has just arrived at thanks to the concept of 'physical real costs', namely that, essentially, the physical conditions of production of the commodities and the need to allow production to be repeated are sufficient to determine relative prices quite independently of what are generally understood as "demand and supply forces"' (Garegnani, 2005: 469). As 'this idea was totally new for his contemporaries, and for Sraffa himself' (Garegnani, 2005: 469–70), it may be guessed that this was the source of Sraffa's great *intellectual ferment and excitement*, as Keynes wrote to his wife, in late November 1927.

To Garegnani's interpretation of Sraffa's *pre-lectures* we would like to add some discussion of one of its premises, namely the idea that in both the 1925–6 articles and in the plan he had in mind when he started to prepare the *pre-lectures*, notwithstanding the detailed criticisms they both contain, Sraffa accepted the general validity of a supply and demand approach to price determination and also accepted – albeit only implicitly – Marshall's depiction of Classical economists as early representatives of that very approach (Garegnani, 2005: 453–4, 456). Garegnani cites as evidence in support of this interpretation a passage from Sraffa's 1926 article[39] and the text of the introductory parts of the manuscript of the *pre-lectures*, where Marshall's demand and supply equilibrium is presented as a synthesis of Classical and Marginalist theories of value.[40]

Garegnani's interpretation might appear to be at variance with passages in the 1925–6 articles where Sraffa emphatically stressed that the Classics were completely alien (both logically and chronologically) to the approach connecting price determination to symmetric forces of supply and demand;[41] it may also appear to be at odds with the critique of both demand and supply curves based on the concepts of utility and disutility developed in the *pre-lectures*.[42] Nevertheless, paradoxically, even Sraffa's manifest hostility to Marshall's analysis and to the Marginalist approach in general, which often emerges from his papers (see Rosselli, 2004, 2005; Marcuzzo and Rosselli, 2006), could not but be based upon supply and demand categories so long as Sraffa had no other interpretative category at his disposal except that very apparatus. In this sense, therefore, we agree with Garegnani's interpretation. But if the latter leads quite naturally to interpret the text of the *pre-lectures* as reflecting Sraffa's growing awareness that his own point of view – his *1925–6 synthesis* (Garegnani, 2005: 461) – was defective, we would suggest that that particular text by Sraffa, fragmentary as it is, also reveals a fairly clear plan designed to show how limited was the validity of a demand and supply apparatus based on the concepts of utility and disutility, and to highlight the rational basis of the Classical approach to the analysis of value. This conclusion, however, far from solving all the interpretative problems, raises other questions: when did Sraffa conceive this plan? Did he see it from the outset in terms of direct criticism of his previous position? When and why did he come to regard the text he had prepared as unsuitable for the lectures he was to deliver?

We will not be able to provide a full answer to these questions in this chapter, but all the same we would like to put forward some considerations. First of all, we would like to note that in the *pre-lectures* Sraffa also introduced an element which points directly to a fundamental difference between the Classical approach on the one hand and the Marginalist and Marshallian on the other. Elaborating upon the idea that there is something to be said for a conception of real cost based on a hypothetical *absolutely necessary commodity* (Sraffa Papers D3/12/3/46), that is to say, setting out to highlight the rational basis of the Classical approach to the analysis of value, led Sraffa to state that:

> to Ricardo's T[heory of] V[alue], based on amount of labour, two interpretations can be given: 1) the subjective psycholog., disutility one, 2) the objective, physical necessaries of existence one. He probably had not always clear in mind the distinction, but I believe that the latter is the one that underlies his T[heory of] V[alue].
> (Sraffa Papers D3/12/3/47)

This interpretation of Ricardo's theory of value as based on *objective* rather than *subjective* magnitudes marked a step forward from his 1925–6 articles and possibly also from the original plan of his lectures. Certainly, it opened the way to the idea that Classical and Marginalist approaches (with no distinction, in this sense, between Marshall on the one hand, and Jevons, Menger and Walras on the other hand) could be distinguished from one another as resting on radically different foundations. In fact this idea appears to be in contrast with the premise of the *pre-lectures* that the Marshallian equilibrium approach embodied the doctrines of both Classical and Marginalist schools of thought (Sraffa Papers D3/12/3/8)[43] and was to be the main characteristic of the view adopted by Sraffa in the text he later prepared for the lectures on Advanced Theory of Value actually delivered from Michaelmas 1928 to Easter 1931. We may therefore wonder exactly what role was played by this new understanding in leading Sraffa to doubt the basic structure he had conceived for his lectures. Certainly it provided an important substratum to the development of his new and more strictly theoretical analysis of the determination of exchange ratios directly expressing physical real costs which he seems to have first approached in late November 1927.

But there is yet another item that merits a place within the compass of our attempt to clarify the grounds of Sraffa's dissatisfaction with the lectures he had prepared in summer 1927 and the evolution of his thought towards the breakthrough of late November 1927. Indeed, if we are to take at face value what Sraffa wrote to Angelo Tasca in a letter dated 22 September 1927, we are led to believe that in late September Sraffa was still essentially untroubled by theoretical difficulties or novelties: 'Mi scusi se non faccio niente per lo S[tato] O[peraio]; fra 15 giorni qui cominciano le lezioni, e io mi accorgo che il far lezione in inglese è molto più difficile di quanto credessi e sono indietro nel lavoro' (FGGF).[44] In fact, the text of the *pre-lectures*, which possibly has reached us after dispersion of some of its parts,[45] might have been intended to provide only a relatively rough guide to the lecturer (as, we may presume, had been Sraffa's wont when he lectured in Italy), and the letter to Tasca probably shows that at that time Sraffa perceived that he could not comfortably lecture from this text filling in the gaps on the spot. This could have been the main reason which prompted Sraffa to ask to postpone the beginning of his course by a term, as he did in October 1927.[46] Such being the case, Sraffa may have meant to rewrite his previous text in a more complete form. At this point it seems likely that his reflections on the differences between Classical, Marginalist and Marshallian approaches and on their respective limitations, together with his analysis of the reduction of various inputs of a production process to a hypothetical *absolutely necessary commodity*, led Sraffa to conduct his research in a new direction and devote most of his time to the new approach he had discovered. He would then soon have realised, in light of his new insight, that he could not satisfactorily prepare his lectures (that is, write them down as a text which could be read to the students) unless he had several months ahead. Unfortunately, we may search in vain through a draft letter addressed by Sraffa to the Secretary to the General Board dated 11 January 1928,[47] another addressed to Pigou on 14 January 1928,[48] and Pigou's reply to Sraffa,[49] for conclusive evidence on the nature of Sraffa's difficulties and on the chronology of their development. In fact, if it emerges quite clearly from Sraffa's letters that *the difficulties* which had prevented him from lecturing in October and again in January were not connected with the progress of his work on his *equations*,[50] the former still gives us cause to wonder when it suggests that only *now* (that is to say, in January 1928) had Sraffa realized that the subject he had chosen for his lectures was *really quite unsuitable*,[51] while no help comes from Sraffa's references in the letter to Pigou where he mentions 'the difficulties which have prevented my lecturing on that subject at present' and remarks that overcoming them had nothing to do with his work on his *equations*. Certainly, with respect to the *pre-lectures*, the actual lectures had to conform with Sraffa's new understanding of the difference between the Classics and the Marginalists, now including Marshall, but they could not incorporate the core of Sraffa's new research, as it turned out to be still very much in embryo and – as Keynes had written to his wife – probably too difficult for his students to grasp.

The methodological foundations of Sraffa's *equations*

Archival researches on the path followed by Sraffa from the first formulation of his equations to the development of the complex structure that formed *Production of Commodities* have been presented in several papers (see in particular de Vivo, 2000, 2003; Garegnani, 2004, 2005; Gehrke and Kurz, 2006; Kurz and Salvadori, 2004, 2005a, 2005b), focusing mainly on certain points. In particular, they dwell on the general philosophical basis of Sraffa's research – that is, Sraffa's *objectivism* and the evolution it underwent in the process of defining and refining the analytical structure of *Production of Commodities* (Kurz and Salvadori, 2005b); on the analytical evolution of specific parts of *Production of Commodities* and the way Sraffa dealt with a number of difficulties and complemented his own logical discussion of those difficulties with the advice of mathematicians (Kurz and Salvadori, 2001, 2004, 2005a); on the evolution of Sraffa's interpretation of the Classical economists and Marx from 1927 to the completion of his book (de Vivo, 2000, 2003; Garegnani, 2004, 2005; Kurz and Salvadori, 2005b; Gehrke and Kurz, 2006; Signorino, 2005); and finally on the relationship between the origin of Sraffa's *equations* and the text of the lectures on *Advanced Theory of Value* which he read in Cambridge between 1928 and 1931 (Garegnani, 2004, 2005).

Of these themes, we would like to discuss briefly only two points, and – in both cases – Kurz and Salvadori's research will be our main reference. First of all, we intend to discuss the development of Sraffa's *objectivism*. Secondly, we shall draw attention to the evolution of Sraffa's treatment of labour and wages.

As pointed out by Kurz and Salvadori, Sraffa's *objectivism* may be depicted as based on adherence to the general idea that only *objective quantities* – that is, quantities measurable with ordinary instruments and units – should enter as data or unknowns into his system, and on the adoption of the concepts of *physical real costs* and *physical social surplus* as keystones of the same system. We will not discuss here how Sraffa came to adopt this conception,[52] but will confine our attention to the observation that, according to Kurz and Salvadori, from 1927 onwards this conception was developed through at least two phases, which it may prove interesting to distinguish chronologically. In both phases, adherence to an *objectivist* approach meant for Sraffa introducing among the data of his system only 'quantities [that] have an objective, independent existence at every or some instants of the natural (i.e. not interfered with by the experimenter) process of production and distribution; they can therefore be measured physically, with the ordinary instruments of measuring number, weight, time, etc.' (Sraffa Papers D3/12/13/2, quoted in Kurz and Salvadori, 2005b: 426). But in the first phase, dating from Autumn 1927 to August 1931, Sraffa associated this conception with the idea, which he seems to have derived from his readings in the epistemology of natural sciences, that for every *effect* in his system a *sufficient cause* had to be indicated. The latter conception was particularly important in Sraffa's attempt to develop the equations describing a no-surplus economy into a set of equations describing an economy producing a surplus. In fact, in the latter case, Sraffa tried to find *a cause* within his system – that is, a cost – capable of explaining the existence of rents and profits just as values in the no-surplus case could be explained by physical real costs. But he soon realized that magnitudes of a subjectivist and psychological nature could not be excluded from his analysis if it was to include an attempt to explain the distribution of social surplus between rents and profits (Kurz and Salvadori, 2005b: 431). If he was to remain faithful to what may be considered the essential basis of his objectivist stance, Sraffa could not accept this conclusion, and decided that the line of his approach had to be redefined: the requirement that the analysis be self-contained should be dropped, and the existence of causes acting from outside the system admitted. We may interpret this point as suggesting that Sraffa came to understand that he could not rule out subjective influences on the determination of distributive variables or of any other magnitude in his system, but that he could limit the object of his analysis to a core of relations where subjective influences could be said to have no role and which, nevertheless, would remain meaningful as it would describe a system open to influences from other economic and social spheres.[53] This led Sraffa to a deeper understanding of the meaning of his assumption of *given quantities*, which turned out to be a crucial feature of his analysis. In this respect, we would suggest that Sraffa's methodological problem of deciding which conception of *objectivism* he had to follow (as pointed out by Kurz and Salvadori, – 2005b: 432, these are the terms used by Sraffa himself to describe his concern – Sraffa Papers D3/12/7/161/3-4) reflected the question of how he should locate his own analysis within economic discourse.

Another point that marked the evolution of Sraffa's analysis in the early stages of his work on his *equations* relates to the treatment of labour input and wages. Initially Sraffa did not treat the quantity of labour employed in the production of a single commodity as a datum of his system: in its place he considered the commodities consumed by the labourers, assuming that they were necessary to enable them to perform their activity (Kurz and Salvadori, 2005b: 417–19, 420–1). The reason for this choice may be rooted in part in Sraffa's dislike for magnitudes defined in terms of subjective motives or which could be interpreted in that sense (such was the case of labour, which had been interpreted as *effort* or *sacrifice*) and in part in the fact that, as long as wages were conceived as paid in physical terms, explicitly introducing labour quantities was not necessary. In this context, as far as the determination of the value of commodities was concerned, the work of a waged labourer, that of a slave and that of a horse turned out to be homogeneous, because no *objective* element differentiated them (Sraffa Papers D3/12/9/89; Kurz and Salvadori, 2005b: 419). Interestingly enough, this conception was gradually abandoned between summer 1928 and the end of 1929 when Sraffa, considering the case of workers who participate in the distribution of the surplus product, concluded that he had no choice but explicitly to introduce labour and wages into his system (Kurz and Salvadori, 2005b: 419, 422) (the latter were introduced considering various possibilities and eventually through the concept of *proportional wages* – see Gehrke, 2003; Kurz and Salvadori, 2005b: 421–4). Evidently, Sraffa came to the conviction that his previous misgivings could be laid to rest; on the one hand, that is, that he should not be bothered by the fact that labour *could* be interpreted as a non-objective magnitude and, on the other hand, he seems to have convinced himself that wages could be regarded as objectively measurable just like workers' consumption and that with respect to the latter they had the advantage of allowing for a description of the functioning of economic systems closer to observable reality, and in particular with regard to the fact that workers are often rewarded with wages which may be expended with discretion and that labour is generally heterogeneous (relative wages – taken as given – being apt to be used to represent such heterogeneity). This led Sraffa to reverse his previous conclusion: workers could not be treated on the same footing as slaves and horses – as he will later put it: 'men . . . (and in this they are distinguished from horses) kick' (Sraffa Papers D3/12/16/18; quoted in Kurz and Salvadori, 2005b: 423).

V. Years of uncertainty

The intuition that inspired so much excitement in Sraffa in November 1927 opened a period that was certainly fruitful in terms of research, but also rife with difficulties.

In October 1928, a year after the date initially agreed upon, Sraffa finally started lecturing on *Advanced Theory of Value* and on *Continental Banking*. His lectureship was to expire at the end of 1930, but on

15 March 1930 it was extended for three more years. Shortly before that date, on 13 February 1930, the Royal Economic Society, doubtless on Keynes's suggestion, decided to entrust Sraffa with the preparation of an edition of the complete writings of David Ricardo (BLPES RES/2/1/2, Minute Book 1921–1938).[54] Teaching in Cambridge and, presumably, giving his course on *Advanced Theory of Value* in particular, proved to be very exacting for Sraffa, and we may guess that one of the reasons why Keynes thought of the job on the Ricardo edition was to entice Sraffa to stay on in Cambridge beyond the original three-year proposition. At the end of May 1930, Sraffa requested a sabbatical term, as was his right after having taught for six terms, expressing the intention to 'finish my work for the Royal Economic Society edition of Ricardo by the end of the year '(draft letter from Piero Sraffa to Gerald Shove, 31 May 1930, Sraffa Papers B9/1/10, quoted in Naldi, 2005: 391; see also Sraffa Papers B9/1/15, 19; and UL Faculty Board Minutes). After the sabbatical term, in January 1931, Sraffa resumed lecturing, but by May he had handed in his resignation (accepted by the General Board of the University of Cambridge on 27 May 1931 – Sraffa Papers B9/1/13), thus forgoing his lectureship permanently. However, abandonment of his Cambridge lectureship came right on the heels of his assignment to the post of librarian in the Marshall Library (4 May 1931, UL Faculty Board Minutes)[55] – a decision that, we may guess, was consistent with his work on the edition of the writings of Ricardo. In fact, by this time we may say that Sraffa's scientific activity concentrated on editing Ricardo, and that he put aside the work on the *equations* begun in late 1927.

Just a few months after having given up his Cambridge lectureship, on 1 November 1931, just on the very day when a new Italian law required that university professors pledge their allegiance not only to the king, to the *Statuto* (Constitution) and the other laws of the kingdom, as had thus far been the case, but also to the Fascist regime,[56] Sraffa resigned from his Political Economy chair – a life tenure – at the University of Cagliari.[57] Within the compass of six months Sraffa had renounced two university lectureships. Writing his second resignation he had it with a false declaration: 'as a result of being nominated for a professorship at Cambridge University . . . he feels it is his duty to no longer occupy the chair at Cagliari' (Sraffa Papers B7/10, quoted in Naldi, 2005: 399). In fact, at that time he only held the position of Marshall librarian, and a year later on 23 May 1932, the same post was assigned to Charles Ryle Fay, who was to take it on as from 1 January 1933 (UL Faculty Board Minutes).[58] We may suppose that it was Sraffa himself who had chosen to give it up, perhaps with a view to concluding his work for the Royal Economic Society and leaving Cambridge with a grant from the Rockefeller Foundation which, at least at the outset (that is, approximately between September 1932 and February 1933 – Sraffa Papers B12/1/5-7, 10), he had hoped to be able to use in Italy,[59] but later on (that is, at least from February 1933 – Sraffa Papers B12/1/13) he realised it could only be used in the United States.

But if in 1932–3 Piero Sraffa still believed he could rapidly finish his work for the Royal Economic Society and take up research on his *equations* once again (Sraffa Papers B12/1/12, letter from P. Sraffa to N.F. Hall, 10 March 1933), by February 1934 he saw that the work on Ricardo could not be concluded before October 1934 or February 1935 (Sraffa Papers B12/1/2).

The condition of uncertainty in which Piero Sraffa found himself obviously meant a smaller and less reliable income.[60] If the position of librarian at the Marshall Library provided any salary at all, it would surely have been relatively modest. He may have supplemented this income with compensation related to the direct supervision of a few students, but even if this had been the case the sum would have been paltry.[61] Under such circumstances, keeping in mind that, as we mentioned, as of January 1933 Sraffa no longer held any position, the Royal Economic Society's decision in 17 March 1933 (BLPES RES/2/1/2 Minute Book 1921–38) to grant him an advance of £350 on the royalties due to him for editing Ricardo's writings must have been very welcome indeed. This advance, roughly equivalent to a lecturer's annual salary, was to be paid in two instalments, but the actual payment, or at least Sraffa's willingness to accept it, is not entirely clear: among the Sraffa Papers is a cheque stamped *paid* written by Sraffa himself, made out to the Royal Economic Society and dated 16 May 1933, for the exact amount of one of the advances (Sraffa Papers A2/6). It is therefore possible that some difficulty arose or that Sraffa had initially refused payment, but that later the difficulty was overcome or Sraffa was persuaded to go back on his decision and accept payment. The fact remains that the decision to pay out this sum was confirmed by the Royal Economic Society Council, 18 September 1933.

In short, the chain of events linking Sraffa's decisions with regard to his lectureship at Cambridge, his chair at Cagliari, his post as librarian at Cambridge and his fellowship with the Rockefeller Foundation on the one hand and the development of his editing work of Ricardo's writings on the other, map out an uncertain path between the desire to leave Cambridge and return to Italy, or to go to America, and the desire to remain in Great Britain. It is quite clear that Keynes actively supported the latter option, but it seems that protraction of the work on the edition of Ricardo also moved Sraffa to modify his plans to leave Cambridge.

Meanwhile, in May 1933 the Board of the Faculty of Economics and Politics considered re-nominating Sraffa as lecturer or appointing him Assistant Director of Research (UL, Faulty Board Minutes). The latter solution was to prove the more congenial to Sraffa; in fact, he kept this post – which was on his request associated with that of librarian at the Marshall Library – until the 1960s. But the definitive decision of the General Board of Cambridge University was not made until October 1935 – and we may assume that Sraffa's own uncertainty as to whether to move to the USA on the Rockefeller Fellowship was a factor in delaying this decision. Although Sraffa had remained without any official position for almost three years, even accepting the nomination to Assistant Director of Research was no simple matter for him. Both Keynes and Robertson were involved in urging him to accept the terms established by the General Board. Particularly significant are the words Keynes used to communicate to his wife the result of his attempt to convince him: 'Piero has signed on at the last moment, will take the job, and all is over. What a troublesome fellow' (letter from J.M. Keynes to Lydia Lopokova Keynes, 11 March 1935, JMK/PP/45/190/7/33-4, quoted in Skidelsky, 1986: 79).[62] Keynes's success, however, was not complete: in May 1935 negotiations with the General Board were still open,[63] but in the end Sraffa accepted.[64]

References

Accademia Nazionale dei Lincei (2004) *Convegno internazionale Piero Sraffa*, Rome, 11–12 February 2003, Atti dei Convegni Lincei, no. 200, Rome: Accademia Nazionale dei Lincei.

Ciccone, R., C. Gehrke and G. Mongiovi (2007) *Sraffa and Modern Economics*. London: Routledge.

Ciuffoletti, Z. (ed.) (1979) *Epistolario famigliare. Carlo, Nello Rosselli e la madre (1914–1937)*, Milan: SugarCo Edizioni.

Cozzi, T., and R. Marchionatti (eds) (2001) *Piero Sraffa's Political Economy. A centenary estimate*, London: Routledge.

de Vivo, G. (2000) 'Produzione di merci a mezzo di merci': note sul percorso intellettuale di Sraffa. in M. Pivetti (ed.), *Piero Sraffa. Contributi per una biografia intellettuale*, Rome: Carocci, pp. 265–95.

de Vivo, G. (2003) Sraffa's path to "Production of commodities by means of commodities": An interpretation. *Contributions to Political Economy*, vol. 22: pp. 1–25.

Eatwell, J., and C. Panico (1987) Piero Sraffa, in *New Palgrave Dictionary of Economics*, London: Macmillan, pp. 445–51.

Garegnani, P. (2004) Di una svolta nella posizione teorica e nella interpretazione dei classici in Sraffa nei tardi anni Venti. Atti dei Convegni Lincei, *Convegno internazionale Piero Sraffa*, Rome: Accademia Nazionale dei Lincei, pp. 159–94.

Garegnani, P. (2005) On a turning point in Sraffa's theoretical and interpretative position in the late 1920s, *European Journal of the History of Economic Thought*, vol. 12, no. 3: 453–92.

Gehrke, C. (2003) More on the Sraffa-Dobb collaboration in Piero Sraffa's edition of *The Works and Correspondence of David Ricardo*, mimeo, Graz.

Gehrke, C. (2005) Bringing the edition of Ricardo's works to completion: The making of the General Index, 1951–73. *Review of Political Economy*, vol. 17, no. 3: pp. 443–64.

Gehrke, C., and H. Kurz (2002) Keynes and Sraffa's 'Difficulties with J.H. Hollander', *European Journal of the History of Economic Thought*, 9: 644–71.

Gehrke, C., and H. Kurz (2006). Sraffa on von Bortkiewicz: Reconstructing the Classical Theory of Value and Distribution, *History of Political Economy*, vol. 38, no. 1: 91–149.

Harcourt, G.C. (1983) On Piero Sraffa's contribution to economics, in P. Groenewegen and J. Halevi (eds), *Altro Polo. Italian economics past and present*, Sidney: University of Sidney, pp. 117–28.

Keynes, J.M. (1944) Mary Paley Marshall, *Economic Journal*, 54: 268–84.

King's College (1984) Piero Sraffa, *Annual Report* (October): 74–6.

Kurz, H., and N. Salvadori (2001) Sraffa and the mathematicians: Frank Ramsey and Alister Watson, in Cozzi and Marchionatti (2001), pp. 254–84.

Kurz, H., and N. Salvadori (2004) On the collaboration between Sraffa and Besicovitc: the cases of fixed capital and non-basics in joint production. Convegno internazionale Piero Sraffa, Rome, 11–12 February 2003, Atti dei Convegni Lincei, no. 200, Accademia Nazionale dei Lincei, pp. 255–301, Rome.

Kurz, H., and N. Salvadori (2005a) Removing an 'insuperable obstacle' in the way of an objectivist analysis: Sraffa's attempts at fixed capital. *European Journal of the History of Economic Thought*, vol. 12, no. 3: pp. 493–523.

Kurz, H., and N. Salvadori (2005b) Representing the production and circulation of commodities in material terms: On Sraffa's objectivism. *Review of Political Economy*, vol. 17, no. 3: pp. 413–41.

Marcuzzo, M.C. (2004) Sraffa all'Università di Cambridge, *Convegno internazionale Piero Sraffa*, Rome, 11–12 February 2003, Atti dei Convegni Lincei, no. 200, Rome: Accademia Nazionale dei Lincei, pp. 123–55.

Marcuzzo, M.C. (2005) Piero Sraffa at the University of Cambridge, *European Journal of the History of Economic Thought*, vol. 12, no. 3, pp. 425–52.

Marcuzzo, M.C., and A. Rosselli (2006) Sraffa and his reasons against 'marginism'. in *The Cambridge Approach to Economics: A Re-Invented Tradition?*, M.C. Marcuzzo (ed.), Quaderni del Dipartimento di Scienze Economiche, Rome, pp. 69–83.

Marshall, A. (1920) *Principles of Economics*, London: Macmillan.

Meldolesi, L. (1982) *L'utopia realmente esistente*. Bari: Laterza.

Naldi, N. (1998a) Some notes on Piero Sraffa's biography, 1917–1927, *Review of Political Economy*, vol. 10, no. 4: 493–515.

Naldi, N. (1998b) Dicembre 1922: Piero Sraffa e Benito Mussolini, *Rivista Italiana degli Economisti*, vol. 3, no. 2: 269–97.

Naldi, N. (2000) The friendship between Piero Sraffa and Antonio Gramsci in the years 1919–1927, *European Journal of the History of Economic Thought*, vol. 7, no. 1: 79–114.

Naldi, N. (2001) Piero Sraffa's early approach to political economy: From the gymnasium to the beginning of his academic career; in Cozzi – Marchionatti (2001) pp. 23–40.

Naldi, N. (2002) Infanzia, adolescenza e prima giovinezza di Piero Sraffa: 1898–1916, Quaderni del Dipartimento di Scienze Economiche, Rome.

Naldi, N. (2004) Piero Sraffa: emigrazione, attività scientifica e rapporti di amicizia fra gli anni Venti e gli anni Quaranta, *Convegno internazionale Piero Sraffa*, Rome, 11–12 February 2003, Atti dei Convegni Lincei, no. 200, Rome: Accademia Nazionale dei Lincei, pp. 81–121.

Naldi, N. (2005) Piero Sraffa: emigration and scientific activity (1921–1945), *European Journal of the History of Economic Thought*, vol. 12, no. 3: 379–402.

Naldi, N. (2006) 6 November 1924: Piero Sraffa and Keynes's *new theory* and *social policy*, in M.C. Marcuzzo (ed.), *The Cambridge Approach to Economics: A Re-invented Tradition*. Quaderni del Dipartimento di Scienze Economiche, Rome.

Pasinetti, L. (1983) In memoria di Piero Sraffa: economista italiano a Cambridge, *Economia Politica*, no. 3: 315–32.

Pasinetti, L. (2001) Continuity and change in Sraffa's thought: an archival excursus, in T. Cozzi and R. Marchionatti (eds), *Piero Sraffa's Political Economy. A Centenary Estimate*, London: Routledge, pp. 139–56.

Pivetti, M. (ed.) (2000) *Piero Sraffa. Contributi per una biografia intellettuale*. Rome: Carocci.

Pollit, B.H. (1988) The collaboration of Maurice Dobb in Sraffa's edition of Ricardo, in *Cambridge Journal of Economics*, no. 12: pp. 55–65.

Potier, J.-P. (1987) *Piero Sraffa*, Italian edition 1990, Rome: Editori Riuniti.

Robinson, A. (1977) Keynes and his Cambridge Colleagues, in *Keynes, Cambridge and 'The General Theory'*, D. Patinkin and J.C. Leith (eds), London: Macmillan, pp. 25–38.

Roncaglia, A. (1981) *Sraffa e la teoria dei prezzi*, Bari: Laterza.

Rosselli, A. (2001) Sraffa's edition of Ricardo's *Works*: reconstruction of a reconstruction, in T. Cozzi and R. Marchionatti (eds), *Piero Sraffa's Political Economy. A Centenary Estimate*, London: Routledge, pp. 187–206.

Rosselli, A. (2004) Sraffa e la tradizione marshalliana, *Convegno internazionale Piero Sraffa*, Rome, 11–12 February 2003, Atti dei Convegni Lincei, no. 200, Rome: Accademia Nazionale dei Lincei, pp. 195–214.

Rosselli, A. (2005) Sraffa and the Marshallian tradition, *European Journal of the History of Economic Thought*, vol. 12, no. 3: 403–23.

Servadio, G. (1993) *Incontri*, Catanzaro: Abramo.

Signorino, R. (2005) 'Piero Sraffa's *Lectures on the Advanced Theory of Value 1928–31* and the rediscovery of the Classical approach, *Review of Political Economy*, vol. 17: 359–80.

Skidelsky, R. (1986) Keynes e Sraffa: un caso di non-comunicazione, in R. Bellofiore (ed.), *Tra teoria economica e grande cultura europea: Piero Sraffa*, Milan: Angeli, pp. 73–84.

Spriano, P. (1958) *Storia di Torino operaia e socialista. Da De Amicis a Gramsci*, Turin: Einaudi.

Sraffa, P. (1921a) Open Shop Drive, *L'Ordine Nuovo*, (5 July).

Sraffa, P. (1921b) Industriali e governo inglese contro i lavoratori, *L'Ordine Nuovo*, (24 July).

Sraffa, P. (1921c) I *Labour Leaders*, *L'Ordine Nuovo*, (4 August).

Sraffa, P. (1922a). The Bank Crisis in Italy. *Economic Journal*, 32: 178–97.

Sraffa, P. (1922b). Italian Banking Today. *Manchester Guardian Commercial Recostruction in Europe*, (11): 675–6.

Sraffa, P. (1924) 'Problemi di oggi e di domani, *L'Ordine Nuovo*, 1–15 April (English translation in Naldi, 2000).

Sraffa, P. (1925) Sulle relazioni tra costo e quantità prodotta, *Annali di economia*, 2: 277–328; English translation in L.L. Pasinetti (ed.), *Italian economic papers* (vol. III), Il Mulino-Oxford University Press, (1998), pp. 323–63.
Sraffa, P. (1926) The laws of returns under competitive conditions, *The Economic Journal*, 36: 535–50.
Sraffa, P. (1960). *Production of Commodities by means of Commodities*. Cambridge: Cambridge University Press.
Turati, F., and A. Kuliscioff (1977) *Carteggio 1923–1925*, vol. VI, ed. A. Schiavi, Torino: Einaudi.
Valiani, L. (1984) Ricordo di Piero Sraffa. *Quaderni di Nuova Antologia*, 21: 81–4.
Vita-Finzi, P. (1989) *Giorni lontani. Appunti e ricordi*. Bologna: Il Mulino.

Notes

1 Earlier drafts of this paper were presented in May 2006 at the Conference 'Wittgenstein and Sraffa' (University of Graz) and in June 2006 at the III annual STOREP conference (University of Lecce). I would like to thank P. Garegnani, H. Kurz, M.C. Marcuzzo, F. Ranchetti and A. Rosselli for their comments and criticisms, the institutions mentioned in the text for the support they provided to my research, and P. Garegnani for giving me permission to quote previously unpublished passages from the Sraffa Papers. The following archival sources are referred to in abbreviated form: Sraffa Papers (Sraffa Papers, Wren Library, Trinity College, Cambridge); JMK (Keynes Papers, Modern Archive Centre, King's College, Cambridge); AFLE (Archivio Fondazione Luigi Einaudi, Turin); FGGF (Fondazione Giangiacomo Feltrinelli, Milan); BLPES (British Library of Political and Economic Sciences Archive Division, London), UL (University Library, Cambridge), CSDPS (Centro Studi e Documentazione Piero Sraffa, Roma). Responsibility for any inaccuracy lies entirely with the author. The research was funded by a contribution by the MIUR (Cofin, 2004).
2 We may also add that in 1914–15 and in 1915–16, because of the war, the requirements to be admitted to the following year were less stringent.
3 The information given above concerning Sraffa's family and childhood is taken from Naldi (2002).
4 Angelo Sraffa's attention to economic themes was an essential basis of his understanding of commercial law (see his 1894 paper on *La lotta commerciale*, and also Turati and Kuliscioff (1977), 276 where we find a reference to Angelo Sraffa's position on the possibility that factories were subject to workers' control and its relation to competition). For a short curriculum vitae of Angelo Sraffa and a list of his published works see Naldi (2002).
5 According to the information we have been able to gather, Domenico Re (1861–1948) was a socialist, but the main centre of his activity was teaching. He edited some collections of Greek and Latin texts and published lyrics, short novels and essays on literature. Of these texts we have been able to trace a short article on the Italian novelist Alessandro Manzoni (*Emporio Pittoresco*, March 1865) which proves particularly interesting as it tells us

much about how Domenico Re was able to transpose his political passion to his activity as a teacher (our information on Domenico Re was collected at the Archivio Storico of Liceo G. Parini, at the *Comune* of Sartirana Lomellina, and in a conversation with Maria Pia Re).

6   Piero Sraffa followed his family from Parma to Milan in 1906 and from Milan to Turin in 1913. His family moved back to Milan in 1917 but he remained in Turin as a university student.

7   In the end, notwithstanding Salvemini's speech and another speech delivered by Mussolini (who at that time was still a socialist) shortly before, Bonetto was defeated and Bevione won the seat (Spriano, 1958).

8   Letters from Angelo Sraffa to Piero Sraffa, 10 July 1911 and 18 July 1912, Sraffa Papers C300/5, 28.

9   Letter from Piero Sraffa to Giulio Einaudi, 18 July 1949 (CSDPS).

10 Some books by Ciccotti are among those left by Sraffa to Trinity College: *Il tramonto della schiavitù nel mondo antico*, 1899; *La guerra e la pace nel mondo antico*, 1901; *Psicologia del movimento socialista*, 1903; and an Italian edition of writings of Marx, Engels, and Lassalle, in eight volumes, 1914–21 (but volume two, Marx's *Per la critica dell'economia politica*, was probably published in 1903).

11 In the library of Paolo Vita-Finzi we also find two books which testify to his interest in socialism and Marxism: Marx's *Il capitale* and *La democrazia industriale* by Sydney and Beatrice Webb (titles of the Italian translations); on the former Paolo Vita-Finzi wrote 'Torino 5.6.20' and on the latter 'Torino giugno 1920'. A further volume on Marx's political economy – *La teoria del valore di C. Marx* by Arturo Labriola – was bought by Paolo Vita-Finzi's father in 1902, and given to Paolo Vita-Finzi as a present in 1921. To the same period, which is slightly later than the one considered here, belongs also another relevant observation by Paolo Vita-Finzi, who, referring to the years 1920–1, wrote: 'at that time my political opinion was mainly influenced by the lectures of Luigi Einaudi and by the reading of classical economists' (Vita-Finzi, 1989: 139).

12 The books we refer to are: N.G. Pierson, *Trattato di economia politica* (1905 edition); V. Pareto, *Manuale di economia politica. Con una introduzione alla scienza sociale* (1909 edition); G. Valenti, *Principi di scienza economica* (1909 edition); A. Loria, *Corso completo di economia politica* (1910 edition); C. Supino, *Principi di economia politica* (1914 edition); C. Gide, *Principi di economia politica* (1915 edition); A. Segrè, *Manuale di storia del commercio* (1915 edition); G. Ricca Salerno, *Scienza delle finanze* (1916 edition).

13 With reference to this decision Pierangelo Garegnani, in a conversation with the present author, also stressed the role played by Piero Sraffa's love for law as an intellectual discipline and the importance of the fact that Sraffa's father was an eminent jurist. Garegnani also recalled that Piero Sraffa seriously considered the possibility of matriculating in the Faculty of Mathematics.

14 Luigi Einaudi is recorded as *relatore* of Piero Sraffa's thesis but he seems to have discussed its content with him only when it was already written.

15 'I suggested to Sraffa junior that he study for his graduate thesis (which he will be presenting in November) the issue of revaluation of money, and whether it will be in the interest of continental Europe to go back to gold as numeraire. The young man is very bright, and the topic appeals to him

greatly, but the idea of going through it with Loria annoys him: would you have any objections if he discussed it with you? And is there anything to be done to this end? Sraffa junior is in Turin at the moment: if you should wish to tell him anything, write to me and I'll pass it on!'

16 'Sraffa junior, Dr. Piero, is going to London and he would appreciate a letter of introduction to one of the big economists. If you could do one for him, his father would be very grateful to you, too'.

17 'I hope that my son – whom I place under your high Paretian protection – will be back here for your arrival'.

18 A hint of the radicalization of Piero Sraffa's political position may be found in a letter he wrote to Antonio Gramsci in 1923–4: 'The [present] situation bears a striking resemblance to that of 1916–17, as does my state of mind . . . My political opinions remain unchanged – worse, I have become fixed in them, fixed as I was, until 1917, in the pacifist socialism of 1914–15, from which I was shaken out when I made the discovery, after Caporetto and the Russian revolution of November, that it was precisely the worker-soldiers whose hands held the guns' (Sraffa, 1924).

19 During a conversation with the present author, Pierangelo Garegnani recalled that Sraffa mentioned to him a rather unconventional aspect of his activity at the *Ufficio provinciale del lavoro*: he was engaged in coordinating the efforts of cooperatives and of other workers' organizations to defend themselves from fascists' assaults.

20 Unfortunately the file on Piero Sraffa originally kept by that institution has been destroyed, but useful information has been gathered from the minutes of the *Consiglio Provinciale* and from the records of the correspondence (*registri di protocollo*) of the Province of Milan.

21 Detailed reconstruction of this episode in Sraffa's life can be found in Naldi (1998a), 498–9.

22 This definition of the *Partito Socialista Unitario* (P.S.U.) can be found in a line handwritten, most probably by Piero Sraffa, on the first page of the copy of a book on the first year of activity of the Italian fascist government published in 1923 by the P.S.U. now in the library of the *Associazione Sandro Pertini* (Florence). The P.S.U. was formed in October 1922, when the Italian Socialist Party split into a leftwing party (*Partito Socialista Italiano*) and a rightwing one (*Partito Socialista Unitario*).

23 Nino Levi was also president of the abovementioned committee, of which Attilio Cabiati was a member.

24 The resignation was prompted by the fact that the votes of the socialist majority proved insufficient to pass the budget, while the president of the council and the members of the *Deputazione*, following tradition, did not vote (see Naldi, 1998a: 499).

25 We may also recall that in the same period Piero Sraffa had suffered a direct attack by Mussolini, immediately after the publication of his December 1922 article on Italian banking (Sraffa, 1922b). Subsequently, in January 1923, in Dover, he had been denied permission of entry in Britain and before returning to Italy he probably thought it better to wait some months in France (Naldi, 1998a, b). In light of this we may imagine that in 1923–4 Sraffa might have been forced to reduce contacts with the Italian communists (as Meldolesi reported to have been told by Sraffa: Meldolesi, 1982: 110).

26   'The urgent question, taking priority above all else, is that of "freedom" and "order": the others will come later, but for now they cannot even interest the workers. I do not think the Communist Party can succeed at this time in decreasing Fascist pressure: now is the time for democratic opposition and I believe it is necessary to let them do it, and perhaps help them. First of all we need a "bourgeois revolution", which will then allow the development of a worker-oriented politics' (Sraffa, 1924). This letter was reproduced and discussed in detail in Naldi (2000).

27   In this letter Gramsci also noted that, after early contacts with the communist movement in Turin, Sraffa had *remained isolated*, which would explain the views he was expressing (see Naldi, 2000).

28   'I was honoured and pleased by being among the first to hear from your own mouth your great new theory of the credit cycle and the outlines of the social policy which, I hope, will direct progress in the near future' (letter from Sraffa to Keynes, 6 November 1924, JMK/L/S/18-19). This letter was discussed in detail in Naldi (2006).

29   In a draft letter to Kingsley Martin written in Cambridge in October 1927, Sraffa stated: 'I certainly do not want to throw in my lot with the emigrated "rebels", in fact they are much more légitimistes than rebels, and are quite as hopelessly on the shelf as the Russian White émigrés. Besides, they have entirely lost touch with the masses in Italy, that is with the only serious chance of ever overthrowing Fascism' (Sraffa Papers C181/1).

30   'If I could better define my doubts, they would not concern the answer to the question, whether it should be yes or no, but the very nature of the question'.

31   Letter from John M. Keynes to Lydia Lopokova Keynes: 'Monday Nov. 28 1927 . . . On Sunday I had a long talk with Sraffa about his work. It is very interesting and *original* – but I wonder if his class will understand it when he lectures. I think he is now getting on very well. . . . Sraffa is in so much intellectual ferment and excitement about his ideas since I said that I thought there was something in them that he walks very fast up and down his room all day thinking about them' (JMK/PP/45/190/3/268–9, quoted in Naldi, 1998a: 513).

32   On 26 November 1927 Sraffa's diary records this entry: 'K approves 1st eq.' (Sraffa Papers E1; see also Naldi, 1998a); most probably Sraffa was referring to a meeting he had had with Keynes and to the set of *equations* he had conceived describing a no-surplus economy.

33   'Layout of the book. The only way is to make history in reverse, that is: present state of ec.; how it has been reached, showing the difference and the superiority of the old theories. Then, present the theory. If I go in chronol. order, Petty, Physiocr., Ric., Marx, Jevons, Marsh., it is necessary to make first a statement of my theory to explain where I "drive at": which means to present first *all* the theory. And then there is the danger to end up like Marx, who published Cap., and then did not succeed to finish the Histoire des Doctr. And the worse is that he has not succeeded to make himself understood without historical explanation. My purpose is: to present history, which is really the essential thing. To make myself understood: for which what is required is that I go straight to the unknown, from Marshall to Marx, from disutility to material cost.' English translation from Pasinetti, 2001: 152–3. The document is undated but was probably written in November–December 1927.

34   This note continues as follows: 'The typical case of Marx's metaphysics is his statement that "only human labour produces (causes) values", "values are

embodied human energy (crystallized)": there is no doubt that he attached
to it some metaphysical meaning. The extraordinary thing is that the same
metaphysical notion is held by such an anti-Marxian as Cannan (Theories,
p. 380). The metaphysics of the modern economists is that 'a commodity . . . is
the embodiment of measurable efforts and sacrifices' (Marshall, Memorials
126); on the same plane as Marx's 'cristallized labour'. And much more
Clark's notion that marginal distribution being equal to product of each is
'just'. Clark's metaphysics is much more grossolana than Marx's: it is equal to
Proudhon's, Hodgkin's etc who believed (*against* Marx) that since labour produces the whole it must get the whole. All the inquiry about value has always
been (and still is and probably always will be) a purely metaphysical quest.
When the old economists asked for the "causes" or the "measure" of value,
they really were looking – as in fact we are, under the illusion of our equations "determining" value – for the "nature" of value (it is not an accident, as
Cannan . . . says that the word is in A. Smith's title) in the same metaphysical sense in which we look for the nature of "matter" or of "mind". In fact,
we want to "explain" in terms of familiar words or notions (i.e. to which we
are used) the "new" thing that we meet: but when we have got used to them
(as now economists have with prices) we take them for granted and require
no further explanation. The explanation has simply to be "satisfactory" that
is provide the accommodation suited for our mental habits, and prove rest-
ful to the mind – cool down the fever of quest and sate the thirst for explanation' (Sraffa Papers D3/12/4/16).

35 The cover of this document bears the following title, written by Sraffa himself: 'Notes – London, Summer 1927 – (Physical real costs etc.)' (Sraffa Papers
D3/12/3/77). See also document B9/1/16, reproduced and discussed in notes
47 and 51 below.

36 'The "cost of production" principle and the "final utility" principle are
undoubtedly component parts of the one all-ruling law of supply and
demand; each may be compared to one blade of a pair of scissors' (Marshall,
1920, Appendix I.3).

37 Sraffa attributed to Classical and Marginalist (pre-Marshallian) theories also
philosophical, ideological, or political biases, and referred to an anti-landlords
complex in the case of Ricardo's theory of cost-value, and to anti-socialism as
the explanation of the success of the theories based on the concept of utility.
In this sense, the introduction of the concept of equilibrium was depicted by
Sraffa as a shift from politics to science (Sraffa Papers D3/12/3/1, 2, 8, 14, 15;
Garegnani, 2005: 456–7).

38 Heinz Kurz pointed out to me that a note added by Sraffa in a margin of document D3/12/3/44 may anticipate this development.

39 'In normal cases the cost of production of commodities produced competi-
tively – as we are not entitled to take into consideration the causes which
may make it rise or fall – must be regarded as constant in respect of small variations in the quantity produced . . . And so, as a simple way of approaching
the problem of competitive value, the old and now obsolete theory which
makes it depend on the cost of production alone appears to hold its ground as
the best available' (Sraffa, 1926: 540–1, quoted in Garegnani, 2005: 455).

40 'The introduction of the concept of equilibrium . . . brought with it the great
practical advantage that, being to a certain extent compatible with both
schools of thought (since it embodied their doctrines), it closed the old

controversy and brought back the T[heory of] V[alue] from the field of politics to that of economic theory' (Sraffa Papers D3/12/3/8, quoted in Garegnani, 2005: 456).

41 'The idea of interdependence between quantity produced and the cost of production of a commodity produced under competitive conditions is not suggested by experience at all and could not arise spontaneously. It can be said that all classical writers accept implicitly, as an obvious fact, that cost is independent of quantity, and they do not bother to discuss the contrary hypothesis. . . . The importance of the laws of variation of cost in relation to the determination of the price of single commodities has appeared only in consequence of the "fundamental symmetry of the general relations in which demand and supply stand to value" ' (Sraffa, 1925: 325). 'A striking feature of the present position of economic science is the almost unanimous agreement at which economists have arrived regarding the theory of competitive value, which is inspired by the fundamental symmetry existing between the forces of demand and those of supply, and is based upon the assumption that the essential causes determining the price of particular commodities may be simplified and grouped together so as to be represented by a pair of intersecting curves of collective demand and supply. This state of things is in . . . marked contrast with the controversies on the theory of value by which political economy was characterised during the past century' (Sraffa, 1926: 535; see also p. 537).

42 In the *pre-lectures* Sraffa combined the line of his criticism of the construction of Marshallian supply curves which pointed to constant costs as the only consistent way of introducing cost curves in partial equilibrium analysis with a critique of utility as the basis of demand curves which stressed how the latter should rather be considered as founded on empirical relations (Sraffa Papers D3/12/3/19). This evidence, together with a remark in Sraffa's letter to Keynes of 6 June 1927 ('although I believe that Ricardo's assumption is the best available for a simple theory of competition (viz., a first approximation), of course in reality the connection between cost and quantity produced is obvious' – JMK/L/S/21-4) suggests that Sraffa conceived the possibility of treating both demand and supply curves as empirical relations.

43 For the passage referred to see note 40 above. The qualification *to a certain extent* introduced by Sraffa may deserve some attention.

44 'Excuse me for not doing anything for *Lo Stato Operaio* [a communist journal edited by Tasca]; here in 15 days lessons begin, and I am discovering that giving lessons in English is far more difficult than I expected and I am late with the work'.

45 Interestingly enough, a manuscript kept in folder D1/30 of the Sraffa Papers could have originally been part of Sraffa's *pre-lectures* (document D1/30/2/1-2, bearing the title 'Measure of influence of causes on value (anti-symmetry)', was written on the same paper and with the same spacing as the *pre-lectures*) and could have been later moved by Sraffa himself to that folder. In this sense it is also important to note that we do not know if the present order of the documents which form Sraffa's *pre-lectures* is the one they had in summer 1927 (as noted in the manuscript, the page numbers from 4 to 71 were added after Sraffa's death and reflect their order at that time).

46 The *Cambridge University Reporter* of 18 October 1927 announced that the beginning of Sraffa's lectures would be postponed to Lent term.

47 'I put off last term delivering the lectures which I was due to give . . . Unfortunately, however, I find that I am still not ready to give them. This is partly due to the fact that now that I have prepared a certain number of lectures I am convinced that the subject I have chosen is really quite unsuitable. It is also partly due to the fact that I have been engaged on a piece of research which has so much occupied my mind as to interfere with everything else; and also, of course, there are difficulties of language' (Sraffa Papers B9/1/16).

48 'With reference to our conversation yesterday, I should like to state say that, if the General Board were to grant me leave of absence for the present academic year, I would undertake definitely to lecture in October. This would be quite independent of the progress of the work which I mentioned to you. Should lecture, if possible on the theory of value, or else if I could not in the near future overcome the difficulties which have prevented my lecturing on that subject at present, on some subject unconnected with it, which I should be able to prepare and put in writing in the meantime' (Sraffa Papers B9/1/11).

49 'I am sure you greatly exaggerate the standard of lecturing required. It is perfectly certain that you could say a great deal about Value that would be very useful to students, even if you have not yet completely satisfied yourself on all parts of the subject. I think that at least you should try and make a start. If the worst came to the worst, you might have to abandon your course halfway through. But that would be better than not trying at all. You will probably find it very much easier than you expect' (Sraffa Papers C239/2).

50 This is certainly what 'the work which I mentioned to you' refers to, as emerges from another letter from Pigou to Sraffa of January 1928 (Sraffa Papers C239/1, reproduced in Naldi, 1998a: 514).

51 The sentence by Sraffa ('now that I have prepared a certain number of lectures I am convinced that the subject I have chosen is really quite unsuitable') is surprising also because it implies that he had prepared no lectures before October. This sentence may be explained in different ways. On the one hand, it is possible that Sraffa did not consider what we have called *pre-lectures* as lecture notes at all, and that by January 1928 he had prepared a *proper* set of lecture notes which has not survived among his papers. On the other hand it could reflect a statement which had justified his first request to delay the beginning of his lectures with the fact that he had not had enough time to prepare them.

52 Most probably Sraffa's description, in his *pre-lectures*, of Ricardo's theory of value as based on 'the objective, physical necessaries of existence' (Sraffa Papers D3/12/3/47) is the first instance of his use of the term *objective* in the sense considered above.

53 This we may take to have been implicit in a remark by Sraffa, in private correspondence with A. Bose, referring to the case of the determination of prices. In fact, after the publication of *Production of commodities* he wrote that his book was not meant to maintain that demand has no role in price determination: 'You write: "It is a basic proposition of the Sraffa theory that prices are determined exclusively by the physical requirements of production and the social wage-profit division, with consumer demand playing a purely passive role." Never have I said this . . . Nothing, in my view, could be more suicidal than to make such a statement' (Sraffa Papers C32/3).

54 The early history of the Royal Economic Society edition of Ricardo's writings is studied in Gehrke and Kurz (2002: 645–6).

55   According to Sraffa's obituary in the 1984 *Annual Report* of King's College
(possibly by Nicholas Kaldor), the position of librarian of the Marshall
Library was an innovation introduced intentionally at that moment by
Keynes' initiative (King's College, 1984: 75). But from a letter sent by Dennis
Robertson to Piero Sraffa on 6 March 1931 (Sraffa Papers C 264/2) we deduce
that it was Robertson himself who was responsible at that time for the man-
agement of the Marshall Library (just as stated by Keynes in his obituary of
Mary Paley Marshall, Keynes, 1944: 283).

56   On this point see Naldi (2000; 2004).

57   A draft of a letter of resignation dated *Milan, January 9* (Sraffa Papers B7/9/3)
suggests that he had already considered giving up his lectureship in Italy
before November 1931.

58   One may wonder whether the letter sent by Paul Rosenstein Rodan to Luigi
Einaudi on 5 February 1932 related to Sraffa's resignation from his lectureship or from the post of librarian: 'the sensational news here is that Sraffa
resigned from Cambridge, nobody knows why; they know that after his resignation was announced they immediately offered him a position "for life"
with a higher salary, but he wrote directly to the Chancellor of the University
in order to avoid any argument, and did not change his mind' (AFLE; our
translation from the Italian original).

59   Oddly enough, on 12 April 1932, from Stockholm, Joseph Schumpeter wrote
to Sraffa: 'I hear you have definitely resigned, and are going to Chicago'
(Sraffa Papers C281/1).

60   A letter from Angelo Sraffa to Raffaele Mattioli and a letter from Raffaele
Mattioli to Piero Sraffa (Archivio Storico Banca Intesa, Milan) show that in
February 1934 Piero Sraffa received a large amount of money (£428) from his
father. It is also quite likely that during this period Piero Sraffa was able to
obtain an income from the management of a share of his family's resources.
In a letter postmarked Chiasso dated 29 May 1933 Angelo Sraffa mentions
the transfer of some gold, arranged by Piero, who in doing so had anticipated
his father's decision (letter from Angelo Sraffa to Piero Sraffa, Sraffa Papers
C300/2). In a letter postmarked Lugano 28 April 1934 Irma Sraffa tells her
son how some relatives were 'sorry to have only in part carried out your
advice to sell their stocks' (Sraffa Papers C115). In 1979, in a draft letter to the
London office of the Swiss Bank Corporation, Piero Sraffa wrote 'from [1927]
up to the beginning of the war I had a very active account (in stocks and
bonds) with the SBC of London . . . After the war, perhaps due to my age, I
no longer enjoyed speculating on the Market' (Sraffa Papers C1/19, quoted in
Naldi, 2005: 400). An interesting passage on the same subject is also contained in the draft of a letter addressed by Sraffa to Livio Catullo Stecchini,
the oldest son of his friend Nino Levi, a few months after the death of the latter: 'The only thing in which I might be of some little use to you having [had
a good deal of] some experience of [American bonds and stocks] the matter,
is your investments. In a general way, I should strongly advise you to keep
away from speculation, even if (or rather, specially if) you are given "tips" as
to impending rises or falls, however reliable the source' (2 September 1941,
Sraffa Papers A5/1/25, quoted in Naldi, 2005: 400; words within brackets had
been crossed out by Sraffa).

61 None of Sraffa's pocket diaries kept at Cambridge shows any indication that he had been supervising any students in the period between 1933 and 1938 (Sraffa Papers E1-10).

62 In this respect we may also quote some letters written by Keynes shortly before 11 March: 'Piero is in his most defeatistic mood, wants to throw in his hand and leave Cambridge, although really longing to stay; and he won't lift a finger to help me to save the position for him. Even Ludwig [Wittgenstein] says that he is like a troublesome child' (letter from J.M. Keynes to Lydia Lopokova Keynes, 4 March 1935, JMK/PP/45/190/7/28-9, quoted in Skidelsky, 1986: 79); '[Piero] thinks that life in Cambridge is sapping his moral fibre and that he ought to throw himself on the bleak world again' (letter from J.M. Keynes to Lydia Lopokova Keynes, 10 March 1935, JMK/PP/45/190/7/31-2, quoted in Skidelsky, 1986: 79).

63 On this occasion it was Dennis Robertson's turn to be involved. The letters he sent to Sraffa are particularly interesting and are reproduced in the Appendix to this chapter.

64 From a document dated March 1936 we can deduce that in the course of 1935 Piero Sraffa definitively renounced the Rockefeller fellowship he had effectively been granted, albeit informally (Rockefeller Archive Center).

Appendix

Two letters from Dennis Robertson to Piero Sraffa relating to his acceptance of the post of Assistant Director of Research.

Trinity, 1.5.35
My dear Piero,
I have continued in touch with the G.B. [General Board] since our conversation. It seems quite clear that they share your view (and mine) that the contact with research students (in the extended sense which you explained to me) is to be by far the major part of the proposed post, the Librarianship as such being a relatively subordinate affair.

Where they differ from you is in their estimate of the efficacy, for the purpose of initiating contacts which might be developed in the main elsewhere, of your being known to be accessible, during 1 hour per day on x days per week, in the Library, – or rather in the Faculty Home, i.e. either in the main Library itself as in your Librarian's room at the threshold, according as convenient to you at the moment. I.e. the purpose of the proposed conditions is not to magnify the Librarianship side of the job, but to contribute (in their view) to the effective fulfilment of the 'directorship' side.

My own view, for what it is worth, is that some arrangement of the kind would be likely to do something in bringing to your notice a certain number of undergraduates who would be too shy or too slack to find their way to your rooms (even if you succeed in finding as central ones as St. Edward's Passage) in the first instance, and who might well not be members of Keynes' Club or, even if they were, not find a chance to speak to you there. And if so, it would be, from the University's point of view, a good investment of some small part of your time, even though it led to some moments of irksomeness for you, and seemed at first to bring in small results. For, as I said on Monday, it is evidently a case in which either a vicious or a virtuous circle might easily develop! (You know how easily young men are put off by even one fruitless journey, and how apt to generalise, – 'Prof Pigou seems to be always in the Lakes, Prof. Hilton seems to be always broadcasting, – Mr. Sraffa seems to be always in bed, or else talking to Bulgarian professors')

I don't know at all what the G.B. will finally decide. I've tried tactfully to hint that I hope they won't make rules just because they are rules without thinking out clearly what purpose they are intended to serve: and I should like, if I may, equally tactfully to hint to you that I hope you won't reject rules just because they are rules, without considering carefully whether they may not serve some end! I think it is conceivable that the final offer will contain a stipulation that you should notify, at the beginning of each term, your intention to be present

in the Library Building for one (specified) hour on x (specified) days per week, –
this condition to be reconsidered in the light of experience after (say) two years.
If this should be so, I hope very much that you will feel able to accept it.

I think, by the way, that I misinformed you about the tenure of the proposed
appointment. Like other ass.t-directorships of research, it is for five years in the
first instance. This, I think, is notional in view of the novelty of the post.

Please forgive the formal and frigid style of this letter, – the result of an
attempt, not to be dictatorial, but both to get my own mind clear and to make
it so to you!

Yours ever
Dennis Robertson
(Sraffa Papers B 9/3/2-3)

Trinity, 3.5.35
My dear Piero,
The G.B. have sent me a copy of their letter to you of today. I feel sure that in
it 'Research Students' is to be read in the sense explained by you to me and by
me to them, viz to include 'serious-minded undergraduates'.

I hope very much you will accept. I have got bunged up with engagements
tomorrow up to 7 p.m., but would be v. glad to come and see you after that in
case you care to think it over again. Or would you come and see me then, and
stay and dine in Hall at 8.0!

The Faculty Board is to be asked to report on the working of the scheme after
2 years experience.

Yours ever
Dennis Robertson
(Sraffa Papers B 9/3/1)

3
The Collaboration between Keynes and Robertson during the Second World War: A Perspective from the National Archives

*Eleonora Sanfilippo**

To my father

1.   Introduction

The relationship between John Maynard Keynes and Dennis Robertson has been widely examined in the literature,[1] and three periods are commonly distinguished: intensive scientific partnership in the 1920s, a drift apart following the publication of the *Treatise on Money* and widening during work on the *General Theory*, and finally renewed collaboration during the Second World War.[2]

The Robertson–Keynes scientific cooperation started very early, in 1913 to be precise, on the occasion of Robertson's Fellowship Dissertation and relative discussions on business fluctuations, and continued throughout the 1920s. During that period they influenced each other greatly in their respective works (see Robertson 1915, 1922, 1926, 1928a and 1928b; and Keynes 1923, 1925, 1930). In 1931, for theoretical and personal reasons their paths started to diverge, the drift apart culminating in the mid-1930s during the drafting and publication of the *General Theory*, which made it clear that they belonged to opposite camps. When, in 1938, Robertson decided to leave Cambridge for the London School of Economics (LSE), everyone in the Cambridge Faculty of Economics was convinced it was the right decision, given the difficult climate, in particular, between Robertson and Keynes's disciples. From 1941, Keynes and Robertson returned to intensive cooperation in the context of their common work at the Treasury.

A fundamental source of knowledge on their activities (and relations) during this third period is the material – including letters, notes and memoranda – they exchanged, which is conserved at the British National Archives.

This chapter uses this (mostly unpublished) material[3] to clarify Robertson's role in the crucial years in which Keynes engaged in various fields, ranging from war financing and national income accounting to international trade policy and, above all, shaping and building a 'new' international monetary order.

Section 2 provides a brief description of the kinds of documents kept in the National Archives.[4] Section 3 examines some selected examples (mostly from the unpublished correspondence) to show: (i) how Robertson supported Keynes in his work at the Treasury; (ii) what their relations were like in that period; (iii) what kind of collaboration they developed in those peculiar circumstances; and (iv) how distant some of their theoretical positions remained. Section 4 provides an analysis of the possible reasons for their renewed partnership.

2. The material conserved at the National Archives and its importance

Almost all the correspondence between Keynes and Robertson in the National Archives[5] dates from the period 1941–4.[6] In those years both economists were at the Treasury: Robertson, from the outbreak of war (September 1939), as a 'temporary' civil servant, and Keynes, (from July 1940), as a member of the Chancellor's Consultative Council.[7] Perusal of this archival material clearly shows that during that time they collaborated intensively on all the major issues in which Keynes was involved: from drafting the Clearing Union Plan to the Bretton Woods agreements; from analysis of the British external position to the Lend-Lease negotiations with the Dominions and the US; from trade policy to foreign investment, public finance, and even diplomatic strategies, to offer but a few examples.

The documents considered in this analysis are all kept in the Treasury Series T 247 'Papers of Lord Keynes' (which contains 130 files) and amount to at least 112 exchanges between Keynes and Robertson, but there are other Series,[8] also relevant to this correspondence, in which other material could be found.[9] The letters are not included in a single file of the above Series but are scattered (together with other kinds of documents) through many subsections or files, according to the subject dealt with, the circumstances in which they were exchanged and the extent to which they circulated inside and outside the Treasury offices. Quite often they also took the form of 'circular' letters or notes, which went through a series of correspondents[10] besides Keynes and Robertson, each inserting handwritten comments or suggestions in the margin of the same sheet, testifying the exchanges of ideas and views within the Treasury.

As far as the relationship between Keynes and Robertson is concerned, the importance of this material mainly lies in showing the fundamental role that Robertson played in that period as careful reader, commenter and reviser of Keynes's work – as we shall see below – notwithstanding the marked theoretical opposition that divided them as from the early 1930s. The second relevant point is that their positions on (national and international) economic policy appear less distant than those on economic theory, and this element seems to have contributed to their renewed collaboration during the war.

3.   Keynes and Robertson working at the Treasury

An account of all the subjects dealt with in this correspondence is beyond the scope of this work. In the following paragraphs, however, we shall be looking into some specific exchanges – arranged by subject and dates – particularly telling of the kind of everyday collaboration that Keynes and Robertson achieved during their common experience at the Treasury.

The first exchange we consider concerns the preparation of the 1941 Budget, the second deals with the British external position for the Lend-Lease negotiations in 1942–3, the third is on the drafting of the Clearing Union Plan for an international monetary unit in 1941–2, the fourth is on trade policy in 1942–3, and the last on the negotiations for the Bretton Woods agreements in 1943–4.

3.1   The 1941 National Income White Paper

In two articles published in *The Times* on 14 and 15 November 1939, Keynes (1939a) approached the problem of how to finance the war without excessively reducing the reserves in foreign currencies and increasing the level of prices. Keynes's suggestion (which is more or less the same as what he proposed a few months later in his book *How to Pay for the War*) was compulsory savings, which had – he held – the great advantage of avoiding inflation and, at the same time, favouring a better redistribution of revenues. This proposal came in for immediate criticism from colleagues and politicians,[11] to which Keynes replied with another article[12] in *The Times* on 28 November (Keynes 1939b) and with a paper – 'The income and fiscal potential of Great Britain' – and a supplementary note in the *Economic Journal* respectively in December 1939 and March 1940 (Keynes 1939c, 1940b).

One of the problems related to the above question concerned exact and reliable estimation of the National Income – which was also fundamental for decisions about the measures of economic policy to be implemented by the government. This is why in June 1940, when Keynes was invited to join the Treasury, James Meade and Richard Stone were entrusted with the task of producing official calculations for the national income, aggregate consumption and voluntary savings for the years 1938 and 1940. The result was ready by December 1940 in the form of a statistical document on 'National Income, Savings and Consumption'. At the beginning of 1941 Keynes, on the basis of the above statistics, estimated the budgetary gap at 450/500 million pounds sterling.[13] In March 1941 a White Paper entitled 'Analysis of the sources of war finance',[14] prepared by Stone and Meade and revised by Keynes, drawn up to accompany the 1941 April Budget, was ready for circulation. On 23 March 1941 Robertson, who did not fail to understand the importance of this document, sent Keynes a long note. The comments were, as so often in the case of Robertson, very much to the point and well-founded, moved by a constructive spirit in the sole interest of improving the paper. He wrote:

> 1. The question arises, does not the paper fall between two stools? It departs from official precedent in presenting estimates of quantities (such as 'net disinvestment') which are both difficult to define and difficult to evaluate. But it does not, as an article in a learned journal[15] would be expected to do, either examine the conceptual difficulties involved or disclose in any detail the basis of the estimates adopted. Still less does it discuss the economic implications of the statistical results which it purports to establish. 2. To take this last point first. The crucial proposition of the paper is that the annual rate of 'voluntary' personal savings has risen from £ 150 m.[illion] in 1938 to £ 400 m.[illion] in the first year of war and £ 700 m.[illion] in recent months. This might mean either that the official economy campaign has been overwhelmingly successful or that our feet are firmly planted on the high road to inflation. Which does it mean? The paper is silent.
>
> (TNA: PRO T 247/48, in CWK XXII: 338)

These comments made a positive contribution to the final version of the White Paper, which appeared in the second week of April 1941, and also mark the renewed role of Robertson as a careful reader of and commentator on Keynes's work, as had already been the case in the 1920s and, to some extent, in the 1930s.[16] Through the last week of March and the early days of April 1941 their exchanges, relating to imaginary examples and calculations on national accounts and propensities to save and consume, became very intensive (CWK XXII: 342–7). Keynes took Robertson's objections to and estimations on these technical aspects of economic policy very seriously, as he had in the past for economic theory.[17]

3.2   The British external position, 1942–3

Starting in summer 1940, when France was occupied by the Nazis, Keynes's attention began to shift from the domestic to the external side of war financing. The British financial position was deteriorating and the most pressing problem was now to find the resources necessary to sustain the war effort through the country's international relations. At the same time, Keynes was beginning to approach the question of the future pattern of the post-war economic world (Moggridge, 1992: 670). Analysis of the British external position as the benchmark of the Lend-Lease negotiations with the Dominions and the US and drafting a post-war financial and monetary set of international agreements lay at the heart of Keynes's preoccupations. With respect to both issues, which saw Keynes actively engaged through direct involvement in diplomatic efforts in Washington and the writing of various memoranda and official and unofficial papers, Robertson's contribution can by no means be taken as marginal. As this correspondence clearly shows, Robertson's help to Keynes took many different forms. It consisted not only in careful reading and revising of Keynes's documents but also in providing statistical calculations and revisions of Keynes's estimates, shedding light on aspects neglected in Keynes's analyses and finding arguments in support of positions other than Keynes's. In other words, Robertson appears to have been a perfect *alter ego* of Keynes. The marked independence that Robertson showed in his opinions and judgements proved enormously useful to Keynes, who was engaged on several fronts (within and without the British government) defending the soundness of his positions, and suggesting measures of domestic and international economic policy. It is something more than an impression drawn from the correspondence that Keynes 'used' Robertson as a rigorous and competent reader, also for testing the level of 'persuasion' his papers contained.[18]

One example of Robertson's independent and critical attitude can be seen in the analysis of the question of dollar balances. On 10 September 1942[19] a Memorandum on 'Our prospective dollar balances' by Keynes was circulated within the Treasury (CWK XXIII: 243–52). It was a secret document – one of the various studies elaborated within the Treasury as a benchmark for the Lend-Lease negotiations with the US – and included an analysis of the stock and future level of British reserves (both in gold and dollars). Keynes raised the question of how much information it was expedient to give to the American Congress about the effective magnitude of the British reserves. According to his estimation, the amount of both gold and dollar reserves at the end of 1942 could result in a value between 1,500 and 2,000 million dollars, thanks to the reserves transferred from the Dominions to Great Britain and those obtained through the sale of the British assets in US corporations (as in the case of the Viscosa Corporation).[20] Keynes's main preoccupation was that this increase in British liquid assets could give the US public an erroneous impression of the true financial condition of their main ally, inducing a less generous attitude in US relief policy (CWK XXIII: 245). To this document Robertson replied with a letter dated 15 September 1942 (TNA: PRO T 247/74), in which he commented that Keynes was, on the one hand, in favour of a more reticent attitude towards the US Treasury while, on the other – as Robertson put it – 'he holds that it is desirable to adopt certain expedients to <u>damp down</u> the growth in our reserves . . . . These expedients are two in number, viz: (i) the retention, so far as possible, of other quick assets in preference to reserves . . .; (ii) the avoidance of measures which will increase our reserves and liabilities . . . by equal amounts, and the taking of certain measures which will reduce them by equal amounts' (*ibid.*, underlining in the text). Robertson expressed a different opinion, stressing the reasons in favour of a contrary policy and also singling out an element of self-contradiction between the strategy advocated by Keynes and his own Clearing Union design: 'Does not the preliminary ventilation of the Clearing Union plan afford an opportunity for frankly linking up our desire to possess adequate reserves with our anxiety to put ourselves in a position to work a relatively "free" post-war system (in accordance with American desires) rather than with our immediate war-time needs?' (*ibid.*).

In the letter Robertson also attacked Keynes's idea that it would have been 'politically safer', in any case, for Great Britain to increase its reserves (in response to its increased level of liabilities towards foreign countries) in the form of gold instead of dollars. Two arguments were at the bottom of Keynes's claim: first that 'the US Treasury might find it difficult to justify to Congress a considerable increase in our dollar holdings, even though they themselves accepted the reasonableness of an increase in our total reserves in relation to our liabilities' (CWK XXIII: 248); second that the American public had the general conviction – as Keynes puts it – 'that our gold reserves are primarily our affair and our dollar reserves, if not primarily, at least significantly, theirs' (CWK XXIII: 256). Robertson pointed out:

> I cannot help doubting whether ordinary American opinion (e.g. in Congress) distinguishes at all clearly between the two [gold and dollar reserves], or has really accepted the principle that our gold is not

available in any circumstances for shipment to the United States. But in any case our own assertion of the principle has rested largely on the plea that our current purchases of gold are required to fulfil our actual and prospective liabilities to third countries. If we succeeded in arranging a substantial proportion of these gold liabilities to third countries in dollars, should we not be cutting the ground from under our own principle, and running the risk of such acceptance as it has met with in America being withdrawn?

(letter 15 September 1942, TNA: PRO T 247/74,
underlining in the text)

These remarks, which fully reflect Robertson's analytical reasoning, were replied to by Keynes in his supplementary note (CWK XXIII: 252–62). It is difficult to say whether, in this as in other similar cases, Keynes changed his opinion as a consequence of Robertson's criticisms: what is sure is that Keynes considered Robertson's to be valid objections, calling for an answer and some modifications at least in the way in which his point of view was presented. Very often Robertson, when examining Keynes's work, had an extraordinary capacity to put his finger on the weak-point in the argumentation and the aspects of Keynes's analysis more open to criticism. We can well understand, therefore, that in this respect it was in Keynes's interest to take Robertson's critiques into very serious consideration.

On the other hand, Keynes's positive estimation of Robertson's capacities was not limited to appreciation of his ability to criticize other people's work but also regarded his skills as an excellent writer of technical documents, as, for example, the following exchange shows. In March 1943 Robertson sent Keynes a very detailed paper on the 'Mechanics of the Canadian Aid', which examined in depth the main aspects of the British/Canadian position. Keynes had the possibility to appreciate the quality of Robertson's work. He wrote on 24 March 1943: 'What has happened to your excellent paper on this [The Mechanics of the Canadian Aid]? I hope it is being sent as it stands to Canada. If I were . . . Malcolm MacDonald [UK High Commissioner in Canada 1941–6] I should hand it over to the Canadians exactly as it stands, with all its excellent airs and graces' (TNA: PRO T 247/126).

3.3   Drafting the Clearing Union plan, 1941–2

According to Moggridge (1992: 671), in September 1941 Keynes was able in just a few days to write a plan (known afterwards as 'Keynes's plan') for a post-war International Currency Union. At the end of November, Keynes presented the second draft of his plan, which was greatly appreciated

within the Treasury. Robertson greeted Keynes's proposal with extraordinary enthusiasm, declaring that 'the spirit of Burke and Adam Smith is
on earth again . . .' (letter 27 November 1941, TNA: PRO T 247/33, in
CWK XXV: 67). The scheme was based on a very simple idea, even though
the clauses and provisions for the implementation of it were highly complex. The idea consisted in the creation of an International Clearing Bank
which – according to the 'principle of banking' – was to work as a Central
Bank for the National Central Banks of the member countries. The latter
should have their deposits and reserves in the Clearing Bank, which should
operate as a compensation institution, serving for the regulation of international monetary payments. Two aspects seemed particularly original: the
creation of an international currency (the 'bancor') issued by the International Bank and the involvement of creditor countries in the adjustment process.[21] In December Robertson, examining the redraft, advanced
this criticism: 'the scheme is *prima facie* much weakened by the dropping
of the provision in earlier versions for the automatic surrender of credit
balances above a certain sum' (letter 22 December 1941, TNA: PRO T
247/116). To which Keynes replied:

> I do not disagree at all with your point here and had not meant to lay
> myself open to this criticism. I will be more careful of the way in
> which I word the next revise. . . . I dropped with great reluctance my
> previous proposal for automatic surrender of credit balances, but did
> so to meet criticisms from more than one source. My most vehement
> critic was Roy [Harrod], and he is still very discontented because I have
> retained the feature of taxing credit balances at 1 or, in some cases, at
> 2 per cent. I am told both by him and by Waley[22] that I ought to drop
> this too, since it is unfamiliar and will provoke prejudice.
> (letter 29 December 1941; TNA: PRO T 247/116)

Robertson's opinion was that the existence of an automatic mechanism of
surrender of credit balances (above a certain level) could enhance the effec-
tiveness and credibility of the collaboration of creditor countries in the
international process of re-adjustment of balance of payments. To this
point Robertson attached fundamental importance.[23] Indeed, a few years
later, commenting on the international set of monetary regulations which
came out of Bretton Woods, he considered the lack of this provision a
particularly regrettable weakness in the agreements, and one that could
seriously compromise the success of a plan aiming at world financial and
monetary stabilization (Robertson, 1948: 222). It is worth noting that in the
final version of Keynes's plan (of April 1943) a mechanism of penalization

for creditor countries – even though much weakened as compared with the first draft (see Moggridge, 1986: 71–2) – was eventually included.

On 30 December 1941 Robertson replied, raising, among others, the following point: 'In substance I am really in greater danger of disagreement (as you might expect) on grounds of the scheme not being strict enough on the deficiency countries, making it perhaps too easy for them to indulge in the Forbidden Tricks,[24] and ruling out (as I read it) by implication . . . the only real remedy, viz. deflation of money incomes' (TNA: PRO T 247/116). The problem was that in Keynes's Clearing Union scheme no real obligation was contemplated for countries with an adverse balance of payments to reduce and eliminate their disequilibrium. This, Robertson held, meant leaving them the possibility to postpone or, worse, fail to apply a serious and rigorous anti-inflationary policy, the only one – in his opinion – which could ensure the elimination of external imbalances. As had already happened in the 1930s in the case of Robertson's criticisms of the *General Theory* – for example, the undue emphasis Keynes placed on the speculative motive for demanding money in the liquidity preference theory, the 'exceptional' character of the condition of underemployment equilibrium (Robertson, 1936: 168–91) – here, too, Robertson immediately detected the major source of future controversies, namely the inflationary bias that Keynes's Plan would frequently be faulted for in the subsequent debate of 1943–4.

In reality, the question of the Clearing Union Plan and in general of a set of international regulations binding the member countries in their economic policies was quite a complex one and divided the interested parties, both interventionists and supporters of *laissez-faire*. As Toye (2003: 181 and ff.) has underlined, for those who called for an active role of the state in the economy (such as the Labour Party or a Liberal like Keynes himself) there was a contradiction between the favouring of state intervention at a national level and the provision of a sort of delegation of power by the state to certain supranational authorities which were to regulate international trade and financial payments. The same could also apply to the upholders of economic liberalism (like Robertson) who adhered to Keynes's Plan, viewed as a means to implement and favour a free-trade environment. It is not paradoxical, in light of these considerations, that Robertson, as we have seen above, criticized the Clearing Union Plan for not being strict enough towards the countries with foreign imbalances – for not bringing sufficient obligations to bear on national governments, that is.

Robertson's contribution is also evident in the subsequent re-drafting of the plan. The letter dated 7 August 1942 from Robertson to Keynes

(TNA: PRO T 247/33) contains some comments on Keynes's draft of 4 August 1942. Comparison between the 4 August and 28 August 1942 versions of the Plan – which finally went to Harry Dexter White[25] (see CWK XXV: 449–52) – clearly shows that most of Robertson's suggested alterations were in fact introduced in the text, as Keynes himself recognised in his reply of 10 August 1942: 'Dear Dennis, thank you for taking so much trouble about my Clearing Union draft. I am adopting all your miscellaneous suggestions, which are improvements in every case. . . . The real objection, I take it, is concerned with the inflationary possibilities of the system. But this I call attention to and admit on page 24' (TNA: PRO T 247/33). In Robertson's letter a further theoretical point of opposition was also raised:

> My discomfort is doubtless bound up with my having a somewhat different 'slant' from Lord Keynes (and Mr. Harrod) on the whole vexed subject of the strength of the alleged forces tending (after the preliminary period of scarcity generally thought likely) to make for chronic world depression.[26] Without wishing to attempt to impose this slant on the paper as a whole, I indicate below certain changes which would go a considerable, though not the whole, way to remove my discomfort.
>
> (7 August 1942, TNA: PRO T 247/33)

Robertson's suggested changes in this case were only partially accepted by Keynes.

3.4 Trade policy, 1942–3

Their collaboration also saw some moments of difficulty and keen confrontation, not to mention the well-known episode which took place in summer 1944 over interpretation of Article VIII of the Bretton Woods Agreements.[27] Another significant episode came at the end of 1942 and the beginning of 1943, on the occasion of the circulation of the Overton Committee Draft Report.[28] This was based mainly on a memorandum drawn up by James Meade on 4 August 1942 on an 'International Commercial Union', in response to the trade requirements in Article VII of the Lend-Lease Agreement, which set out the clause of non-discrimination in trade towards US commodities and which, in the American intention, would bring about a progressive reduction arriving at elimination of the 'imperial preference' in favour of British products (Skidelsky, 2000: 236–8). Meade's Plan was also framed in the direction of liberalising trade between the two countries: it established (i) that all members of the Union would grant most-favoured-nation treatment to each other, with tariff preferences limited to 10 per cent; (ii) that quantitative import controls be outlawed except in emergencies; (iii) that export subsidies be limited to 10 per cent below domestic prices. Even though this plan was well accepted by the majority of the Overton Committee, it came under heavy fire from Hubert Henderson, and Keynes, on that occasion, was in full agreement with him. His fundamental point was that this plan would have enormously damaged the post-war recovery of Great Britain (see letter from Keynes to Waley, 31 December 1942, TNA: PRO T 247/2; see also Pressnell, 1986: 103–5). Robertson, on the contrary, apart from a matter of a few details that, he believed, could be improved (letter from Robertson to Keynes, 18 December 1942, TNA: PRO T 247/2), showed a favourable attitude towards Meade's plan, which was, from a theoretical point of view, firmly grounded on the doctrine of free trade. A debate followed in the Treasury between protectionist and anti-protectionist views, but favour towards the plan eventually waned. Notwithstanding Keynes's opposition to the plan, Robertson did not stop his campaign for elimination of the protectionist measures in British trade policy, showing here his independence of judgement from Keynes. He courageously denounced the ambiguities of his own country, especially towards its main ally-competitor, the US. In a note on 'Quantitative Restriction of Imports' sent to Keynes on 19 February 1943 he wrote:

> As I understand it, Treasury opinion is hardening in favour of claiming the right to employ import restriction, for an indefinite period and on an indefinite scale, without international sanction or consultation. It is also tending towards planning to use this right for the purpose of establishing, in the domain of the manufacture, a regime of autarky far out-distancing anything ever contemplated, by us or by any non-totalitarian country, in the chaos of the 1930s. Simultaneously we are preparing to broadcast among the European Allies a document which has long been in the hands of the Americans, and which treats quantitative restriction of imports as one of the more dislocating forms of protection, recourse to which should in general be abjured in all commercial treaties (Proposal for an International Clearing Union, p. 11). I do not see how, when our intentions become known, we are to escape indignant charges of hypocrisy and double dealing.
>
> (TNA: PRO T 247/2)

Evident, here, is the theoretical distance between Robertson and Keynes. Robertson was (and remained) fundamentally a 'neoclassical' economist, believing in free trade and perfect competition, viewing state intervention – in all fields – as a temporary measure, justifiable only in specific circumstances. Keynes, on the contrary, had a general bias in favour of management of the economy by the public authorities, and did not regard certain protectionist measures introduced by his own country as a scandal, especially given the expectations of difficult economic conditions at the end of the war. Secondly, according to Keynes – as he put it very clearly one year later replying to Robertson on a similar point – there was a sharp distinction between 'currency multilateralism' and 'commercial multilateralism':

> the former does not imply or require the latter. Indeed, currency multilateralism has been in the past the normal state of affairs without in fact being accompanied by commercial multilateralism. The one no more implies the other in the future than it has done in the past. The fact that those people who have a strong sympathy for the one are likely to have a strong sympathy for the other also seems to me to be beside the point.
>   (letter 31 May 1944, TNA: PRO T 247/35, in CWK XXVI: 25)

Finally, as far as Robertson's complaint about a British double-dealing attitude was concerned, Keynes flatly rejected it, especially because it was clear to him that while a new system of economic relations in the world had been taking shape, at the same time an undeclared 'war' against the economic predominance of the US was being prepared. In this perspective, his positions were perfectly coherent with both aims.

3.5   Bretton Woods: preparation and negotiations, 1943–4

Study of the correspondence dating to 1943 shows how extensive Robertson's contribution was to the revision and improvement of the final draft of the Clearing Union Plan (up to the publication of Keynes's White Paper on 7 April 1943), and to analysis of it and comparison with Harry Dexter White's scheme (the 'Stabilization Fund'). This comparison between the two plans eventually led – one year later – to the publication of the 'Joint Statement by Experts on the Establishment of an International Monetary Fund', the benchmark of the Bretton Woods negotiations.

Moggridge (CWK XXV: 215) reconstructs the steps in Keynes's work on the two schemes thus: 'When the Treasury in London received another revision of White's Stabilisation Fund, the eighth re-draft of the proposal Keynes had first received from Sir Frederick Phillips the previous summer, Keynes turned to a comparison of the Clearing Union and the Stabilization Fund, with a first draft[29] dated 18 February and a revised version . . . that went into circulation on 1 March'. Between the two versions there was a letter from Keynes to Robertson (dated 19 February 1943, TNA: PRO T 247/30C), in which Keynes thanked his colleague for his help in the analysis of these documents. Keynes submitted to him his first draft and received back useful comments, which were renewed by Robertson on the occasion of the 1 March version of the document (see letters 3 and 5 March 1943, TNA: PRO T 247/30A, in CWK XXV: 228–31).

After the publication of Keynes's Plan as the Clearing Union White Paper, which again benefited from Robertson's remarks, Robertson left Great Britain as a member of the British Treasury Delegation in Washington. From May to July 1943 their exchanges were particularly intensive, mainly regarding the issue of the comparison between the American and British plans, their weaknesses and strengths, their internal coherence and, to some extent, also their compatibility. In fact, starting from April 1943 until April 1944 (when the *Joint Statement* finally appeared) all the efforts of the British (but also American) officials were devoted, at the same time: (i) to analysing both texts in order to find errors and difficulties in the other camp; (ii) to developing a common basis upon which they might start drafting a single 'compromise' text; (iii) to waging a political and technical 'battle' to impose their own respective points of views as far as possible.

In this context Robertson's contribution to Keynes's work was, once again, very important, in at least three major respects. First of all, Robertson had access to the American officials' opinions, which he faithfully reported to Keynes, giving him direct insight into the political framework and general moods prevailing in the US Treasury, as for example when he described a conversation he had had with Mr. Bernstein,[30] which Keynes found very interesting and illuminating with regard to the American point of view (letters 28 June and 19 July 1943, TNA: PRO T 247/81, in CWK XXV: 300–4 and letter from Robertson to Keynes 5 July 1943, TNA: PRO T 247/81). Robertson also liaised with US academic environments, and in particular with Jacob Viner, who, for his part, had close relations with US Treasury and Federal Reserve Bank officers. On 24 July Robertson wrote to Keynes:

> My dear Maynard, I had another talk with Viner yesterday. He reverted to the theme of the last pages of his letter to you, i.e. to the difficulty he experiences in discussing the Monetary Plans, notably in banking circles, owing to his uncertainty as to how far they are intended to take care of the non-recurrent, but also non-relief, immediate post-war needs of various countries (e.g. the U.K.). He says that banking opinion is very nervous of being committed to dealing with the latter on the 'anonymous' basis of the Plans (however appropriate that may be

for dealing with 'normal' fluctuations in the balance of payments) – regarding them rather as a proper subject for definite medium or long term loans; and I think he shares that opinion.

(letter 24 July 1943, DHR papers C/2/8/19)

Secondly, Robertson took a hand in the subsequent redrafts of Keynes's paper on comparison between the two plans. In April 1943, in fact, a revised version of the American plan was published. At the end of the month Keynes wrote a note on it (CWK XXV: 258–60), which was the occasion for a long discussion with Robertson on the technical aspects (see letters from 24 May to 14 June 1943, TNA: PRO T 247/30A, in CWK XXV: 287–99). Robertson raised well-founded questions with great competence, winning Keynes's approval and confidence, as can be seen, for instance, in the letter of 1 July 1943 (TNA: PRO T 247/30B) in which Keynes – sending him a further note on the Clearing Union and Stabilization Fund (dated 29 June 1943), wrote:

> My dear Dennis . . . I have been making a first shot at a synthesis of C.[learing]U.[nion] and S.[tabilization]F.[und] in the light of the latest telegrams and other information with which you have kept us so fully and magnificently posted. . . . I send you this copy, purely for your private eye, so as to give more of a chance for any criticisms you may have to reach us in good time.[31]

Thirdly, Robertson had an important role in direct negotiations in Washington for the preparation of the Joint Statement and the Plan for an International Bank (see Moggridge, 1992: 742; Skidelsky, 2000: 300–1). When, in September 1943, Keynes arrived in Washington for confrontation with the Americans about the two plans, many aspects were debated and discussed. Robertson was also part of the British Treasury delegation and in this capacity participated in all the discussions and meetings with US Treasury officials, which eventually, on 9 October 1943, gave birth to a document which took into consideration both points of view in all cases of disagreement.[32] In December 1943 – when Keynes had already returned to London – Robertson provided his comments on the subsequent version of the *Joint Statement* drawn up by Keynes (letter 6 December 1943, TNA: PRO T 247/30B).

Meanwhile the preparatory work for the Bretton Woods Conference went ahead. When Keynes prepared a memorandum 'Conference on International Monetary Fund', once again it was Robertson who provided a detailed list of comments (letter 8 June 1944, TNA: PRO T 247/28), which helped Keynes anticipate the possible reactions to his own work.

4.   What is at the bottom of the Keynes–Robertson wartime partnership?

Analysis of the material conserved in the National Archives reveals the considerable extent and systematic nature of their cooperation during the war: indeed, without the help of the archival sources it would have been impossible to appreciate the real proportions of this collaboration. This appears all the more surprising if we remember the deep theoretical and personal rift that divided them in October 1938, when Robertson, after a long period of difficult relations with Keynes and Keynes's disciples, and after exclusion from a research project under Keynes's direction,[33] decided to leave Cambridge for the Cassel Chair 'with special reference to banking' at the LSE.[34]

A factor which doubtless played a role in their rapprochement was the sense of loyalty to their country, which both economists felt particularly keenly during the war, although this alone cannot suffice to explain the manner and intensity of their renewed collaboration, as is suggested below.

In that period Keynes's attention was attracted by national and international aspects of economic policy, as well as urgent and concrete problems calling for solutions in terms of state intervention and regulations. In this context, as we have seen, he regularly requested Robertson's advice on the more crucial questions, evidently considering him a valuable collaborator for analysis of all these aspects. What seems more likely is that they found a common ground on economic policy prescriptions in the specific context of the war, notwithstanding their theoretical distance. In fact, the issues in which Keynes was involved in the 1940s were largely related to immediate measures of economic policy and far-reaching questions of designing international economic institutions, and in this respect their positions were not as distant as in matters of theory. On the role of the state, too, Robertson (like Alfred Marshall and Arthur Pigou) had a very pragmatic position, and was not totally against 'managed' economies but claimed that government intervention had to be limited to cases in which economic fluctuations during the cycle take on abnormal amplitude; outside this hypothesis, 'appropriate' fluctuations of business activities have to be allowed for by the economic authorities because they are the only means through which the system can adjust (Robertson, 1926).

In the 1948 edition of his book *Money* he wrote, more explicitly: '. . . it is, in the author's view, unlikely that the monetary system will ever be able to cope unaided with a trade slump . . . as efficiently as with a trade boom . . . . It is likely to require the assistance of a more powerful ally – the Government of the country itself' (Robertson, 1948: 178).

Furthermore, the fundamental point in Robertson's opposition to the theoretical framework of the *General Theory* – besides their contrasting theories of the interest rate and their differences in methods of analysis – had to do with the existence of a permanent condition of underemployment equilibrium in the economic system. Robertson (1936: 174; 1948: 214) denied this pessimistic conclusion reached by Keynes (which constituted the theoretical justification for 'permanent' state intervention), in favour of the 'old' idea of business fluctuations, according to which the system oscillates around a position of full employment equilibrium. In the war economy, however, the problems to be faced by the state appeared completely different from underemployment or insufficient aggregate (or effective) demand: on the contrary, there was the pressure of high demand from the strategic war sectors that, summed with the demand for consumption goods, could create inflation (Keynes, 1940a). So the real danger was that of an excessive use of a given productive capacity – a *scenario* in sharp contrast with the situation assumed in the *General Theory*. The risk of high inflation in a context of high aggregate demand found Robertson (1922, 1928a, 1928b) particularly sensitive, and it is not surprising that he was on the same side as Keynes.[35] We may, therefore, conclude that the particular historical circumstances in which they worked favoured their collaboration.

It has also been argued (Hirai, 2004) that, as far as social policy was concerned, leading Cambridge economists (like Pigou, Keynes, Robertson and Ralph Hawtrey) had many points in common, in the sense that they all shared a position of so-called 'Liberal Interventionism' – as Robertson (1947) put it. Their political views were in favour of a state which should assume the role of redistributing resources, sustaining the working classes, and improving, in general, the economic conditions of the majority of people.[36]

As for the titanic effort made by Keynes in shaping an international monetary framework to guarantee world monetary and financial stability, at the same time retaining a leading position for Great Britain, it is evident that Keynes attributed a far-reaching role to state intervention. Why, then, did Robertson agree to participate actively in this immense labour and effort? Why was he so involved in this ambitious project? Not simply because of his sense of loyalty: in fact he did not simply participate, but gave Keynes great help in the construction of his international monetary system proposal. We should, therefore, look for the reason in some kind of adhesion by Robertson to Keynes's great plan. A possible explanation can be suggested by the speech that Robertson delivered in Chicago to a meeting with the US bankers and published in the *Economic Journal* (Robertson, 1943), in which he briefly presented the Clearing Union Plan.

Interestingly enough, not only does Robertson's attitude reveal a profound sympathy with the structure and general objectives of Keynes's scheme, but it also shows the peculiar view Robertson took of it. Unlike Keynes, who attributed particularly to the Plan the task of avoiding the great monetary crises of the previous years associated with difficulties in international payments, Robertson insisted more on the positive effects that the future set of monetary regulations could have in enhancing the liberalization of commerce and establishing a future free trade international framework, which was, according to Robertson's theoretical background, of the greatest benefit to the world economy.

A further element has been underlined in the literature: that in the interwar period the theoretical paradigm in economics had changed and the idea of state monetary regulations, especially after the great depression, had started to make its way in governmental and academic environments (see Cesarano, 2000). The position in favour of the gold standard had lost ground; the gold exchange standard had shown its limits and failures. The times were ready for acceptance of an idea of a new monetary system regulated at the international level as a means to tackle the problem of world financial instability. Possibly, Robertson was also influenced by this new approach to international monetary policy.

5.   Conclusion

Writing to Sir Richard Hopkins on 22 July 1944 (at the end of the Bretton Woods negotiations), Keynes gave his own evaluation of Robertson's role:

> Everyone in our team has played together splendidly. If anyone is picked out I think it would have to be Dennis, whose help has been absolutely indispensable. He alone had the intellectual subtlety and patience of mind and tenacity of character to grasp and hold on to all details and fight them through Bernstein (who adores Dennis), so that I, frequently occupied otherwise, could feel completely happy about the situation. . . . Some of the Americans told me that they had particularly appreciated his [Sir W. Eady] work and Dennis.
>
> (Moggridge, 1992: 742)

Examination of this unpublished correspondence provides a better understanding of Keynes's claim. It shows that the Robertson–Keynes collaboration during the war – notwithstanding their divergences on pure economic theory – was real, renewed intellectual cooperation, aiming at providing solutions for the difficult issues of national and international economic policy of their times.

References

Aslainbeigui, N., and G. Oakes (2002) 'The theory arsenal: The Cambridge Circus and the origins of the Keynesian revolution', *Journal of The History of Economic Thought*, 24: 5–37.

Bordo, M.D., and B. Eichengreen (eds) (1993) *A Retrospective on the Bretton Woods System*, Chicago: The University of Chicago Press.

Bridel, P., and B. Ingrao (2005) 'Managing Cambridge Economics. The correspondence between Keynes and Pigou', in M.C. Marcuzzo and A. Rosselli (eds) (2005), pp. 149–66.

Cesarano, F. (2000) *Gli Accordi di Bretton Woods. La costruzione di un ordine monetario internazionale*, Collana storica della Banca d'Italia, Roma–Bari: Laterza.

De Cecco, M. (1979) 'The origins of the post-war payments system', *Cambridge Journal of Economics*, 1: 49–61.

De Cecco, M. (1985) 'The international debt problem in the interwar period', *BNL Quarterly Review*, 152: 45–64.

De Cecco, M. (1987) 'Gold standard', in J. Eatwell, M. Milgate and P. Newman (eds), *The New Palgrave. A Dictionary of Economics*, London: Macmillan, pp. 539–544.

van Dormael, A. (1978) *Bretton Woods. Birth of a Monetary System*, London: Macmillan.

Fletcher, G. (2000) *Understanding Dennis Robertson*, Cheltenham and Northampton: Edward Elgar.

Hirai, T. (2004) 'The social philosophy in the interwar Cambridge: Pigou, Robertson and Hawtrey', *Sophia Economic Review*, 49: 45–89.

Howson, S. and D.E. Moggridge (eds) (1990) *The Collected Papers of James Meade: The Cabinet Office Diary: 1944–46*, London: Unwin Hyman.

Howson, S. and D. Winch (1977) *The Economic Advisory Council, 1930–1939: A Study in Economic Advice during Depression and Recovery*, Cambridge: Cambridge University Press.

Johnson, E., and H.C. Johnson (1978) *The Shadow of Keynes*, Chicago: University of Chicago Press.

Kahn, R.F. (1976) 'Historical origins of the International Monetary Fund', in A.P. Thirlwall (ed.)(1976) *Keynes and the International Monetary Relations*, London: Macmillan, pp. 3–35.

Kaldor, N. (1941) 'The White Paper on National Income and Expenditure', *Economic Journal*, 202–3: 181–91.

Keynes, J.M. (1923) *A Tract on Monetary Reform*, London: Macmillan.

Keynes, J.M. (1925) *The Economic Consequences of Mr. Churchill*, London: Hogarth Press.

Keynes, J.M. (1930) *A Treatise on Money*, London: Macmillan.

Keynes, J.M. (1939a) 'The control of consumption' and 'Compulsory savings', *The Times*, 14 and 15 November 1939; reprinted in CWK XXII: 41–51.

Keynes, J.M. (1939b) 'Mr Keynes and his critics. A reply and some questions. The alternative to inflation', *The Times*, 28 November 1939; reprinted in CWK XXII: 74–81.

Keynes, J.M. (1939c) 'The income and fiscal potential of Great Britain', *Economic Journal*, 49: 626–35; reprinted in CWK XXII: 52–66.

Keynes, J.M. (1940a) *How to Pay for the War*, London: Macmillan.

Keynes, J.M. (1940b) 'The concept of national income: a supplementary note', *Economic Journal*, 50: 60–5, reprinted in CWK XXII: 66–73.

Keynes, J.M. (1943) 'The objective of international price stability', *Economic Journal*, 210–211: 185–87; reprinted in CWK XXVI: 30–33.

Keynes, J.M. (1971–1989) *The Collected Writings of J.M.Keynes*, (CWK) D. Moggridge (ed.), London: Macmillan,

Vol. XXII *Activities 1939–1945. Internal War Finance;*

Vol. XXIII, *Activities 1940–1943. External War Finance;*

Vol. XXV, *Activities 1940–1944. Shaping the Post-War World. The Clearing Union;*

Vol. XXVI, *Activities 1941–1946. Shaping the Post-War World. Bretton Woods and Reparations.*

Lüke, R.E. (1985) 'The Schacht and the Keynes Plan', *BNL Quarterly Review*, 152: 65–76.

Marcuzzo, M.C. (2005) 'Keynes and his favourite pupil. The correspondence between Keynes and Kahn', in M.C. Marcuzzo and A. Rosselli (eds) (2005), pp. 21–35.

Marcuzzo, M.C. and A. Rosselli (eds) (2005) *Economists in Cambridge. A Study through their Correspondence, 1907–1946*, London: Routledge.

Marcuzzo, M.C. and A. Rosselli (2005a) 'Introduction', in M.C. Marcuzzo and A. Rosselli (eds) (2005), pp. 1–18.

Meade, J. and R. Stone (1941) 'The construction of tables of national income, expenditure, savings and investment', *Economic Journal*, 202–203: 216–233.

Moggridge, D. (1986) 'Keynes and the international monetary system, 1909–1946', in J.S. Cohen and G.C. Harcourt (eds), *International Monetary Problems and Supply-side Economics*, London: Macmillan, pp. 56–83.

Moggridge, D.E. (1992) *Maynard Keynes. An Economist's Biography*, London: Routledge.

Moggridge, D.E. (2006) 'Keynes and his Correspondence', in R.E. Backhouse and B.W. Bateman (eds), *The Cambridge Companion to Keynes*, Cambridge: Cambridge University Press, pp. 136–59.

Moggridge, D.E. and S. Howson (1974) 'Keynes on Monetary Policy, 1910–1946', *Oxford Economic Papers*, 26: 226–47.

Opie, R. (1944) 'Can national and international monetary policy be reconciled', *American Economic Review, Papers and Proceedings*, 34: 396–99.

Patinkin, D., and J.C. Leith (eds) (1977) *Keynes, Cambridge and the General Theory*, London: Macmillan.

Presley, J.R. (1978) *Robertsonian Economics*, London and Basingstoke: Macmillan.

Presley, J.R. (1992) 'J.M. Keynes and D.H. Robertson: three phases of collaboration', in J.R. Presley (ed.), (1992a) *Essays on Robertsonian Economics*, London and Basingstoke: Macmillan.

Pressnell, L.S. (1986) *External Economic Policy since the War, I, The Post-War Financial Settlement*, London: Her Majesty's Stationary Office.

Pressnell, L.S. (2003) 'Keynes and wartime finance: a clarification', *History of Political Economy*, 35: 679–84.

Robertson, D.H. (1915) *A Study of Industrial Fluctuation*, London: P.S. King.

Robertson, D.H. (1922) *Money*, Cambridge Economic Handbooks II, London: Nisbet.

Robertson, D.H. (1923) *The Control of Industry*, Cambridge Economic Handbooks IV, London: Nisbet.

Robertson, D.H. (1926) *Banking Policy and the Price Level*, London: P.S. King.

Robertson, D.H. (1928a) *Money*, Cambridge Economic Handbooks II, Revised edition, London: Nisbet.

Robertson, D.H. (1928b) 'Theories of banking policy', *Economica*, 7: 131–46.

Robertson, D.H. (1936) 'Some notes on Mr. Keynes' General Theory of Employment', *Quarterly Journal of Economics*, 51: 168–91.

Robertson, D.H. (1938) 'The future of international trade', *Economic Journal*, 189: 1–14.
Robertson, D.H. (1939a) 'Indemnity payments and gold movements', *Quarterly Journal of Economics*, 53: 312–14.
Robertson, D.H. (1939b) 'British monetary policy', *Lloyds Bank Review*, May 1939: 146–57.
Robertson, D.H. (1943) 'The post-war monetary plans', *Economic Journal*, 212: 352–60.
Robertson, D.H. (1947) 'The economic outlook', *Economic Journal*, 228: 1947: 421–437.
Robertson, D.H. [1922](1948) *Money, Cambridge Economic Handbook*, 4th edn, revised with additional chapters, London: Nisbet and Cambridge: The University Press.
Robertson, D.H. (1963) *Lectures on Economic Principles*, London: Fontana Library.
Robinson, J. (1943) 'The international currency proposals', *Economic Journal*, 210–211: 161–75.
Sanfilippo, E. (2005) 'D.H. Robertson: Keynes's valuable opponent and collaborator', in M.C. Marcuzzo and A. Rosselli (eds) (2005), pp. 58–74.
Sayers, R.S. (1956) *Financial Policy 1939–45*, London: Her Majesty's Stationary Office.
Shimodaira, H. (2005) 'Dennis Robertson on industrialized society: The *Control of industry* reexamined', *The History of Economic Thought*, 47: 45–56.
Skidelsky, R. (1992) *John Maynard Keynes. The Economist as Saviour 1920–1937*, London: Macmillan.
Skidelsky, R. (2000) *John Maynard Keynes. Fighting for Britain 1937–1946*, London: Macmillan.
Toye, R. (2003) *The Labour Party and the Planned Economy, 1931–1951*, Royal Historical Society, Woodbridge, Suffolk: Boydell & Brewer.
Viner, J. (1943) 'Two plans for the international economic stabilization', *Yale Review*, XXXIII (September).
Viner, J. (1951) *International Economics*, Glencoe-Illinois: The Free Press.
Williamson, J. (1983) 'Keynes and the International Economic Order', in D. Worswick and J. Trevithick (eds), *Keynes and the Modern World*, Cambridge: Cambridge University Press, pp. 87–113.

Notes

* This paper was presented at the Conference on 'Keynes's Influence on Macroeconomic Policy', held at Hitotsubashi University, 23 March 2006; I would like to thank all the participants, and in particular, R. Backhouse, M. Boianosky, T. Hirai, H. Shimodaira and R. Toye for their useful comments. I am also indebted to M.C. Marcuzzo, N. Naldi, A. Rosselli and, in particular, D. Moggridge for their precious comments on a previous draft. Any remaining errors are, obviously, mine.
1 See Moggridge (1992), Skidelsky (1992, 2000) and Fletcher (2000), but also Patinkin and Leith (1977), Johnson and Johnson (1978), Presley (1978, 1992), Aslainbeigui and Oakes (2002) and, recently, Sanfilippo (2005).

2   Interesting insights into the Keynes–Robertson wartime collaboration deriving from analyses of the National Archives material can also be found in Sayers (1956), Pressnell (1986) and, very recently, in Moggridge (2006).

3   Apart from 26 letters in the *Collected Writings of John Maynard Keynes* – CWK hereafter – (Vols. XXII, XXV, XXVI).

4   The National Archives, former Public Record Office, are located near London, at Kew. Many collections and papers are held there: not only of historical relevance (such as British Government documents from the eleventh century to the present day and material on military history, as well as historical maps) but also of a biographical and genealogical nature (Family Records). Detailed information as well as an online Catalogue are available on the website www.nationalarchives.gov.uk.

5   For archival references in this work the following abbreviations are adopted: TNA for the National Archives and PRO for Public Record Office; JMK papers for Keynes Papers in the Modern Archives Collection, King's College, Cambridge; DHR papers for Robertson Papers, Trinity College, Cambridge.

6   A few letters relating to the wartime period are also held in the JMK papers and DHR papers.

7   'Robertson was made "temporary administrative officer" at the Treasury to Sir Frederick Phillips, head of the Finance Division' (Skidelsky, 2000: 46). Then he left the Treasury by Fall 1944 to take the Chair of Political Economy at the Cambridge Faculty – left vacant with Pigou's retirement. Keynes, despite his very influential role, 'held no official position. He was merely an unpaid adviser to the Chancellor of the Exchequer, with a room in the Treasury' (Skidelsky, 2000: xv) and worked for the Treasury until his death in April 1946. (See also Moggridge, 1992: 638 and 2006: 147–8.)

8   For example, the 'Overseas Finance Division' (T 236) Series amounting to 6793 files, the Series 'Cabinet Office, Economic Section, and Treasury, Economic Advisory Section' (T 230) consisting of 1077 files, the 'Financial Enquiries Branch' (T 208) Series containing 206 files and the 'Finance Department' (T 160) Series with its 1418 boxes or files.

9   The total amount of this exchange is also pending the forthcoming full edition of Robertson's correspondence edited by D. Moggridge.

10   Including Henderson, Hawtrey, Sir Frederick Phillips, Sir Richard Hopkins, Lord Catto, Sir W. Eady, Mr Waley, by then all officials or advisers at the Treasury.

11   A highly critical position was subsequently taken by John Hicks (who complained about the redistributive effect of family allowances in Keynes's scheme) and, for different reasons (see fn. 12), the leaders of the Labour Party (see CWK XXII: 107–10, Moggridge, 1992: 629 ff.; Skidelsky, 2000: 52–61). This is why in the following months Keynes was actively engaged in persuading the trade union leaders, also adding some changes to his scheme in order to gain the approval of the working classes.

12   In the article Keynes (1939b) replied to one of the criticisms brought against him (that of depriving workers of their freedom to choose between consumption and savings) that in fact workers 'will have no such choice. If they try (as, left to themselves, they will) to exercise their apparent freedom of choice to consume, they will be defeated, if not by taxes, by an inflationary rise of prices, just as they were in the last war. My proposal to credit them with deposits in the Post Office Saving Banks will mean for the workers as a whole an absolute

net addition to their wealth, something which otherwise they will just not receive' (CWK XXII: 76).

13 This was the provision made in the subsequent 1941 April Budget, where it was indicated that the gap was to be filled with taxes and voluntary savings. Keynes's idea of compulsory savings (Keynes, 1940a) was, in fact, not accepted, but the warning about the risk of inflation and the method of calculation of national accounts as the basis for economic policy entered as general principles into government finance, revolutionising the way the Budget Bill was conceived (CWK XXII: 325–6; see also Moggridge, 1992: 645–7; Skidelsky, 2000: 83–5).

14 An interesting analysis of this document can also be found in Kaldor (1941).

15 Meade and Stone subsequently published their statistics in the *Economic Journal* (June–September 1941).

16 Another element to be considered is that during this period Richard Kahn, Keynes's preferred reader and commentator, was very much engaged with his work at the Board of Trade, and this circumstance can also explain why Robertson regained his central role as Keynes's adviser. In the mid-1930s he had lost this position in favour of Kahn (see Sanfilippo, 2005: 66).

17 See Moggridge (1992), p. 597; Skidelsky (1992), p. 272; but also Sanfilippo (2005), p. 59.

18 Keynes 'used' Robertson more or less in the same way in the 1930s to revise the drafts of his theoretical works – the *Treatise* and the *General Theory* – but in the latter case the level of criticism and opposition shown by Robertson rose so high that collaboration no longer seemed possible to Keynes. (See also Sanfilippo, 2005: 70.)

19 In the previous July Keynes and Robertson had worked on the figures provided by the Bank of England on the gold liquidity of Great Britain in relation to its external position with the Dominions and other countries (see letters between 13 and 16 July 1942, TNA: PRO T 247/73).

20 This was one of the means by which the British government was trying to increase its reserves. (For data on the British gold and dollars reserves in the 1939–45 period see Sayers, 1956: 496). Another was to obtain loans secured against British assets. Keynes had negotiated two of these loans during his 1941 visit to Washington (see Moggridge, 1992: 665 ff.).

21 For analysis of the technical aspects of the plan see, for example, van Dormael (1978), De Cecco (1979), pp. 49–52, Bordo and Eichengreen (1993), and Cesarano (2000), pp. 103–12.

22 Civil servant and principal assistant secretary at the British Treasury from 1939 to 1946.

23 In the analyses of the subsequent years, this element was considered peculiar to Keynes's Plan and a plus marking out Keynes's from White's Plan (see, for example, Viner, 1943).

24 By this expression Robertson meant that deficiency countries are not induced to adopt virtuous behaviours to eliminate their deficits.

25 Director of Monetary Research at the US Treasury from 1938 to 1945, he was the author of the American plan.

26 This had been one of the fundamental theoretical points of disagreement between them since the times of their discussions around the *General Theory* (see Sanfilippo, 2005: 69; see also Robertson, 1963: 375–92).

27 The close of the Bretton Woods Conference saw Robertson and Keynes discussing the interpretation of Article VIII, clause (2) and (4), on the obligations of each member regarding the convertibility of foreign held balances. (For a detailed reconstruction see Moggridge, 1992: 748–53 and 2006: 150–4, but also Pressnell, 1986, I: 170 and ff. and Skidelsky, 2000: 357–8).

28 A Committee on post-war commercial policy set up by Hugh Dalton, President of the Board of Trade. (See also the files TNA: PRO T 230/125 and T 230/126).

29 The document also received interesting and detailed comments from Harrod (see CWK XXV: 226–32).

30 Assistant Director of Monetary Research in the US Treasury from 1941 to 1946.

31 In July–September 1943 they also were involved in discussion on the exchange rates that would again be discussed in the subsequent meetings with US officials (see letters 5 July 1943, TNA: PRO T 247/81 and 17 September 1943, TNA: PRO T 247/82).

32 For clear, detailed analysis and comparison between the two plans see Viner (1943).

33 A project involving Kahn, Joan and Austin Robinson, Pierro Sraffa, Michel Kalecki and David Champernowne to be carried out in the Cambridge Faculty in cooperation with the National Institute of Economic and Social Research. (For more details see Marcuzzo, 2005: 30.)

34 See letter 7 October 1938 from Robertson to Keynes, JMK papers L/R/137–8; see also Moggridge, (1992), pp. 601–2; Aslainbeigui and Oakes (2002), pp. 28–32, Bridel and Ingrao (2005), pp. 152–3 and Sanfilippo (2005), pp. 70–2.

35 Commenting on the book *How to Pay for the War* Robertson wrote to Keynes: '. . . you won't be surprised to hear that at first blush I think it your best work since E.C.P. [Economic Consequences of the Peace] (letter 6 March 1940, JMK papers HP/4/414–15).

36 As far as Robertson's social philosophy is concerned, useful insights can be drawn from analysis of *The Control of Industry* (Robertson, 1923). (See Hirai, 2004; Shimodaira, 2005).

4
Harrod's Discontent with Harrodian Growth Theory[1]

*Daniele Besomi**

1. Introduction

The 'Harrod-Domar growth model' is traditionally seen as the starting point of modern growth theory. Its core is found in two similar equations. The first (describing the growth rate of the economic system in terms of the proportion of income saved and the capital/output ratio) was expounded by Roy Harrod in 'An Essay in Dynamic Theory' (1939); the second (expressing the growth rate in terms of the society's productive capacity and of the propensity to save) was formulated by Evsey Domar in "Capital Expansion, Rate of Growth, and Employment" (1946) and "Expansion and Employment" (1947).

Harrod complained that the interpretation of his theory as a growth path model was reductive and sometimes plainly wrong. At first, however, he seemed quite satisfied with his idea receiving at last some kind of recognition, and directed his criticisms to specific points of dissent with the use that was made of his model. Having failed to reject this interpretation as a whole, Harrod's mild reaction did not discourage growth theorists from pursuing their interpretative line, which therefore consolidated fairly quickly. By the early 1960s, Harrod's equation (originally formulated in 1939) was widely considered as the starting point of the modern theory of growth. At some point, Harrod's dissatisfaction with this state of things prevailed over the gratification of having his name linked with an all-important branch of economic theory but eponymously attached to an idea he could not share. Beginning from the mid-1960s, Harrod expressed his dissent in stronger words, openly quarreled with Joan Robinson on the interpretation of his writings, and eventually in 1973 published a new edition of his 1948 book in which he explicitly emphasized the aspects that were misinterpreted in the literature.

This chapter is concerned with Harrod's increasing awareness of the distortion of the textbook interpretation of his views in the decade 1964–73. While in his published writings the break becomes apparent all of a sudden, his correspondence and unpublished notes reveal specific incidents that triggered Harrod's reaction, and bear witness to the steps he took to counteract the misinterpretation of which he was a victim.[2]

In Section 2, Harrod's dynamic theory is outlined, in Harrod's own version and through the eyes of his contemporary commentators. Section 3 describes, in Harrod's words as sent to Robin Matthews in 1964, his gratification for the recognition that was given to his pet idea. Section 4 illustrates how, a year later, Harrod was perplexed by some letters by Joan Robinson showing a complete lack of understanding of the core of his theory, but also how he failed to point to the precise reason for this misunderstanding. The following Section reports an exchange with George Shackle (almost contemporary to the one with Robinson) that instead left Harrod quite satisfied: Shackle, in his *Scheme of Economic Theory*, by correctly characterizing the peculiar time dimensionality in Harrod's dynamics and stressing the role of the three different interpretations of his growth equation, pointed to the features that Robinson (and most other commentators) had missed. In Section 6 Harrod's first attempts are documented to give emphasis to the interplay of the actual, warranted and natural growth rates, in a series of lectures he delivered in Russia and in America. Section 7 discusses a further exchange with Joan Robinson, where she reiterated her previous misunderstandings, the causes of which, this time, Harrod could identify. In the concluding section Harrod's restatement of his theory in his book on *Economic Dynamics* is examined in light of the preceding developments.

2.   Harrod and growth theory

The essential part of the story of Harrod's dynamics begins in 1934, when he published two articles, originally devoted to other subjects but containing two essential ingredients on which he continued building in the following years. The first is a methodological principle, according to which a moving equilibrium should be analysed in terms of the consistency of growth rates of various magnitudes. The appropriate approach for such a task is to take a cross-section of the system at one point in time, as one would do when examining the movement of a train in motion at constant speed as distinct from the phases of acceleration and deceleration (Harrod, 1934c: 478, and 1934b: 296).

In another article published in the same year, Harrod outlined his instability principle. This was not originally thought of as a *result*, for

Harrod had not yet devised the analytical mechanism capable of giving rise to fluctuations, but concerned the very possibility of trade cycle theorizing. Harrod argued that in a system with stable equilibrium, fluctuations could only be explained by means of some exogenous force bringing the system away from a state of rest; this would be unsatisfactory, for a proper theory of the cycle should be capable of explaining movement in terms of its own dynamics. The instability of equilibrium should therefore be postulated at the outset (Harrod 1934a: 468–70).[3] Harrod's instability principle had an epistemic rather than analytical origin, and defines a condition the model should incorporate.

Although in 1934 Harrod's ideas as how to organize his preliminary thoughts into an analytical frame were still 'amorphous in the extreme' (letter to James Meade, 4 October 1934, in Harrod (2003), 295), he soon found the additional ingredients. On reading a memorandum by Gottfried Haberler (autumn 1934), Harrod became aware of the possible application of the acceleration principle to business cycle analysis (Haberler, 1934).[4] The reading of the proofs of John Maynard Keynes's *General Theory*, during summer 1935, made him aware of the implications of the multiplier. By the end of 1935, the two principles were chained together producing a mechanism capable of describing self-sustained growth, and by early 1936 Harrod could start writing *The Trade Cycle*, which was in the bookshops by September of the same year.

The mechanism of economic fluctuations expounded in *The Trade Cycle* relies on the instability principle and on the nonlinearity of relationships. One of the possible outcomes of the multiplier–accelerator interaction is a state of moving equilibrium: if the income generated, via the multiplier, by the investment undertaken to meet an expected increase in demand for consumption goods (the proportion being determined by the acceleration coefficient), gives rise to additional consumption matching the increase entrepreneurs expected at the outset, entrepreneurs as a whole feel justified in their decisions. Nothing, however, guarantees such an outcome: if, for any reason, investment is short of the equilibrium level, a cumulative downfall ensues. Low investment means low income, therefore consumption is less than expected and entrepreneurs are disappointed and find their investment was too high (rather than too low), and therefore further reduce their accumulation rate. The moving equilibrium is thus an unstable state, and this instability is the engine of the cumulative upward and downward movements. Even if the equilibrium rate is reached, growth itself will trigger a deviation (with cumulative effects) from equilibrium. As income increases and people grow richer, in fact, the propensity to save increases and the multiplier correspondingly diminishes. As a consequence, the income generated by a rate of investment previously sufficient to justify expectations is now too low, and the deviation from equilibrium tends to amplify. Fluctuations in the value of parameters is also an ingredient making for revival in the opposite situation: not only when income is decreasing does the multiplier increase, but the rate of interest also diminishes, thus favouring the introduction of more capital intensive techniques, which are reflected in a higher value of the acceleration coefficient. An expected increase in consumption thus determines a higher rate of investment, which increases income and thereby actually generates additional demand for consumption goods.

Three years later, *The Economic Journal* published 'An essay in dynamic theory', later to become famous for the inclusion of the growth rate formulas at the core of the 'Harrod-Domar model'. These formulas were meant to recast Harrod's multiplier–acceleration mechanism in a different form, although this explicit aim was largely concealed by the shift of emphasis Harrod introduced in order to meet Keynes's criticism of an earlier version. Harrod presented three equations representing growth rates in terms of the proportion of income saved (as a determinant of the multiplier) and the capital/output ratio (depicting the accelerator[5]). The first is a truism: $G = s/C_p$, where G is the *actual* (ex-post) rate of growth of output, s is the recorded proportion of income saved, and C_p is the 'value of the increment of capital per unit increment of output actually produced' (Harrod, 1939: 17–18).[6]

The second equation, $G_w = s/C$, is analogous to the first but has a different meaning. s is again 'the fraction of income people choose to save' (p. 16; Harrod declined to express precise views as to the possible causes of divergence between actual and ex-ante saving). C is 'the value of the capital goods required for the production of a unit increment of output' (p. 16); its value 'depends on the state of technology and the nature of the goods constituting the increment of output. It may be expected to vary as income grows and in different phases of the trade cycle; it may be somewhat dependent on the rate of interest' (p. 17). G_w, the unknown in this equation, is the warranted rate of growth. It is 'that rate of growth which, if it occurs, will leave all parties satisfied that they have produced neither more nor less than the right amount. Or, to state the matter otherwise, it will put them into a frame of mind which will cause them to give such orders as will maintain the same rate of growth'. Harrod used 'the unprofessional term warranted instead of equilibrium, or moving equilibrium, because every point on the path of output described by G_w is an equilibrium point in the sense that producers, if they remain on it, will be satisfied, and be induced to keep the same rate of growth in being' because 'the equilibrium is . . . a highly unstable one' (p. 16).

These statements are problematic, as these notions of 'equilibrium' are not equivalent to each other;[7] this paved the way for numerous discussions as to how equilibrium is characterized and what the behaviour of the system in equilibrium really is – with obvious implications for the definition of the reactions to disequilibrium states.[8]

The possibility (and indeed the necessity) that parameters change in the course of the cycle is fully consistent with the position expressed in *The Trade Cycle*; and if one looks at the first draft of the 'Essay', it becomes obvious at a glance that Harrod's main interest is in the deviations from equilibrium rather than in equilibrium itself. His discussion, however, is problematic. The description of how parameters change is rather vague and not expressed in mathematical terms, and could not be incorporated in the fundamental equations. We are thus told that the warranted rate chases the actual rate, for the propensity to save increases as income grows (the movement of the required capital/output ratio is not described in detail for the phase of expansion), but the equations describing the chase are missing. Moreover, Harrod failed to specify how one state of the system is connected to the next, for example, by specifying how the system reacts to the difference between G and G_w. In spite of having defined a one-instant world, Harrod tried to argue that the system is unstable, that is, that a difference between the actual and the warranted rate tends to amplify, pointing out that if at any point in time the actual rate is higher than the warranted one, the actual capital/output ratio is lower than the 'required' one, thereby inducing entrepreneurs to further accumulate in order to fill the gap; the accelerated investment drives the actual rate even higher. In spite of being intuitively appealing, this argument is fallacious, as the system is one equation short, as commentators were quick to point out (this will be discussed later).

Again as in *The Trade Cycle*, the movement of the parameters is the key for the turning point. However, a further ingredient is necessary in the new formulation. This involves Harrod's third growth rate, the natural one (G_n): 'This is the maximum rate of growth allowed by the increase of population, accumulation of capital, technological improvement and the work/leisure preference schedule, supposing that there is always full employment in some sense' (p. 15). When the actual rate is larger than the warranted one, G increases and, after some delay, drags G_w along. At some point, G will reach the ceiling of the natural rate, and cannot grow further. Such a constraint, however, does not apply to G_w, which can increase beyond G and G_n. But at that point $G_w > G$, which initiates a cumulative downward movement. This, in turn, will only cease when the fall of G_w (attributed to the decrease of the propensity to save as income declines, to long-range capital outlays and exports holding back the fall of G, and to C being abnormally depressed due to the difficulties in liquidating fixed equipment[9]) brings the warranted rate below the actual one. The movement will then be reversed, and a new cycle can begin.[10]

Although Harrod gave an outline of his theory of the cycle and a few hints regarding policy implications, of the three stages of which he thought dynamics consist only the first – 'dynamic proper', the study of the mutual consistency of growth rates at one instant – was discussed in full, while stages two and three – the succession of events, where lags belong to, and the question of remedies – were only touched upon.[11] This is perhaps natural, as Harrod was always adamant that his aim was to lay the foundations of dynamic economics,[12] rather than to develop a full-blown theory of growth or cycles. Accordingly, the same bias is present in *Towards a Dynamic Economics*, where the discussion of the trade cycle is limited to three pages (Harrod, 1948: 89–91). Harrod, however, makes it clear that the assumption of fixed coefficients (pp. 82 and 86), which he introduces for the purpose of analysing steady advance (p. 84), is temporary only, and indeed he removes it when discussing the cycle.[13]

The secondary literature on Harrod's equation focussed very soon on the problem of stability. Harrod's equation could not answer the question due to the lack of an explicit link between states.[14] Interpreters therefore began by filling in the missing relationship, in the form of some behavioural equations, drawing from one or another of Harrod's statements, often including the lags that Harrod had carefully relegated to the second stage of dynamics. In this setting, Harrod's distinction between different rates of growth became redundant, for the dynamic formulation only needed a single functional equation. Harrod's instantaneous rates of growth turned into paths of growth. His emphasis on the changes in the values of the parameters became redundant, partly because by shifting the emphasis on growth the need for factors explaining fluctuations disappeared and linear equations served the purpose, partly because only a handful of economists knew how to deal with nonlinearities. Finally, Harrod's claim that the system is unstable was attributed to the rigidity of parameters: neoclassical growth theorists argued that flexibility in the capital/output ratio in response to changes in interest rates would suffice to bring the actual growth rate in line with the natural rate (thereby attributing to the system not only stability, but also full employment of labour and resources).[15] Post-Keynesian growth theorists argued instead that Harrod failed to consider fluctuations in the propensity to save as linked to changes in the share of profit, and elaborated alternative models where the distribution of income is at the centre of the accumulation process (for a brief survey see Besomi 1998, 61–63).

3. From cycles to growth

By the mid-1960s, the view of Harrod's theory as the proto-model describing balanced growth was codified in the literature. Robert Matthews and Frank Hahn, in their celebrated survey of growth theory, took the Harrod–Domar model as the starting point of their classification, precisely in terms of the possible variants on 'the various assumptions on which it is based' (Hahn and Matthews, 1964: 783).

By that time, Harrod had mildly complained of misinterpretation, but seems to have been satisfied overall with the recognition his formulas were receiving.[16] The following exchange with Matthews is enlightening in this respect. When Matthews and Hahn were writing their survey, they asked Harrod what redirected his mind from a theory of the cycle to a theory of growth:

> In your book on the trade cycle, published immediately after the General Theory, you introduced, as everyone knows, the notion of a cycle model based on the acceleration principle and the multiplier. In 1939 you gave the theory an entirely different twist by using much the same ingredients as the basis of a theory of growth. What we were wondering was what led you to transfer your thinking onto this second tack.
> (Matthews to Harrod, 2 January 1964)

The hypothesis under inspection was whether Harrod was influenced by Jan Tinbergen's (1937) review of *The Trade Cycle* in the *Weltwirtschaftliches Archiv*, where he reformulated Harrod's theory in terms of a first order linear functional equation, which is of course only capable of describing exponential growth rather than fluctuations. Harrod could not recollect having seen Tinbergen's review (although he certainly did, as he and Tinbergen exchanged correspondence on the subject[17]), he denied it had influenced the evolution of his ideas,[18] and gave an account of the evolution of his dynamics into a theory of growth:

> It is natural that they should take that turn. For some time I had become convinced that certain problems could be solved only by considering the concomitant movement of variables in a phase of steady growth. What brought this forcibly to my mind were the inconclusive, but very sharp, controversies between Hayek & Keynes about the theories of bank credit, and there is evidence of this in my *Economica* article of 1934 (August) about the expansion of credit in an advancing community (re-published in my "Economic Essays"). This is not concerned with the Keynesian analysis of saving and investment, but does analyse

certain monetary problems in terms of a growing economy. I went on thinking about what more could be done by that type of approach.

I think that the use of the expression 'dynamic determinants' in the Trade Cycle shows that I was feeling my way towards a growth theory that should complement a static theory.

In my Trade Cycle I say of Keynes: 'Mr. Keynes does not formally set out the proper method of dynamic analysis. This method should proceed by asking the following question. What is the rate of growth which, if maintained, will leave the parties content to continue behaving in a way consistent with it?' (p. 150). This surely gives the kernel of thought in my later Essay. [. . .]

The passage in the Trade Cycle on the foreign balance (pp. 151 & ff) is as much on growth as such as in the Trade Cycle & is better than anything incorporated in my International Economics.

(Harrod to Matthews, 7 January 1964)

On the following day, he added that, as he met Tinbergen shortly after the publication of *The Trade Cycle*, it could be possible

that it was I who suggested to T[inbergen] that my thought had a closer relation to growth theory than to trade cycle theory, rather than the other way round.

(Harrod to Matthews, 8 January 1964)[19]

On previous occasions Harrod had given several definitions of dynamics, each emphasizing a different aspect but all part of the same general view: he had stressed that savings and investment entail growth; that statics determines the level of output, while dynamics relates to its rate of growth; that statics deals with *per saltum* changes and dynamics with continuous change; that in dynamics the unknown are rates of growth of variables; that dynamics concerns the consistency of these rates of growth at one point in time; that while static equilibria are stable, dynamic ones are unstable (Besomi, 2001: 88–9). From this somewhat grandiose view, in his letters to Matthews he chose one aspect only: dynamics as growth theory, indicating that at that point he was content with his name being associated with the growth formula, no longer interpreted as a set of instantaneous rates of growth but as describing a growth path. The various interpretations were only a matter of detail, to be individually rebutted without it being necessary to revise the whole story.

At the time of publication of Hahn's and Matthews's survey, the only misinterpretation about which Harrod had systematically complained regarded the attempt to insert lags into his formula. Many commentators found this necessary in order to unfold the time path of the main variables by means of difference equations, while Harrod insisted that his dynamic method consisted in analysing the consistency at one point of time of the growth of the system's components during a period of regular advance, and stressed that lags come into play only when the economy does not progress steadily but undergoes fluctuations.[20]

4. Joan Robinson on the meaning of the growth formula

At the end of 1965 an exchange between Harrod and Joan Robinson took place that is likely to have indicated to Harrod that there was something wrong with the dominant interpretation of his growth rate formula. Although only part of the correspondence survives, what is preserved in Harrod's archives gives the gist of the problem he was envisaging.[21]

With reference to Harrod's review of Nicholas Kaldor's *Essays on Economic Policy* (Harrod, 1965), Robinson commented as follows:

> I was disconcerted by your remarks about $P/K = G/\alpha$. I have always maintained that altho' your formula *seemed* to be saying that "the rate of growth depends on the fraction of income saved" you never intended to throw the General Theory out and say that saving governs investment.
>
> I thought your last piece admitted the necessity for an independent propensity to accumulate. Combining this with the Treatise view of profits, you get [the] idea that accumulation *causes* the share of saving to be what is required *via* its effect on the rate of profit.
>
> (Robinson to Harrod, 8 December [1965])

Harrod does not seem to have understood what Robinson was talking about, as she had to point to the precise passage she was referring to. She thus specified:

> your original formula $g = s/v$,[22] appears to support the view that saving governs investment, which is certainly not what you mean. I thought that in your last contribution to the subject you agreed that a separate propensity to accumulate is needed to make the system work. Our formula for the rate of profit is a most useful and necessary development of your theory. It is not mere formalism but a causal relation. If g or $(1 - Sp)$ [Sp indicates savings out of profits] were greater the rate of profit would be greater, and it cannot be greater unless.
>
> (Robinson to Harrod, 20 December 1965)

Harrod's reply, as reported by Robinson, seems to have run in the following terms: 'You say that a high s requires a high g (v being given) but it does nothing to cause a high g'. The point was lost on Robinson, who argued: 'I rescue you from this dilemma by saying that g is the independent factor and s will be accommodate [sic] to it via the share of profits. Your theory is a projection into the long run of the paradox of the General Theory, not a reversal of it' (Robinson to Harrod, 10 January 1966).

Harrod thus pointed out that the paradox was apparent, for the growth rate equation is not meant to depict a growth path, but to provide a reference system for a dynamic theory:

> I agree fully that a high s does nothing to cause a high g.
>
> I am never quite sure what relation my steady growth has to your golden age. Anyhow, it is an abstract construction like the stable equilibrium of static economics. It may never actually occur.
>
> What I say is that a high s determines a high value for g in this abstract construction. To determine the value of a term in an ideal construction is quite different from causing something to happen.
>
> The ideal construction relates, of course, to a fully capitalist system, in which there is no public tinkering with s.
>
> (Harrod to Robinson, 1 February 1966)

Again, Robinson did not understand:

> The difference is that with your s there is only one steady rate of growth possible, whereas with ours steady growth is possible at any rate provided that the real wage is not too low.
>
> What is the point of making a less natural assumption which leads to logical difference when the more natural assumption is free from them.
>
> (Robinson to Harrod, 2 February 1966)

At this point, Harrod must have been quite desperate about not being able to have his method understood, and it is not surprising that within a few years he changed his attitude towards the established interpretation of his theory and reverted from a substantial gratification with having his name attached to the foundation of growth theory to an explicit expression of dissatisfaction with Harrodian dynamics as cristallized in the textbooks: he felt the need to deny that he had produced a 'model' (Harrod, 1968), he explicitly stated that Joan Robinson failed to understand what his theory was about (Harrod, 1970), and published a completely revised edition of *Towards a Dynamic Economics* where he restated his 'original' intention (Harrod, 1973).

As an intermediate step, Harrod had to understand precisely at what point Robinson and the textbook interpretation of his dynamics went wrong. Harrod's bibliography does not help in understanding how this occurred, for his published writings just show this break having taken place without giving a pointer to the reason why. The extant correspondence, however, points to a precise event that seems to have triggered Harrod's reaction.

5. The Keynesesque model

In 1965, G.L.S. Shackle's *A Scheme of Economic Theory* was published.[23] One of the chapters was largely dedicated to Harrod's first 'Keynesesque' model of coherent growth.[24] While Keynes produced an ' "open" or non self-contained model . . . deliberately [leaving] out some of the linkages which would be needed in order to calculate the future from the past', notably refusing to give a formal specification of decisions to invest, the 'Keynesesque' models used Keynesian components to produce a closed system (Shackle, 1965: 98–9). In particular, Harrod supplied an investment equation based on the acceleration principle.

Harrod praised Shackle's reading of his theory as

> much the more carefully considered and understanding treatment that my views have had. I like particularly your analysis of the part that *time* plays in my theory. I have found difficulty in getting this apprehended by others.
>
> (Harrod to Shackle, 11 January 1966)

Although the correspondence on Shackle's interpretation of Harrod focussed on some aspects of (mild) disagreement (to which I shall return later in this section), it is clear that Harrod was impressed by Shackle's 'perfect understanding of my views' (ibid.), surely more because of the overall perspective than for matters of details.

Shackle resurrected most of the elements Harrod had emphasized in his early formulation of dynamics that were overlooked by most postwar commentators. Shackle stressed at the outset that Harrod's description relates to a 'cycle-prone' economy rather than one growing at a regular pace: the instability of equilibrium inevitably throws the system 'into explosive expansion or decline' which, if stopped by obstacles at the top and at the bottom, give it cyclical movement:

> Harrod thus provided the bones of a business cycle theory, but through a desire for simplicity, generalness and compactness comparable with

those of static equilibrium models, he refused to articulate his argument by an explicit consideration of lagged responses, and so in effect asks us to agree that there must be a cycle, without showing us its sequential pattern of phases.

(Shackle, 1965: 100)

This description captures Harrod's awareness of having only given the outline of a theory, and rather acutely renders Harrod's division in stages, with the deviation from equilibrium, cycles and lags belonging to the second stage while the first only concerns the dynamic equilibrium and its stability at one point of time.[25] Shackle points out that such a concept is obtained by telescoping a time-interval into a point,[26] and is therefore intrinsically different from a timeless equilibrium where actions are taken simultaneously (ibid., 100–2). Harrod's problem is

what internal structure of this moment [in the economy's life], what set of relations amongst its various groups of decisions and upshots, will be self-consistent and self-satisfying and lead to a repetition of similar growth in the 'next' moment.

(ibid., 102)

Shackle thus stressed that Harrod was concerned with the 'condition, which may or may not in any instance be fulfilled, of "equilibrium growth" ' (p. 107), which requires the statement of different formulas describing the actual and the 'warranted' growth rates. This emphasis on equilibrium conditions, and consequently on the existence and interplay of different growth rates in Harrod's conception, further distances Shackle's interpretation from the textbook reading of Harrod's formula (Shackle also considered the categorization of states of the economy based on the relative positions of natural, actual and warranted growth rates: p. 122). This is how he avoided falling into the misunderstanding that characterized Joan Robinson's reading of Harrod's formula as describing a growth path: Harrod seems to have understood that here lies the crux of the matter and accordingly (as will be seen in section 6 below) in turn emphasized the role of each of the three growth rates in his construction.

Shackle went even further and also admitted that coefficients in the warranted rate equation are not given once and for all (p. 108), but are subject to change in the course of the cycle (although he did not pause to consider the role this plays in the explanation of the turning points); but he rightly stressed that this is not relevant at the stage of the determination of the equilibrium instantaneous rate, for 'at *any* particular moment, which we choose as the "present", . . . the stock of equipment which exists is a legacy from past history and is hence a datum' (p. 109).

Shackle pointed out that this passage introduces a gap between the mechanistic and symbolic form in which Harrod's model is cast and its economic significance, at the crucial point where the stability of equilibrium is discussed. Stability depends on the system's reaction to a difference between actual and warranted rates. Harrod's argument is based on the implication that a divergence between growth rates is equivalent to a divergence between actual and required capital/output ratios, on which entrepreneurs react. If there is no divergence, and if entrepreneurs taken as a whole 'take as their test of reasonable future action, not the *level* of output which in the immediate past has been successfully absorbed, but the *increase* of output which has successfully matched by increasing sales, growth at a constant percentage per time-unit can be indefinitely sustained' (p. 114). But if there is a divergence – for example, if the actual rate is below the warranted one – they will find that there is excess equipment, and will accordingly reduce orders, thereby further decreasing the actual rate. Shackle points out that at any one instant, the desired capital/output ratio is not a variable, but is taken to be given. Harrod's argument is therefore adapted to describe, on the given assumption, how growth can persist, but is not suited to analyse how it breaks down: for that purpose, a 'period' or 'sequence' analysis is necessary, and Harrod introduces it by means of a 'switch to the psychic', referring to the entrepreneurs' satisfaction with what they are doing by reference to the outcome of their previous actions (pp. 115–16). Harrod's argument on instability is thus based on the lack of simultaneity between action, its result and responsive reaction (p. 120).

Harrod's 'only one complaint' on Shackle's reading of his views concerned Shackle's failure to keep the required and actual capital coefficients apart (this passage requires a warning: while in 1939 C with suffix $_p$ indicated the actual capital/output ratio and the symbol C without a suffix indicated the required ratio, in 1948 Harrod changed symbolism and affixed the suffix $_r$ to the required capital coefficient and left without suffix the actual coefficient):

I cant understand <how>[27] you can say (p. 108) that the suffix in C_r is superfluous. Again on p. 115 you say that C is a technical fact. C (*my* C) certainly isnt a technical fact. C_r (subject to what you say about the possible influence of the rate of interest, with which I agree) is a technical fact. In the identity $G = s/C$, C is the accretion of capital actually occurring. It may be in excess or deficient in relation to what is required (whether in the form of fixed cap. or stocks). *C* represents what happens, if it did not, $G = s/C$ would not necessarily be true. But the whole point of my method of analysis is that it is necessarily true. *C* and C_r are, so to say, poles apart. I really think that you have slipped up here; but I dont think this vitiates most of what you say about me.

(Harrod to Shackle, 11 January 1966)

Shackle explained that understanding the warranted rate as a *condition* to be fulfilled requires that 'there must be some one or more variables which can assume values in agreement, or not in agreement, with the condition':

Where my presentation of your theory differs from your own is in the selection of this variable. I find it difficult to regard the capital–output ratio as one such variable. For if there exists more equipment than is required for the prevailing output, the mechanism of growth-induced investment does not work. On the other side, output cannot exceed what the full employment of the existing equipment can supply. Now let me admit at once that of course these statements assume a fixed technical coefficient linking general output with general equipment: so and so many megawatts of electricity, so and so many dynamos of given capacity. I made this assumption, in my attempt to present your theory, because it seemed to me necessary to simplify away all non-essential difficulties in order to make the exposition *brief* and *swift*, and thus clear. I realize of course that we can take the capital–output ratio to be that ratio which corresponds to the minimum point of a unit-cost-of-product curve, and that then there can be a departure from this optimum, and that such a departure, if on the side of over-use of existing capacity, will have an investment-inducing tendency.

(Shackle to Harrod, 11 January 1966)

Shackle here makes explicit an hypothesis underlying Harrod's model, which does not seem to have been stressed in the literature:[28] the acceleration principle, as used by Harrod, requires that the degree of utilization of capital is constant.[29] Others (Michal Kalecki, for instance) have convincingly argued that it changes in the course of the cycle, and that these variations play a part in the explanation of the phenomenon.

Shackle's next point took up a remark by Harrod, who had reported that he was pointing out 'that in the equilibrium equation $G_w = s/C_r$, I should have given *s* a suffix, e.g. s_d for desired saving thus $G_w = s_d/C_r$'[30] and recalled that in his original E.J. article [Harrod, 1939] I definitely said that, when $G \neq G_w$, either capital formation would deviate from what was required, or saving would deviate from what people wished, and, adding that these two alterations would have the same dynamic effect on instability, whichever way <production> went, I concentrated on the $C \neq C_r$ alternative, & I traced its consequences. But I always had in mind that the effect if $G \neq G_w$ might be concentrated on s, viz. is the result of s_d not being equal to s. That it is why s ought to have had a suffix, such as s_d, in the G_w equation.

(Harrod to Shackle, 11 January 1966)

Shackle replied:

Your own recent suggestion is that the marginal propensity to save may be treated as a variable. If we do not adopt some one or other possibility, viz. a variable saving function, a variable capital–output ratio, or the flexibility introduced by the consideration of price, then we have to accept, what I think was your original contention, that there is just one and only one growth rate which will match demand and supply in the regularly growing economy, given a rigid technological capital–output ratio and a rigid saving propensity; and the regular growth path will even then only be followed if we start from fully employed equipment.

Here we find the only limit of Shackle's rendition of Harrod's theory. Harrod's original contention did not regard the uniqueness of equilibrium, which was instead supposed to change: and fluctuations in G_w, following changes in the parameters, was at the heart of the cycle mechanism as described in *The Trade Cycle* and very clearly taken up in the preliminary draft of the 'Essay'. Shackle clearly failed to see this aspect: quite excusably, as it was only very briefly sketched in the published version of the 'Essay' (1939, Section 15) and in *Towards a Dynamic Economics* (1948: 89–91), and only resumed at length in *Economic Dynamics* (1973, 36–41).

6.   Harrod's lectures on growth

Harrod soon took up some of the topics discussed by Shackle. In a lecture delivered in Moscow in 1966, he carefully characterized the different natures of the three growth rates, pointing out that the comparison between the actual and the warranted rates, by giving rise to cumulative growth or decay, is at the heart of a theory of the trade cycle. In a series of lectures on growth delivered in 1969 and 1970 in the US Harrod stressed this point with more force, digging into further detail as to the implications of the relative positions of the three growth rates, and better specifying his view of the instability principle.

The lecture notes and text of these lectures provide evidence of a shift of emphasis taking place, from a substantial acceptance of his role as founder of growth theory back to the stress on instability and cycles.

6.1   Harrod in Russia

Talk of Harrod visiting Russia had taken place since 1961, when Harrod met some Russian colleagues at the International Economic Association Conference in Brissago. In 1962 Harrod had proposed two or three subjects for lectures, but eventually had to cancel due to overcommitment. The Plovdiv IEA Conference in 1964 on the problems of development for socialist countries further whetted Harrod's appetite for Russia. In a couple of exchanges with Soviet economists, Harrod pointed out that there seems 'there could be a meeting of minds on an objective plane between scientific economists, despite ideological differences' (letter to Anushavan Agafonovich Arzumanyan, 15 December 1964), and that some 'topics within the pure theory of growth . . . can be kept entirely free of ideological considerations' (letter to Stanislav Menshikov, 2 March 1965, in HP IV/B/C).[31]

Harrod's lecture[32] accordingly opened with some considerations on the universality of certain economic laws, 'to which man has to accommodate himself, like the laws of physics themselves'. In spite of having 'devoted part of [his] life's work to studying specifically capitalist manifestations, like imperfect competition and the trade cycle', Harrod's 'major effort' was devoted 'to the study of dynamic or growth economies', the subject of which are economic relations that 'operate in all forms of society' ('tribal, feudal, capitalist, socialist') (p. 1).

Following this premise, Harrod expounded his equation describing the actual rate of growth $G = s/C$,[33] explained that 'this equation is an absolute truism, or tautology', and commented:

> What value can there be in a tautology, you may ask? The value consists, presumably, in the right selection of the variables that one groups together in it, with a view to its leading on to relevant lines of enquiry. There is an infinite number of possible tautologies, but only a few of these are what may be called fruitful. (p. 3)

The second version of Harrod's formula, describing the warranted rate $G_w = s_d/C_r$, is also, 'definitionally, a tautology', for 'G_w is *defined* as the value that G assumes when it is governed by the right hand terms', namely s_d ('the fraction of income (output) that people desire to save') and C_r ('the amount of capital that, in the existing state of technology, is *required* to produce an increment of total output' (pp. 5–6). This equation has a 'capitalistic – or shall we say *laissez-faire* – application' (p. 4) with reference to trade cycle theory (although Harrod envisages that it 'could possibly have a counterpart, on a smaller scale, in socialist economies also', p. 6). The connection offered by Harrod lies in the instability principle: a divergence of G from G_w, that is, of s from s_d or C from C_r, will induce people to further increase (decrease) orders, leading to inflationary (deflationary) pressure which will eventually interrupt the development (or the recession). 'I believe that this is the most viable explanation of the tendency to cyclical fluctuations in *laissez-faire* economies' (pp. 6–7).

The third version of the fundamental equation describes the 'growth *potential* of the economy'. This is suitable to reinterpretation for planned economies, if written in the form $s_r = G_n C_r$.

> On the right hand side G_n stands for the highest growth rate that is achievable, having regard to population growth and technical progress. The determinant, on the left hand side, now stands for the proportion of productive resources that it is *required* to devote to fresh capital accumulation. Instead of sustainable growth being governed by what private individuals and enterprises happen to want to save, we have a *requirement* for saving (= proportion of productive resources that ought to be be devoted to capital accumulation) being governed by the *potential* growth rate of the economy as determined by the population increase and the maximum achievable technical progress in output per person. (pp. 7–8)

6.2 American lectures on growth

The careful distinction of the three growth rate equations was also taken up in a series of lectures on growth and other subjects delivered in 1969 and 1970 in some American universities. A set of lecture notes survives:[34] albeit rough and sketchy, these notes witness of Harrod's dissent with the mainstream interpretation of his theory on a number of aspects. Most of the lectures on growth were very much centred on Harrod's own contribution:

> Why the 3 subjects chosen.[35] Deal with 2 & 3 first. *One.* Largely me. Vast development mainly since war. See E. J. Dec. 1964. So must, in any case, be selective.
> Relation of myself to Domar <+> etc.

The first theme regards the very notion of 'dynamics'. His notes for the lectures at Rutgers, 1969, open as follows:

> Refer to Hahn & Matthews. Dec. 1964. and since.
> Not quite happy. Fundamental equations: mutual consistency of growth rates. (some constant's. E.g. H. J.'s elasticities *or* make them change at steady rate). Steady acceleration or dec. Time lags *only* if discontinuities.

Similarly at Claremont:

> Dynamic axioms concern the mutual consistency of growth rates at a particular point of time, given the dynamic determinants operating at that point (cf. statics). Analysis containing time lags should be excluded except when there is an inflection in the determinants. This important, but subordinate. V. important to conjugate correctly. E.g. increase in X may be conjugated with acceleration of increase in Y, etc.

Harrod thus chose to stress a different aspect of dynamics than that emphasized in the correspondence with Matthews (Section 3 above), and focussed on the consistency of growth rates at one point of time in a state of steady advance, and relegated once more the study of lags to stage two of dynamics, where deviations from steady advance (cycles, in particular) are admitted.

A second reason for complaint concerns the qualification of 'model' attached to his formula. At Penn he took up the point with reference to a recently published methodological paper of his (a subject already discussed with Shackle: see footnote 24):

> Model. Festschrift for J. R. Hicks. 1968. What is a Model? Dont like term much. True or false? Need for connection. How different from hypothesis? Adjustable parameters? e.g. for different countries. Neglects <foreign> influences; so inexact? Contrasted uses in physics and maths.

The following point concerns the interpretation of his three equations. At Rutgers he explained as follows:

> 3 equations. 1. Truism. 2. L[aissez-]. f.[aire] 3. Planned
> 1. Tautology – dont like word. E.g. Q[uantity] T[heory]. Cambridge more tautological than Fisher. Book-keeping identity. Infinite number of tautologies. Is a particular one *useful*? Fact that equations with suffixes helped indicates usefulness.

2. Safe if def. Ambition to make it equilibrium condition. Alexander's objection. Dec. 1950. First reaction June 51 was to alter right hand term. question whether (E.J. 64) if steady growth requires inflationary pressure, price inflation will also result. Behavioural parameter of entrepreneur (Joan's animal spirits). Scope for field work or econometrics. Question of indicative planning. [...]

3. s_0 more important than s_d. Explain G_n.

Similarly at Penn 1969:

1. $G = s/C$. 2. $G_w = s_d/C_r$. 3. $s_0 = G_n/C_r$

1. Tautology. Pause on word again. Necessary truth. Dynamized $I = S$. Book-keeping identity. Infinite number of these. Merit if any depends on choice. But can also raise question if s and C are meaningful.

2. Relates to laissez-faire capitalism. 3 is a welfare <opt[imum].>

Is G_w def or equilibrium? Alexander's objection. Ref. in E.J. bibliography. I give it you. E.J. Dec. 1950. If G_w definition, that gets us some way. We cant assert equilibrium, without examining behavioural propensities of representative entrepreneur. Joan Robinson, quoting Keynes, refers to animal spirits. If not enough policy may have to be such that $s > s_d$ and/or $C < C_r$, in order to prod entrepreneurs, and conversely. This means keeping growth of agg. demand above growth of supply potential and conversely. This may lead to inflation (or defl.). Nothing whatever to do with possible need for inflation to get full employment owing to Phillips curve.

Alexander <+> indicative planning (to avoid inflation). My E.J. art Dec. 1964.[36]

Harrod's discussion of the meaning of G_w originates from the reflections in Harrod 1964.[37] Sidney Alexander (1950) had pointed out that Harrod's notion of the warranted rate as originally formulated required some implicit assumption as to how entrepreneurs would behave.[38] Harrod (1951a, 273) replied by resorting to the notion of a representative entrepreneur, but had to admit that if different postulates as to his behaviour were assumed the path of warranted growth would change accordingly. Harrod (1964, 904) so summarized the argument: 'once the representative entrepreneur's behavioural parameter was defined, there must be *some* sustainable warranted rate of growth, given that the determining forces [that is, s and C_p] remained unchanged'. Now Harrod suggests that to circumvent the problem it is safe to take G_w as a definition, although it is still not clear what he means precisely.

This is specified in the 1973 volume. The equation $G_w = s_d/C_r$ defines G_w as the rate of growth that is consistent with people saving as they desire to save and with the amount of capital, fixed and circulating, being just what people find convenient (pp. 17–19). Whether this is an equilibrium rate – that is, whether the system remains in the same state – still depends on the behavioural parameters of the entrepreneurs. The problem is far from being solved, for the evolution of the system is not defined unless this behavioural parameter is specified: Harrod's dynamics still cannot escape from the single instant to which it was confined.

Finally, Harrod takes issues with the neoclassical criticism of the instability principle.[39] At Penn 1969:

> Instability Princ. If $G > G_w$ either $s > s_d$ *or* $C < C_r$; either way, orders will be increased & G will move further from G_w. Similar downward course. Contrast this with statics.
>
> Neo-classicals argue that if $G > G_w$, interest thus raising s_d or reducing C_r. This quite absurd. It means that every chance deviation will be justified by a sufficient change in the governing variables. There is no principle of this sort in classical statics. On the contrary chance deviations are corrected by steadiness in the governing variables.
>
> Draw attention to analysis with Keynes v. Say's Law in macro-statics. By Say's Law full employment would be maintained without policy measures.

At Rutgers:

> Instability princ. If $G > G_w$ either $s > s_d$ *or* $C < C_r$
> Deny assumption of fixed co-efficients. Refute neo-classicals (Keynes).

At Claremont:

> Instability princ. If $G > G_w$ either $s > s_d$ *or* $C < C_r$ or both. Either way adjustment $+G$. Repudiate knife-edge. Only place where I have talked about, I suggest 6 months.[40]

And at Princeton:

> Neo-classicals say implies fixed co-efficients. Nothing in this at all. Said in my first essay that C_r depends on interest. That in turn determined by general system.

At Rutgers, Keio and Claremont, Harrod noted: 'Go over 7 cases', referring to analysis of disequilibrium in terms of the comparison of the possible relative positions of the actual, warranted and natural growth rates, their effect on employment, inflation and long-run equilibrium later presented in *Economic dynamics*[41] (1973, 104).

In spite of the problem of the still missing connection between states (which Harrod seems to have thought he had resolved), the emphasis on instability is a prelude to the discussion of the amplification of deviations between actual and warranted rate, which Harrod explicitly discussed in the book he was writing (see Section 8 below). In these lectures on growth, however, there are still no references to the trade cycle, nor does Harrod reply to the post-Keynesian criticism of his theories. He was, however, soon dragged into the matter by a paper by Joan Robinson.

7. Harrod and Joan Robinson on saving and growth

In 1969–70, Harrod and Joan Robinson had a further prolonged exchange of views concerning the interpretation of Harrod's growth equation, which is illuminating both as confirming Robinson's reading a few years hence (see Section 4) and as to Harrod's new reaction to it.[42] The exchange was occasioned by a draft of Robinson's 'Harrod after twenty years',[43] that was sent to Harrod on 22 August 1969 by the Editor of the *Economic Journal* to check if it contained misinterpretations. Harrod's first reaction does not seem to have survived, but he preserved a set of reading notes. His first point of disagreement concerned Robinson's first two paragraphs (1970, 731–2), where she failed to appropriately distinguish the three growth rates:

> The "fluke" relates not to the "natural" or desirable rate, but to the "warranted" or equilibrium rate.
>
> [. . .] In my book these terms s and v . . . determine the warranted, not the possible rate. . . . Both were intended to express equilibrium positions. Absolutely indispensable for my argument was another equation expressing what actually happens at any time and is a bookkeeping identity. It must be true.
>
> Para 3 is true provided that possible growth is taken to mean equilibrium growth and not natural growth. (Untitled notes)

A second complaint regarded Robinson's reference to K, the volume of capital ('I do not use the concept K in my <+> treatment. It does not come into my reasonings'; the argument is fully taken up in Harrod's comment: 1970: 739), and the identification of the capital coefficient as a capital/output ratio, rather than as an incremental capital/output ratio.

Joan Robinson's reply introduced the recurrent theme of her own (and Nicholas Kaldor's and Luigi Pasinetti's) treatment of growth, the distribution of income: 'I have to introduce K because I have introduced into your system the rate of profit on capital which you do not mention' (letter to Harrod, 2 September 1969). To this remark, Harrod (1970: 737–8) pointed out (in print) that he had indeed referred to the rate of profit in *The Trade Cycle*, where this variable was one of the dynamic determinants.

Another observation by Robinson is of interest: she pointed out that 'I am concerned entirely with the formula for steady growth whereas you seem to be thinking rather of the trade-cycle aspect'. Harrod himself confirmed this interpretation, as he wrote to Charles Carter that the so-called 'knife-edge' 'is of more importance to cycle theory than to the theory of steady growth' (letter undated [probably 7 November 1969]). This emphasis on cycle theory is quite interesting, as in the reply in print Harrod (1970, 740–1) dropped the point and disputed instead the 'sharpness' of the edge, stressing that there is a breathing space of about six months.

At the end of 1969 'something has happened' that worried Harrod as to the general acceptance of Robinson's view as expressed in the article, for 'although it uses my name, has very little reference at all to my ideas':

> I have read the earlier sections of Morishima's book on growth theory, which may prove to be a work of some importance. He there attributes to me views that have a family resemblance to those which you have attributed to me, but which have no relation to the views that I hold and have published. Now, I am sure that what you write is more important than what Morishima may write. But there is this all important difference. Morishima is a third party who has based his ideas about me on what you have said that I think and not on what I have said that I think. Thus an outside scholar uses you as authority for what I hold instead of studying my own works. Thus the situation is becoming intolerable, especially as you have so greatly misrepresented my view – doubtless unwillingly.
>
> I have of course written to Morishima pointing out that I am not responsible for the views attributed to me by him in his book.
>
> (Harrod to Robinson, 20 December 1969)[44]

At this point, the latent conflict between Harrod and the mainstream interpretation of his dynamics evolved into open war. Harrod himself indicated the point where Robinson's reading failed to interpret him correctly:

> It is impossible to expound my views without using at least three concepts for growth (G, G_w and G_n), three for saving (s, s_d, s_0) and two for the capital output ratio (C and C_r). There is also a C_0 but that is not so central to my theories. Incidentally, I have always used the symbol C, not v, for the capital output ratio.
>
> (letter to Robinson, 27 April 1970)[45]

Joan Robinson commented that she was distinguishing 'between the views of Sir Roy, i.e. what you believe in 1970, and the Harrod model of 1949', and returned to the interpretation of Harrod's growth equation as indicating a causal relationship between saving and growth – thus proving to Harrod that she has actually failed to take his point:

> You now say that the warranted rate of growth represents the desire of firms to accumulate. That is to say, you make s govern accumulation. That is to say, you are trying to turn Harrod's theory into a pre-Keynesian theory. I will not have this at any price. Of course you can criticise me for misunderstanding Harrod. But I maintain that I understand him a lot better than Sir Roy does.[46]
>
> (letter to Harrod, 29 April 1970).

Harrod could only restate the point of the previous letter:

> Your letter continues to ignore the vital distinction between movements in actual growth and movements in warranted growth – both being quite different from natural growth, which is the essence of my theory. An increase at a point of time in the 'desire of firms to accumulate' is a depressant of actual growth. This is Keynes, and I remain a Keynesian in this respect. An increase in the desire of firms to accumulate, to the extent that this is not ephemeral and shortly to be reversed, raises the warranted rate. This is neither Keynesian nor anti-Keynesian, because it is a dynamic principle, and there is no dynamics in Keynes. I explained that there is no dynamics in Keynes in my lecture to the [Econometric] Society (later published in Econometrica), in 1936.[47]

Seeing this continuous misunderstanding, Harrod should probably have explained his point of the distinction of the three rates in detail. The 'desire of firms to accumulate' (that is, their propensity to save) increases (as Robinson pointed out) the warranted rate. But this is not what drives the accumulation rate, which depends instead on the divergence between warranted and actual rate. The increase in the warranted rate brings it above the actual rate, and initiates a depressing cumulative movement.

This exchange left Harrod with the impression that Joan Robinson 'hasn't the faintest idea what my growth theory is about' (letter to Sidney Weintraub, 10 December 1970, cited in John Lodewijks (1990) p. 10), and therefore confirmed to him his suspicion that scholars learning his views second hand would fail to understand his point.

8.   Conclusion: back to fluctuations and instability

The correspondence with Shackle and Joan Robinson, together with the lectures on growth, show how Harrod began taking exception with the two dominant interpretations of his writings, both by neoclassical and post-Keynesian authors. He himself pointed to the locus where the author-ized statement of his dynamics could be found:

> I have given courses on growth theory (including one this term at Penn University) as well as individual lectures in various universi-ties, subjecting myself to lengthy cross-examinations, and a book is in the course of preparation.
>
> (letter to Robinson, 27 April 1970)

The book, Harrod's last, was *Economic Dynamics*. It was meant to be a second edition of *Towards a Dynamic Economics*,[48] but in reality it was completely rewritten (Harrod, 1973, Preface) and expanded. The first chapter takes up and updates Harrod's 1948 plea that foundations for dynamic economics are needed, and distinguishes between the more general 'growth theory' and specific 'economic dynamics'. Of more interest in light of the preceding sections is Harrod's extended discus-sion of the fundamental equation in its three forms (Chapter 2), of the instability principle in its relation to the trade cycle (Chapter 3), and of the policy problems in connection with the relative position of the three growth rates (Chapter 7).

Although some concepts were updated to reflect the debates which had arisen in the meantime (in particular, the warranted rate was rein-terpreted in light of Alexander's 1950 criticism and transformed from an equilibrium into a definitional concept,[49] as indicated in the 1969 Penn lecture cited in Section 6.2 above), Harrod rescued the analytical apparatus developed in the first draft (1938, in Harrod, 2003) of his 1939 'Essay in economic dynamics',[50] where the trade cycle aspect was much more emphasized than it was in the published version.[51] This is one of the most interesting contributions of the book, for it rejects at once the neoclassical and post-Keynesian readings of Harrod's theory as a growth model with fixed parameters (Section 2) by stressing the implications of instability for business cycle theory and the role of nonlinearity in explaining the turning points.

The instability principle states that a divergence between the warranted and the actual rates would be cumulative.[52] But the system's growth or decline triggers changes in the warranted rate. Harrod thus distinguishes between the 'normal' value of the warranted rate – that is, the value pertaining to steady advance – and special warranted rates, capable of fluctuating in the course of the cycle. Both individuals and companies may reduce their saving plans in face of a declining income, thereby reducing G_w (and conversely in a boom). As to the capital coefficient, 'if there is an abatement in the *de facto* rate of recession, for example by the increasing resistance of consumers to a decline in their standard of living [the scrapping of saving plans just discussed], the proportion of existing equipment that needs be replaced goes up', C_r increases and therefore G_w further decreases. The special warranted rate thus chases the actual one, and when actual growth or decline slows down sufficiently or eventually stops (for instance, because it reaches the ceiling of full employment of resources[53]) an overtaking occurs. This inverts the relative position of special warranted and actual rates, and the cumulative movement proceeds in the opposite direction. (1973, 36–41)[54]

Harrod's dynamics, far from being concerned with a rigid description of equilibrium growth determined by immutable parameters, is based instead on fluctuating parameters, suitable for a theory of cycles. Harrod has thus returned to his earliest formulation, although the change is much more a matter of emphasis than of substance (except for the re-introduction of the 'special' warranted rates), for the essentials of a cycle theory, albeit compressed and almost not recognizable, were never blanked out from his 'growth' writings. Without the archival materials, revealing how Harrod's discontent with the 'mainstream' interpretations of his writings grew, how he found the key for the understanding where precisely his readers went astray, and how he attempted to fix the problem, it would seem that his latest formulation came out of the blue, while instead it had its roots in the very first presentation of his 'fundamental equation'. His solution is not without problems: but it is certainly consistent with Harrod's own intellectual history, which is completely different from the rendition textbooks gave of it.

References

Unpublished works

Carter, C.F., Letter to Harrod, 22 August 1969, in Harrod Papers (Chiba University of Commerce), file IV-1089-1107.

Haberler, G., *Systematic Analysis of the Theories of the Business Cycle*, League of Nations: Economic Intelligence Service, August 1934, TD, in League of Nations Archives, Geneva, file 10B/12653/12653, Jacket No 1.

Harrod, R.F., Letter to R.C.O. Matthews, 7 January 1964, Harrod Papers (Chiba University of Commerce), unclassified folder.

Letter to R.C.O. Matthews, 8 January 1964, Harrod Papers (Chiba University of Commerce), unclassified folder.

Letter to A.A. Arzumanyan, 15 December 1964, in Harrod Papers (Chiba University of Commerce), file IV/B/C.

Letter to S. Menshikov, 2 March 1965, in Harrod Papers (Chiba University of Commerce), file IV/B/C.

Letter to the British Council, September 1965, in Harrod Papers (Chiba University of Commerce), file VII/F–5.

Letter to J.V. Robinson, 1 February 1966, carbon copy in Harrod Papers (Chiba University of Commerce), file IV-1089-1107.

Letter to G.L.S. Shackle, 11 January 1966, Shackle Papers (Cambridge University Library), file 9/1/383.

Letter to G.L.S. Shackle, 24 March 1966, Shackle Papers (Cambridge University Library), file 9/1/393.

'Growth theory. Lecture delivered at the State University of Moscow, on April 22, 1966, by R.F. Harrod', initialled typescript, 23 pages, in Harrod Papers (Chiba University of Commerce), file V/326.

Letter to C.F. Carter, undated (but probably 7 November 1969), carbon copy in Harrod Papers (Chiba University of Commerce), file V-124.

Untitled Notes (on J.V. Robinson's "Harrod after twenty years"), 1969, in Harrod Papers (Chiba University of Commerce), file V-124.

Letter to J.V. Robinson, 20 December 1969, marked 'copy', in Harrod Papers (Chiba University of Commerce), file V-124.

Letter to J.V. Robinson, 27 April 1970, carbon copy in Harrod Papers (Chiba University of Commerce), file V-124.

Letter to J.V. Robinson, undated [April or May 1970], carbon copy in Harrod Papers (Chiba University of Commerce), file IV-1089-1107.

Lecture notes in the Harrod Papers (Chiba University of Commerce): Pennsylvania University, 1969: index in file V-128/6, notes in files V-127/1 (1/3) and V-128/2 (1/12, 2–3/12); Pennsylvania 1970, file V-132/6; Rutgers, 1969 (perhaps also delivered at Iowa), file V-132/7; Claremont (probably 1970), Maryland, Waterloo in file V-132/5; Princeton (perhaps 1969), file V-132/11; Keio University, Japan, file V-132/8. All these folders are unfoliated.

Matthews, R.C.O.
Letter to Harrod, 2 January 1964, in Harrod Papers (Chiba University of Commerce), file IV-732-741.
Robinson, J.V.
Letter to Harrod, 8 December [1965], in Harrod Papers (Chiba University of Commerce), file IV-1089-1107.
Letter to Harrod, 20 December 1965, in Harrod Papers (Chiba University of Commerce), file IV-1089-1107.
Letter to Harrod, 10 January 1966, in Harrod Papers (Chiba University of Commerce), file IV-1089-1107.
'Harrod after twenty years', 1969 (draft of Robinson, 1970), in Harrod Papers (Chiba University of Commerce), file IV-1089-1107 and file V-124 (copy).
Letter to Harrod, 2 September 1969, in Harrod Papers (Chiba University of Commerce), file IV-1089-1107.
Letter to Harrod, 29 April 1970, in Harrod Papers (Chiba University of Commerce), file IV-1089-1107.
Shackle, G.L.S.
Letter to Harrod, 11 January 1966, in Harrod Papers (Chiba University of Commerce), file IV-1148-1151.

Published writings

Alexander, S.S. (1950) 'Mr. Harrod's dynamic model', *Economic Journal*, vol. LX, December, pp. 724–39.
Baumol, W.J. (1948) 'Notes on some dynamic models', *Economic Journal*, vol. LVIII, (December): 506–21.
Besomi, D. (1996) 'An additional note on the Harrod-Keynes correspondence', *History of Political Economy*, vol. 28, no. 2: 281–94.
Besomi, D. (1996a) Editorial apparatus to R. F. Harrod, '"An Essay in Dynamic Theory": 1938 draft', *History of Political Economy* 28:2, pp. 245–251.
Besomi, D. (1998) 'Failing to win consent. Harrod's dynamics in the eyes of his readers', in G. Rampa, L. Stella and A. Thirlwall (eds), *Economic Dynamics, Trade and Growth: Essays on Harrodian Themes*, London: Macmillan, pp. 38–88.
Besomi, D. (1998a) 'Harrod and the time-lag theories of the cycle', in G. Rampa, L. Stella and A. Thirlwall (eds), *Economic Dynamics, Trade and Growth: Essays on Harrodian Themes*, London: Macmillan, pp. 107–148.
Besomi, D. (1999) *The Making of Harrod's Dynamics*, London: Macmillan.
Besomi, D. (1999a) 'Harrod's instability principle and trade cycles', in P. O'Hara (ed.), *Encyclopedia of Political Economy*, vol. 1, London: Routledge, pp. 425–7.
Besomi, D. (2001) 'Harrod's dynamics and the theory of growth: the story of a mistaken attribution', *Cambridge Journal of Economics*, vol. 25, no. 1 (January): 79–96.
Besomi, D. (2003) 'The papers of Roy Harrod', *History of Economics Review*, 37 (Winter): 19–40.
Besomi, D. (2005) 'A goodwilling outsider. The correspondence between Keynes and Harrod', in M.C. Marcuzzo and A. Rosselli (eds), *Economists in Cambridge. A Study Through Their Correspondence, 1907–1946*, London: Routledge, pp. 92–118.

Domar, E.D. (1946) 'Capital expansion, rate of growth, and employment', *Econometrica*, 14 (April): 137–47.

Domar, E.D. (1947) 'Expansion and employment', *American Economic Review*, 37 (March): 34–55.

Hahn, F., and R.C.O. Matthews (1964) 'The theory of economic growth: a survey', *Economic Journal*, vol. LXXIV (December): 779–902.

Harrod, R.F. (1934a) 'Doctrines of imperfect competition', *Quarterly Journal of Economics*, 48 (May): 442–70.

Harrod, R.F. (1934b) 'The expansion of credit in an advancing community', *Economica*, NS 1 (August): 287–99.

Harrod, R.F. (1934c) 'Rejoinder to Mr. Robertson', *Economica*, NS 1 (November): 476–8.

Harrod, R.F. (1936) *The Trade Cycle. An Essay*, Oxford: Clarendon Press.

Harrod, R.F. (1937) 'Mr. Keynes and traditional theory', *Econometrica*, vol 5. (January): 74–86.

Harrod, R.F. (1938) 'Scope and method of economics', *Economic Journal*, XLVIII (September): 383–412.

Harrod, R.F. (1939) 'An essay in dynamic theory', *Economic Journal*, XLIX (March): 14–33.

Harrod, R.F. (1948) *Towards a Dynamic Economics*, London: Macmillan.

Harrod, R.F. (1951) *The Life of John Maynard Keynes*, London: Macmillan.

Harrod, R.F. (1951a) 'Notes on trade cycle theory', *Economic Journal*, vol. XLI (June): 261–75.

Harrod, R.F. (1953) 'Comment [to Pilvin]', *Quarterly Journal of Economics*, vol. LXVII, no. 4 (November): 553–9.

Harrod, R.F. (1955) 'Les relations entre l'investissement et la population', *Revue Économique*, vol. 6, no. 3 (May): 356–67.

Harrod, R.F. (1959) 'Domar and dynamic economics', *Economic Journal*, vol. LXIX (September): 451–64.

Harrod, R.F. (1963) 'Themes in dynamic theory', *Economic Journal*, vol. LXXIII (September): 401–21.

Harrod, R.F. (1964) 'Are monetary and fiscal policies enough?', *Economic Journal*, LXXIV (December): 903–15.

Harrod, R.F. (1965) [Review of] '*Essays in economic policy*. By N. Kaldor', *Economic Journal* LXXV (December): 794–803.

Harrod, R.F. (1967) 'Increasing returns', in R.E. Kuenne, *Monopolistic Competition Theory: Studies in Impact. Essays in Honor of Edward H. Chamberlin*, New York: Wiley.

Harrod, R.F. (1968) 'What is a model?', in J.N. Wolfe (ed.), *Value, Capital and Growth: Papers in Honour of Sir John Hicks*, Edinburgh University Press, pp. 173–91.

Harrod, R.F. (1970) 'Harrod after twenty-one years: a comment', *Economic Journal*, vol. LXXX (September): 737–41.

Harrod, R.F. (1971) '[Review of] Kalecki, Michal. *Introduction to the Theory of Growth in a Socialist Economy*', *Kyklos*, 24: 149–52.

Harrod, R.F. (1972) 'Imperfect competition, aggregate demand and inflation', *Economic Journal*, vol. LXXXII (March): 392–401.

Harrod, R.F. (1973) *Economic Dynamics*, London: Macmillan.

Harrod, R.F. (2003) *The Collected Interwar Papers and Correspondence of Roy Harrod*, ed. D. Besomi, 3 volumes, Cheltenham: Edward Elgar.

Harrod, R.F., and J.V. Robinson (2006) 'Correspondence on growth theory, 1965–70', ed. D. Besomi, *History of Economics Review*, 44 (Summer): 16–30.

Jolink, A. (1995) ' "Anecdotal myths": Tinbergen's influence on Harrod's growth theory', *European Journal of the History of Economic Thought*, 2:2 (Autumn): 443–9.

Lodewijks, J. (1990) 'Sidney Weintraub, the English Dons, and an unpublished obituary of Harrod', *The History of Economic Thought Society of Australia Bulletin*, 13 (Winter): 8–17.

McCord Wright, D. (1949) 'Mr. Harrod and growth economics', *Review of Economics and Statistics*, vol. XXXI, no. 4 (November): 322–8.

Moggridge, D.E. (1973) Editorial apparatus to *The Collected Writings of John Maynard Keynes*, vol. XIV, London: Macmillan.

Morishima, M. (1969) *Theory of Economic Growth*, Oxford: Clarendon.

Robinson, J.V. (1970) 'Harrod after twenty-one years', *Economic Journal*, vol. LXXX (September): 731–7.

Robinson, J.V. (1970a) ' "Harrod after twenty-one years": a reply', *Economic Journal*, vol. LXXX (September): 741.

Robinson, J.V. (1971) *Economic Heresies. Some Old-Fashioned Questions in Economic Theory*, London: Macmillan.

Shackle, G.L.S. (1965) *A Scheme of Economic Theory*, Cambridge University Press.

Shackle, G.L.S. (1967) *The Years of High Theory. Invention and Tradition in Economic Thought 1926–1936*, Cambridge: Cambridge University Press.

Tinbergen, J. (1937) '(Review of) Harrod, R.F., *The Trade Cycle. An Essay*', *Weltwirtschaftliches Archiv*, 45.3: 89*–91*.

Young, W. (1989) *Harrod and his Trade Cycle Group. The Origins and Development of the Growth Research Programme*, London: Macmillan.

Notes

* Address for correspondence: c.p. 7, 6950 Gola di Lago, Switzerland. Email: dbesomi@bluewin.ch

1 I am grateful to the following people and institutions for permission to cite passages of unpublished writings: to Chiba University of Commerce, Ichkawa, Japan, for Harrod's writings in their possession; to Dominick Harrod and the late Lady Harrod, for the remainder of Harrod's writings; to the Syndics of Cambridge University Library for permission to use the Shackle Papers, and to Stephen Frowen and two nieces of the late Mrs Catherine Shackle – Frances Ferneyhough and Hilary Law – for permission to use and quote from Shackle's unpublished writings; to Robin Matthews for his letter to Harrod; and to the Provost and Scholars of King's College for permission to cite from the unpublished writings of Joan Robinson, of which they own the copyright.

2 For detailed surveys of the interpretation of Harrod's dynamics see Besomi (1998), while for Harrod's own published reaction to this see Besomi (2001). For a detailed description of the archives where Harrod's papers are preserved see the Editorial Introduction to Harrod (2003) and Besomi (2003), which also assess the significance of these materials for the interpretation of Harrod's writings. For an intellectual biography of Harrod giving special weight to his unpublished papers see the General Introduction to Harrod (2003).

3   See also his correspondence with Haberler in October and November of the same year, in Harrod (2003), pp. 304 and 326. For a discussion see Besomi (1999a).

4   From this, Haberler's *Prosperity and Depression* was eventually to be elaborated. The story is reported in Besomi (1999), pp. 58–60.

5   In spite of the common terminology, the acceleration principle is interpreted in rather different ways in *The Trade Cycle* and in the 'Essay'. In the 1936 book it represented the volume of additions to capital goods necessary to meet a certain expected increase in demand, while in the 1939 article expectations disappeared from view and the link was between investment and the increase in total output, rather than consumption. On the difference between the causal relationships among variables in these two writings by Harrod, see Besomi (1999), Chapter 6.

6   Only the simplest formulas for the rate of growth have been reproduced here; Harrod, however, also included international trade and the part of capital outlays with no direct relation to the current increase of output (1939, 27–8).

7   David McCord Wright (1949, 326) noted that in the 'Essay' Harrod provided six qualifications of the notion of warranted rate: it leaves each entrepreneur satisfied as well as entrepreneurs as a whole, keeps them doing the same thing, equates *ex ante* investment and saving, only concerns the part of investment linked to consumption, and differs from the full employment rate.

8   For a more detailed discussion see Besomi (1998), pp. 53–64.

9   This part of the argument, formulated in the 1938 draft (in Harrod, 2003: 1199–200), is not very convincing, for a drop in C would make G_w higher, not lower.

10 A graphical representation of the relationship between growth rates during the cycle was given by Jacob Marschak in correspondence with Harrod in September 1938. The diagram is reproduced in Harrod (2003), p. 845.

11 On the three stages see Besomi (1999), pp. 126–32, and (1998a), pp. 119–24.

12 Harrod was admirably consistent in maintaining that he was only attempting to devise the tools for thought in dynamic theory: in *The Trade Cycle* he stressed that he was only presenting 'the outline of a theory' (Harrod, 1936: vii and ix; see also 1937: 86, and 1938: 405), in the 'Essay' he invoked 'a new method of approach – indeed, a mental revolution' (1939: 15); the title itself of *Towards a Dynamic Economics* (1948) indicated that Harrod aimed at posing the foundations of the discipline, and accordingly the first chapter was dedicated to 'the need for a dynamic economics'. He later qualified his dynamics as a 'tool of thought', stressing that his analysis 'only claimed to be a preliminary attempt to lay foundations' (1953: 553 and 555; 1973: 2), and that it requires 'far reaching changes in some of our traditional habits of thinking' (1959: 451; see also 1948: 80).

13 'G_w itself fluctuates in the trade cycle' (Harrod, 1948: 89).

14 This was noticed by Marschak on seeing the first draft of the Essay, in August or September 1938 (in Harrod, 2003: 847–8), while after the war it was noticed by William Baumol (1948, 512). The implications drawn by Shackle and Sydney Alexander will be discussed in sections 5 and 6.2 below, respectively.

15 This criticism, besides wrongly assuming that Harrod was postulating constant parameters, also mistakes the working of his dynamics, based on the instability intrinsic in the comparison of actual and warranted rates, not

actual and natural rates. See, for a more detailed survey of the neoclassical criticism, Besomi (1998), pp. 57–61.

16 Harrod was rather frustrated by the lack of recognition of other pet ideas: for instance, he privately complained (in a letter to Dennis Robertson of 8 October 1937, in Harrod, 2003: 724–5) that reviewers did not pay attention to his 'dynamic determinants', and he publicly and repeatedly claimed priority in the discovery of the concept of 'marginal revenue' ('egoistic footnote' to Harrod, 1951: 159–60; 1967: 65n; and 1972: 394; in private, he left a note to future historians of thought to that effect, transcribed in Harrod, 2003: 1067).

17 The correspondence, dated July 1937, was found by Albert Jolink and published in 1995; now also in Harrod (2003), pp. 705–7.

18 For an account of the development of Harrod's dynamics in the early stages see Besomi (1999), in particular chapters 5 and 6 for his methodological reflections on the three stages of dynamics and for the transition from *The Trade Cycle* and the 'Essay', respectively.

19 Other passages of this correspondence, relating to Harrod's sudden discovery of the fundamental equation, are cited in Warren Young (1989), p. 179.

20 See in particular Harrod (1951a), pp. 268–9; (1955), pp. 359–60; (1957), pp. 193; (1963), pp. 402–3. For further references and a detailed commentary on Harrod's view on lags see Besomi (1998a).

21 The extant part of the exchange is published as 'Roy Harrod and Joan Robinson: correspondence on growth theory, 1965–70' (Harrod and Robinson 2006).

22 Robinson's v stands for Harrod's C.

23 This book, and the related correspondence with Harrod, escaped my attention when surveying the secondary literature on Harrod's dynamics (Besomi, 1998), where I only considered Shackle's *Years of High Theory* (1967).

24 In correspondence, Harrod objected to having produced a model, although he admitted not having fully followed Shackle's heuristic notion of a model as 'a form of explanation', a tool 'of insight, not of foresight' (Harrod to Shackle, 11 January 1966, with reference to Shackle, 1965, 96–8). Harrod had instead 'the feeling that a model ought to have adjustable parameters', and therefore denied that his truism could be called a model. This is rather curious, for Harrod in 1938 had explicitly envisaged a heuristic notion of a model (but at the same time failed to appreciate its implications when Keynes took up the subject in correspondence: see, for a discussion, Besomi, 2005, Section 6). Moreover, his explicit aim of devising tools for thought for dynamic problems (see his statements collected in footnote 12 above) should have set him on the right track. Be that as it may, the proposition that a model should have adjustable parameters became the central proposition of Harrod's 'What is a model?' (1968, 174), where Harrod also disputed that a tautology can be a model – due to the lack of adjustable parameters (pp. 183–5) – and took up as an illustration the Cambridge and Fisher equations he had cited in correspondence with Shackle (pp. 184–5, and letter to Shackle of 11 January 1966).

25 Shackle's dichotomy is stressed by the separation of the discussion of stages one and two in separate sections of the book. Although Harrod's idea that knowledge – including the understanding of dynamic systems – should proceed in distinct stages was outlined in his presidential address before the British Association (later published as Harrod, 1938), it only becomes obvious he had

that division in mind when elaborating the 'Essay' if the preliminary draft (written shortly after the presidential address) is considered (see Besomi, 1996: 287–91).

26 Shackle is very careful in defining the time dimension of the various *G, C* and *s* (pp. 106–7).

27 Words within angled bracked are the best guess; <+> indicates an illegible word.

28 Keynes, however, noted it in his March 1937 lecture notes on *The Trade Cycle* (in Harrod, 2003: 648).

29 In his book, Shackle (1965, pp. 104–5) had already stressed that he was deliberately giving a purely technical interpretation of the acceleration principle, ignoring that 'a given machine or factory can be worked more or less intensively, more or less continuously', and that 'when it is a question of creating additional equipment in order to increase general output *Y*, there will ordinarily be available many different technical schemes amongst which the choice may depend on the interest rates at which money can be borrowed or lent for a suitably long term'.

30 Shackle had pointed out in his book that there should have been a distinction between intended and realized saving (1965: 120).

31 Harrod later stressed this point in his review of Kalecki's *Introduction to The Theory of Growth in a Socialist Economy* (Harrod, 1971: 149).

32 'Growth theory. Lecture delivered at the State University of Moscow'. The title originally suggested by Harrod to the British Council, which organized the trip via the British Embassy, was 'Pure theory of economic growth as applicable to socialist and capitalist countries alike' (Correspondence with the British Council, September 1965).

33 Harrod noted: 'I have now adopted the convention, which I did not always observe earlier, of using symbols without suffix for variables in an equation when this equation represents a necessary factual truth' (p. 3). Harrod thus started to follow the rules he set in a letter to Shackle of 24 March 1966: 'As regards my equations, I should like to make it a rule – for my own observance! – that where the symbols are without suffix the equation represents an identity. I am inclined to think, but this I need to brood on a little more, that if any has a suffix they must all have.'

34 The notes, quite rough and sketchy, concern lectures delivered at Pennsylvania University in 1969 and 1970, at Rutgers (and perhaps also Iowa) 1969, Claremont (probably 1970), Maryland, Waterloo, Princeton (perhaps 1969), and Keio University in Japan.

35 Other subjects discussed at Pennsylvania, 1969, were 'U.K. monetary system' and 'International monetary systems'.

36 The article was also cited in correspondence with Shackle, 11 January 1966.

37 There Harrod had also 'conceptually refurbished' the notion of *natural* rate.

38 This is one of the facets of the problem, already cited (section 2), of the missing link between successive states.

39 It is interesting to note that Harrod had already rejected the neoclassical criticism well before anyone could think of it, at the time of drafting his 1939 Essay: 'Application of the static theory has suggested the optimistic view that a system, in which mobility of resources and flexibility of prices were at their maximum, would, given a reasonable allowance for lags and frictions, adjust

itself to this natural rate of increase. Consideration of the dynamic equation suggests (i) that there will be self-aggravating movements away from the equilibrium position. The facts indeed have forced static theorists to admit that there must be present some self-aggravating forces of this kind. But the analysis undertaken in terms of the static equations falls short of full cogency, having to call in aid assumptions with regard to lags supported by what they are intended to prove. Per contra the tendency to a self-aggravating departure follows directly from the dynamic equation. It also suggests (ii), as will presently be shown, that in certain circumstances there may be impediments to full unemployment ever being reached. This seems to go farther than anything which may be legitimately deduced from static theory' (in Harrod, 2003, 1209).

40 It should be noted that Harrod did not mean to repudiate the instability principle, but only the reaction speed. The point is made clear in Harrod (1970), pp. 740–1, and (1973), pp. 32–33.

41 Although Harrod's book was only published in 1973, he was already working at it at the end of 1969, as results from an undated letter to Charles Carter (the editor of the *Economic Journal*), likely to have been written on 7 November 1969 (in HP V-124).

42 This exchange is also to be published in (Harrod and Robinson 2006).

43 Eventually published as 'Harrod after twenty-one years'. The article was originally meant to be published in September 1969, a comment by Harrod should have followed in December. Harrod, however, insisted either that the Comment immediately followed the article, or that Robinson insert a disclaimer, which Robinson refused to do. Both the article and the Comment were eventually published in September 1970, together with a very brief reply by Robinson (1970a). The draft (of which there are two copies in Harrod's papers) is substantially coincident with the published version.

44 Harrod's letter to Michio Morishima is not extant (Morishima, personal communication). Harrod repeated this argument, again with reference to Morishima's *Theory of Economic Growth* (1969), in an undated letter written to Robinson in April or May 1970: 'I suppose that more people read what you write than what I write, so that a number of people, including, for instance, Morishima, attribute to me a quite false version of what I have actually written. This is rather galling. It is not pleasant to have had ideas that one values and have them travestied.' A few months later he wrote to a similar effect to Sidney Weintraub: the passage, from a letter dated December 1970, is cited in Lodewijks (1990), p. 10.

45 Robinson meanwhile had drafted the chapter on "Growth models" for her *Economic Heresies* (1971), on which this letter is a comment.

46 'I think I understand Harrod's theory much better than he does' (Robinson to S. Weintraub, 18 December 1970, cited in Lodewijks (1990), p. 10.

47 Harrod, undated letter (April or May 1970). The *Econometrica* paper was published in 1937, the relevant passages being on pp. 85–6. Harrod maintained that the Keynesian system is static, for it deals only with the consequences of *una tantum* acts of investment on income and saving. Harrod is interested instead in the problem of *continuous* acts of saving (= investment), which entail continuous growth, for the analysis of which it is necessary to work in terms of instantaneous growth rates – cross-section pictures of the relationships among variables. Harrod's definition of dynamics was based on this idea.

48 Letter to Carter, November 1969.
49 An oddly worded passage in Chapter 2, if taken in isolation from the analytical set-up of the dynamic mechanism (based on the movement generated by the divergence between actual and warranted rate) seems to suggest that Harrod had reverted to the position denounced by Robinson in her correspondence with Harrod: the warranted growth equation 'may be regarded as the equation specifying the determinants of growth in a regime of *laissez-faire* capitalism. This is in line with classical economics. What people choose to save, subject to the various institutional arrangements . . . determines the growth rate of the economy' (p. 28). The wording is deceptive, as it suggests that an increase in the propensity to save would determine an increase in the growth rate. The mechanism described in the following pages (reported in the text), however, indicates that an increase in the propensity to save taking place in a situation of equilibrium growth at a steady rate would bring the warranted rate above the actual rate and push the latter downwards.
50 At the time of writing *Economic Dynamics* Harrod had searched his own archives for his correspondence with Keynes, to be included in vols 13 and 14 of Keynes's *Collected Writings* published in 1973, and may therefore have come across and re-read the draft. This, however, is only a conjecture, in favour of which there is the striking similarity of the trade cycle parts in the draft and the 1973 book, against which there is Harrod's declaration to the editor of Keynes's *CW* that the draft had not survived (Moggridge, 1973, in CW XIV, 320); Harrod may not have found it, but the draft definitely *has* survived.
51 For a detailed comparison of the draft and the published version see Besomi (1996a), p. 279.
52 The problem, referred to above, of the impossibility of discussing the stability of a dynamic system within the compass of a single instant has not been solved or even tackled by Harrod.
53 While the 'ceiling' of full employment provides a good reason why actual G should stop increasing, Harrod's discussion of the lower turning point is not so solid, as no reason is given why the decrease in the special G_w should be faster than the decline in G: so far as $G < G_w$, by the instability principle there is a force acting towards a further reduction in G.
54 Harrod (1973: 40) suggested how a time chart of the process should be drawn in the downward movement and early decline. The result matches Marschak's diagram cited in Footnote 10 above.

5
Patinkin's Interpretation of Keynesian Economics: A Genetic Approach

Goulven Rubin

1. Introduction

Don Patinkin's (1922–97) story began in Chicago. He entered Chicago University in 1941 and received his PhD in 1947. He was trained by the members of the Old Chicago School, mostly Frank H. Knight, Lloyd W. Mints, Henry C. Simons and Jacob Viner. But he was also strongly influenced by the mathematical economists of the Cowles Commission. The Commission moved to Chicago in 1939 where it would experience its golden age (Christ, 1952) between 1943 and 1948 under the directorship of Jacob Marschak. Marschak and another eminent member of the Commission, the Polish economist Oskar Lange, were Patinkin's teachers at graduate level. This may explain why he completed his PhD thesis as a research associate of the Cowles Commission. Patinkin became Associate Professor at the University of Illinois in 1948 and emigrated to Israel in 1949. He had been offered a position at the Hebrew University of Jerusalem and stayed there for the rest of his life. It was in the difficult context of the first years of Israel that he wrote his masterpiece, *Money, Interest and Prices* (1956, 1965). This book became the standard reference work in monetary theory in the 1960s and marked the final stage in the codification of the Keynesian Neoclassical Synthesis. About this book, Robert Lucas wrote: 'perhaps the most refined and influential version of what I mean by the term "neo-classical synthesis" ' (1981: 278).

This chapter focuses on the most mysterious part of *Money, Interest and Prices*, namely chapters 13 and 14 on involuntary unemployment and the Keynesian theory. It aims to show how some pieces of evidence taken from Patinkin's archives clarify the meaning and scope of these chapters.

In spite of Patinkin considering chapters 13 and 14 as the crux of *Money, Interest and Prices*, their significance remained unclear. Why did Patinkin believe that Keynesian economics was a disequilibrium theory while everyone else contended that it was about unemployment equilibrium? Patinkin's Keynesianism itself was problematic. On the one hand, he contended that the Keynesian model was an aggregate Walrasian model and considered that Keynesians should admit that the real balance effect made the economy self-adjusting; on the other hand, he defended a radical interpretation of Keynes, saying that involuntary unemployment was not a consequence of nominal wage rigidity. This ambiguity is reflected in the reactions provoked by his works. John R. Hicks (1957), for instance, saw his unemployment theory as a 'modernized version of the theory which Keynes called "classical"' and Robert Clower (1965) presented him as a leader of the 'Keynesian Counterrevolution'. At stake here was the nature of Patinkin's position within the Keynesian camp and of his contribution to the interpretation of Keynes' *General Theory*.

The Don Patinkin Papers, held at the Duke University archives, were opened to the public in 1997. They contain a prolific correspondence with leading economists, drafts and unpublished papers. Together with Patinkin's PhD thesis, this material allows a reconstruction of the genesis of Patinkin's theory of involuntary unemployment. In other words, it allows us to understand and to assess Patinkin's results against the background of his initial intentions and of all the intellectual constraints that he faced from 1947 to the publication of the first edition of *Money, Interest and Prices* in 1956.

In section 2, I will present the main aspects of Patinkin's initial research programme at the doctoral stage. Section 3 presents his first results, that is to say, the second part of his PhD thesis. Section 3 uses the elements gathered previously to analyse some basic characteristics of chapters 13 and 14 of *Money, Interest and Prices*.

2.   Initial ingredients of Patinkin's research programme

Involuntary unemployment

> On the other hand, the economic and social problems of the Depression were part of our everyday experience. My father was in partnership with my uncle in a small business, which succumbed to serious financial difficulties. Fathers of close friends of mine had been unemployed for long periods, if not years. When we went downtown, we would see World War I veterans sitting at street corners behind up-ended empty fruit boxes in the bitter cold of Chicago winters, selling apples and pencils.
>
> (Patinkin, 1995: 360)

Like many Keynesians involved in the neoclassical synthesis, Patinkin was a child of the Great Depression. Hence, even though the choice of his thesis topic was not straightforward, it was not totally by chance that, in the end, he started to work on unemployment.[1] According to Patinkin, unemployment or, more precisely, involuntary unemployment was 'the very question that brought forth the *General Theory*' (1949: 360). Yet Keynes' concept had not been given enough attention.

After the publication of the *General Theory* in 1936, a number of economists tried to capture Keynes' message within formal models of the IS-LM type (see Darity and Young, 1995). Among them, some, like Hicks (1937), completely left aside the concept of involuntary unemployment put forward by Keynes in chapter 2 of his book. The others accounted for it by assuming a horizontal supply curve of labour. The main advocates of this curve were Lange and Franco Modigliani. Time and again (1938: 31; 1942: 61; 1944: 6), Lange stated that:

> Involuntary unemployment in the Keynesian sense is not an excess supply of labor but an equilibrium position obtained by intersection of a demand and a supply curve, the supply curve of labor, however, being infinitely elastic over a wide range with respect to money wages, the point of intersection being to the left of the region where elasticity of supply of labor with respect to money wages becomes finite.
>
> (Lange, 1944: 6)

Likewise, in his 1944 paper on IS-LM, Modigliani asserted that:

> In the Keynesian system, within limits to be specified presently, the supply of labor is assumed to be perfectly elastic at the historically ruling wage rate, say w_0. (1944: 47)

In a report to the Social Sciences Research Council, which financed his doctoral studies, Patinkin claimed that the starting point of his doctoral dissertation was his dissatisfaction in respect of this way of defining and representing unemployment:

> The point taken by my research was that none of the current theories of unemployment had emphasized its involuntary aspect. All of them were expressed in terms of demand and supply curves of labor, and workers were always 'on their supply curve'. From my viewpoint this did not represent involuntary unemployment since workers were acting precisely as they desired, as represented by their supply curve.
>
> (Patinkin, Final report for the Social Sciences Research Council, June 1947)

Here Patinkin clearly attacked the assumption of a horizontal supply curve of labour. The quotation shows that he assimilated the aggregate supply curve of labour and the curve expressing an individual worker's desired supply of labour. Since the labour supply curve expressed the preferences of workers, their situation could hardly be called involuntary when trade was occurring at the intersection of the demand and the supply schedules, whether the latter was horizontal or not. In the conclusion of his dissertation, Patinkin made his point a bit differently by highlighting the absurdity of Lange and Modigliani's approach. In their reasoning, a slight change in the behaviour of workers could turn a situation of 'involuntary unemployment' into a situation of full employment: 'The artificiality of this definition is sufficiently demonstrated if one considers the case in which the supply curve instead of being horizontal in the interval $(0, N_1)$, the supply curve rises with a slope of 0.001!' (1947: 115).

Instead of using Lange and Modigliani's horizontal curve, Patinkin maintained the assumption of a standard 'notional' supply of labour function and defined 'involuntary unemployment' as a situation where workers were 'off their supply curve': 'In order to be acting involuntarily, [workers] must be off their supply curve' (Final Report to the Social Sciences Research Council). In his thesis, Patinkin would thus elaborate upon this idea and try to develop a complete theory accounting for the involuntary character of unemployment.

A Walrasian approach

Patinkin intended to reconstruct Keynes' unemployment theory in a Walrasian perspective. Retrospectively, this approach seems far from obvious. Keynes developed the *General Theory* from within the Marshallian tradition, a tradition that displayed a conception of the market more or less incompatible with the Walrasian conception. However, this issue was understood only recently (see Clower, 1989, and De Vroey, 1999a, 1999b and 2004). The dominant viewpoint, developed by Hicks (1937, 1939) and Lange (1938) was that (1) Alfred Marshall and Léon Walras' conceptions of the market were complementary and that (2) Keynes' apparatus was a special case of the Walrasian general equilibrium framework. Under the influence of Hicks and Lange, Patinkin was thus led to believe that a Walrasian reconstruction of Keynes' theory would deepen his understanding of the *General Theory*.

During his first years as a student of the Department of Economics of the University of Chicago, from 1941 to 1943, Patinkin was barely exposed to the mathematical economics of Walras and the Lausanne school. The main reference as concerns price theory was Marshall, the only exception being the reading of Cassel (1932) who 'reproduced Walras' system without mentioning his name!' (Patinkin, 1995: 362). During his graduate studies (1944–5), Patinkin went into Marshall's *Principles* because it was the basic text of the lectures given by Knight and Viner, the then dominant figures at Chicago University. He discovered mathematical economics only through the courses of Lange:

> But Lange's most valuable course for me was the one on Mathematical Economics (i.e. what was then called mathematical economics!). Here he systematically took us through the Mathematical Appendix of Hicks' *Value and Capital* (1939), as well as Paul Samuelson's path breaking article on 'The stability of equilibrium' (1941), subsequently reproduced as chapter 9 of the latter's *Foundations of Economic Analysis* (1947). My lecture notes from this course served me as a 'reference volume' for many years to come. (1995: 372)

This initiation was continued by a course on mathematical economics and a seminar on Tinbergen's 1939 econometric model of the United States, both dispensed by Marschak. It was completed by Patinkin's immersion in the context of the Cowles Commission, the organization in which he would write his doctoral dissertation. The Cowles Commission, then based at Chicago and directed by Marschak, was initiating a revolution in econometric methodology, its members trying to find new statistical methods to estimate economic systems of simultaneous equations.

Patinkin's enthusiasm for mathematical economics at this stage is reflected in a manuscript probably written in 1948. In it, he stated 'the people who are mathematical economists are mostly the young economists believing that government must play a larger role in the economic sphere'.[2] State intervention required the knowledge of the parameters of the economic system. This could be obtained by estimation of simultaneous equations systems. But the development of these systems implied mathematical economics. Lange's teaching reinforced this belief in an organic link between a Keynesian orientation and the practice of mathematical economics.

In his autobiography, Patinkin (1995) writes that, in a course on business cycle theory, Lange offered a detailed presentation of the *General Theory* based on the paper he had published in 1938 entitled 'The Rate of Interest and the Optimum Propensity to Consume'. In this paper one can read:

> Thus both the Keynesian and the traditional theory of interest are but two limiting cases of what may be regarded to be the general theory of interest.

It is a feature of great historical interest that the essentials of this general theory are contained already in the work of Walras. (1938: 20)

For Lange, Keynes' apparatus was thus a simplified version of the Walrasian model.[3]

Accordingly, in the introduction of his PhD dissertation, Patinkin made clear that his models of reference were the models of the Lausanne school:

The first part consists of an examination of the 'classical system'. As in the examination of any body of thought, the problem of textual interpretation immediately arises. To minimize this problem, I shall concern myself with the mathematical classical school of economics: Walras, Pareto, and certain of their followers. (1947: 5)

In the second part of the thesis, Patinkin intended to show how some limits of the classical system could be overcome by the elaboration of a theory of involuntary unemployment. This approach was Walrasian in that the Keynesian model should take the form of a simultaneous equation system with appropriate microfoundations.[4] Furthermore, this model would be obtained by introducing a series of modifications into a Walrasian model. Yet, as I will show, there was a gap between Patinkin's ambition and the means at his disposal. His mastery of Walrasian economics had nothing to do with the mastery that would be achieved a few years later by Arrow and Debreu. Walras was not translated into English and Patinkin had to read it in French. Moreover, Patinkin's Marshallian training conflicted with his intended Walrasian approach, a problem he was hardly aware of due to the influence of Hicks' *Value and Capital*.

Patinkin vs Lange, Hicks, Modigliani and Klein

When Patinkin began his PhD, he had several interpretations of the Keynesian theory at his disposal. These were the IS-LM models of Hicks, Lange, Modigliani and Lawrence Klein. But the way these models presented Keynes' message did not satisfy him.[5]

Hicks (1937) and Lange (1938) put forward a common interpretation of Keynes' theory in terms of the 'liquidity trap case'. According to them, Keynes' approach differed from the classical one only insofar as he showed that an increase in the inducement to invest could have no effect on the interest rate because the latter had a strictly positive minimum value at which the demand for money became infinitely elastic. Patinkin rejected this interpretation because it implied that the Keynesian theory applied only to a special case. The young Keynesians, Klein, Modigliani and

Patinkin, wanted to show the generality of Keynes approach. Therefore they could not accept Hicks' contention that 'the General Theory of Employment is the Economics of Depression' (1937: 138).

In 'Liquidity Preference and the Theory of Money and Interest' (1944) Franco Modigliani offered an alternative to the interpretation of the Keynesian theory argued by Hicks and Lange. He maintained that the characteristic assumption of Keynes' theory was the assumption of downward nominal wage rigidity:

> It is usually considered as one of the most important achievements of the Keynesian theory that it explains the consistency of economic equilibrium with the presence of involuntary unemployment. It is, however, not sufficiently recognized that, except in a limiting case to be considered later, this result is due entirely to the assumption of 'rigid wages' and not to the Keynesian liquidity preference. (1944: 65)

This approach laid down the standard meaning of the adjective 'Keynesian'. Yet, it did not convince Patinkin. The reason was stated very clearly in a letter written in April 1948 to Franco Modigliani:

> Now, if the whole purpose of Keynes is to say that with rigid wages we can have unemployment 'equilibrium', I really do not see his contribution. This is a point that would have been admitted by classical economists themselves, but Keynes (on page 12, line 9 and following) seems to argue that the classical position on this point was wrong: that there could be unemployment for other reasons.
> (Patinkin, 1948: 2)

According to Patinkin, the explanation of unemployment through wage rigidity was the classical one. If this explanation was ascribed to Keynes, then the *General Theory* brought nothing new. Therefore, a Keynesian theory had to demonstrate that unemployment was not due to wage rigidity but to 'other reasons'.

Patinkin wrote in his 'Training of an Economist' that during his stay at the Cowles Commission 'there were stimulating discussions with Lawrence Klein on the manuscript of his then forthcoming *Keynesian Revolution* (1947)' (1995: 385). In this book, Klein argued that the characteristic assumptions of the Keynesian model were that investment and savings were 'interest inelastic' or 'insensitive' in respect of variations in the rate of interest. Given these assumptions, he asserted that an IS-LM model with flexible prices and wages could have no equilibrium solution.

The problem, in this setting, came from the fact that equilibrium of savings and investment for a full employment outcome could imply a negative rate of interest. Yet such a negative value was excluded. As a result, the aggregate demand remained inferior to the aggregate supply of goods. Klein interpreted this result as a demonstration of the incapacity of the market system to guarantee a perfect coordination of economic activities. But such a situation described a 'hyper-deflationary' system and was not realistic. Therefore, he introduced wage rigidity in his model to guarantee the existence of an unemployment equilibrium. Still, the exogenous wage was not the cause of unemployment in his model: 'In the Keynesian system lower wages need not do any good' (Klein, 1947: 87). Given the psychology of households and entrepreneurs, there was no equilibrium of savings and investment compatible with full employment. Hence, even with the exogenous wage reduced to zero, full employment would not be restored.

Klein was a major source of inspiration for Patinkin's thesis. But while he adopted his explanation of involuntary unemployment, he dismissed his Keynesian version of IS-LM. Patinkin actually jumped from the idea that involuntary unemployment was not a consequence of money-wage rigidity to the contention that wage rigidity, and *a fortiori* price rigidity, had to be excluded from the Keynesian theory. In other words, this theory had to demonstrate that a perfectly competitive system with price and wage flexibility could suffer from chronic unemployment. His correspondence offers clear evidence in support of this interpretation, as the following passage taken from a letter to Wassily Leontief illustrates:

> The second issue, and one with which, as I understand it, Keynes is really concerned is: Is a wage decrease the way to solve the problem of unemployment? The Classical answer is yes; Keynes' answer is no for reasons which he sets out in chapter 19 of the *General Theory*. . . . This position can be maintained without assuming wage rigidity. In fact, what it says is that despite wage flexibility, full employment will not be restored.
>
> (Patinkin to Leontief, 21 February 1950)

In the end, Patinkin's project offered an explosive combination of Walrasian orthodoxy and Keynesian radicalism. Patinkin was more Walrasian than any other young Keynesian. As his doctoral dissertation's bibliography testifies, in 1946–7, he was enthusiastic enough to read the (written in French) work of an obscure disciple of Walras named Divisia. But his correspondence with Modigliani or Leontief also shows how keen he was to preserve the integrity of Keynes' message as he interpreted it.

3.   From intention to realization: the content of Patinkin's thesis

Starting from the preceding ingredients, the problem of involuntary unemployment, the Walrasian perspective and the ambition to find something better than IS-LM with rigid wages, Patinkin developed a bold construction. He actually attempted to model the functioning of the economy on Walrasian equilibrium through the elaboration of a competing concept of general equilibrium with unemployment and flexible prices. Yet this research programme ran into many difficulties.

Microfoundations of the classical macro-model and origins of unemployment

In the introduction of the second part of his thesis, on involuntary unemployment, Patinkin stated that his 'first task [would] be the formation (by aggregation) of these macro-models from the Casselian equations previously considered' (1947, p. 51). In other words, Patinkin intended to derive his macro-models from a Walrasian one. To begin with, he explained how to derive individual demand functions including money income as one of their components. Households' maximization procedure was 'broken up into two steps' (1947: 52), agents making two distinct calculations, as workers and as consumers. This implied that, as consumers, agents considered their money income as an independent variable. Patinkin thus got round the difficulty of inserting income in the demand functions using a method similar to the one that could be found in Klein's *The Keynesian Revolution* (1947). Then he contended that his analysis offered the basis to obtain a 'Casselian system of equations', a set of n equilibrium conditions of the type supply of commodity i equals demand. The aggregation of the supply and demand functions of this system was then supposed to give rise to the following classical macro-model.[6]

$$X^D = G(Y, r) \tag{1}$$

$$X^S = \eta \tag{2}$$

$$X^D = X^S \tag{3}$$

$$Y = X^S \tag{4}$$

$$B(r, p, Y) = 0 \tag{5}$$

$$M(r, p, Y) = 0 \tag{6}$$

The function X^D defined the aggregate demand for goods. It increased in respect of income and decreased in respect of the rate of interest. The aggregate supply of goods was constant. It represented the full employment supply derived from labour market clearing. Eventually, the aggregate income was defined by the aggregate supply. Equations (10) and (11) are respectively the condition for equilibrium on the market for bonds and the condition for equilibrium on the market for money.

Taking up Klein's approach, Patinkin intended to show that this classical system could be 'inconsistent' or that it could have no equilibrium solution:

> The argument is made that the cause of this inconsistency is the insensitivity of savings and investment to fluctuations in the interest rate. This insensitivity creates a situation in which there exists (potentially) more savings at the full employment level than can be offset by investments. Hence this full employment level cannot be brought into existence.
>
> (Patinkin, 1947: 51)

Patinkin assumed that the rate of interest adjusting savings and investment was the money rate.[7] The shape of the investment curve and of the savings curve could be such that the equilibrium rate was negative. But a negative rate of interest was impossible so long as the yield of money was equal to zero.

By definition, in a system without full employment solution, price and wage flexibility cannot bring back full employment. In his dissertation, Patinkin interpreted this result as demonstrating that the problem of involuntary unemployment was inherent in the classical system, which represented a perfectly competitive market economy:

> If the worker is unemployed, it is not because he wants to be, but because the basic inconsistency of the system makes it impossible to satisfy his desires.
>
> (Patinkin, 1947: 116)

The members of the Cowles Commission heavily criticized this theory. Neisser, for instance, a friend of Marschak, asked to comment on Patinkin's work, stated that 'inconsistency indicates that something is wrong with the system, but it is not a guide to what is wrong' (Some Notes on Don Patinkin's on the Consistency of Economic Models, July 1947). In other words, a model without a solution is empty and has nothing to say about the real world. It cannot be interpreted as offering a theory of unemployment. A letter from Marschak to Patinkin confirms that this point 'created most of the criticisms among staff members' (10/11/1948).

But this was only the first stage in the elaboration of the Keynesian model. Patinkin needed an equilibrium concept for, according to him, a system without equilibrium could not 'describe the real world' (1947: 78). The classical model had to be amended to obtain an unemployment equilibrium. Yet Patinkin refused to resort to the assumption of wage rigidity (see Rubin, 2002). Instead, he put forward what he coined as a 'theory of compromise'.

A macro-model based on a 'theory of compromise'

Patinkin interpreted the Keynesian theory in the light of Samuelson's diagonal-cross diagram. From this point of view, one defect of that theory was that it ignored the global supply of goods as derived from the equilibrium on the labour market. Once this supply side was reintroduced in the model, the inconsistency pointed out earlier could appear clearly:

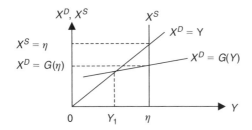

Figure 5.1   (Patinkin, 1947: 85)

The fact that the supply curve and the demand curve did not cut the bisecting line on the same point illustrated the absence of equilibrium. Patinkin simplified the exposition by positing aggregate demand as being completely insensitive in respect of the rate of interest. Hence, in the absence of a real balance effect, the price mechanism failed to adjust both supply and demand. But the Keynesian solution to this 'inconsistency' was revealed in the same way. In the cross-diagram model an equilibrium was obtained by adjusting income independently from the real wage and from the price level. So to obtain an equilibrium outcome, even though the goods market was in excess supply and prices were flexible, Patinkin's (implicit) answer was straightforward: ignore the law of supply and demand and replace the price mechanism by a quantity adjustment mechanism. Yet the author did not ignore the necessity of justifying this new form of adjustment. Therefore, as an alternative to the law of supply and demand he offered his 'theory of compromise'.

The equations of Patinkin's unemployment equilibrium model are presented below:

$$X^D = G(Y) \tag{7}$$

$$X^D = Y \tag{8}$$

$$Y = F(N) \tag{9}$$

$$(W/P)_1 = F'(N) \tag{10}$$

$$(W/P)_2 = \Pi(N) \tag{11}$$

$$W/P = \gamma \, \Pi(N) + (1 - \gamma) \cdot F'(N) \tag{12}$$

Equations (11) and (12) express the Keynesian assumption that makes up for the failure of price adjustment: production follows aggregate demand independently of the real wage, this 'quantity adjustment' allowing the model to find a fixed point. Once production is determined, employment is derived from the production function *F*. Equations (15), (16) and (17) determine the equilibrium real wage.

The 'theory of compromise' twice came into play in the justification of the model.

First of all, it justified the way income was determinate. Patinkin maintained that the initial 'inconsistent system' determined two distinct values for income. The first one, η, was defined by labour market clearing. It expressed the income 'desired' by the suppliers of goods. The second one was defined by the equation $Y = G(Y)$. It was the income Y_1 in Figure 5.1. This value expressed the income 'desired' by the demanders of goods. The 'theory of compromise' explained that when such 'disagreement' occurred between the two sides of the market, a 'compromise' had to be reached the outcome of which depended on the respective 'bargaining powers' of suppliers and demanders. The stronger the 'bargaining power' of demanders, the nearer to their desired income they would get. Thus, a priori, the equilibrium income could take any value between the full employment income and the income determined by the outlet constraint. Happily enough, according to Patinkin, in the 'normal situation' and in a case of excess supply, the demanders were the ones to lay down their conditions:

Assume, for example, that suppliers have no bargaining power. This means that buyers need make no compromise and can force the suppliers to accept the level of *Y* which they (the buyers) desire. . . . *I believe this to be a description of the normal situation in our economy.*

(1947: 84, highlighted by me)

The 'theory of compromise' was used a second time to determine the equilibrium real wage. In a 'normal' economic situation, income was fixed by the demand for goods. To this income corresponded a certain level of employment given by the production function. According to Patinkin there were two different real wages in these conditions. The real wage defined by labour demand (equation 15) was the biggest and, consequently, was the one desired by workers. Inversely, the real wage defined by the labour supply equation was the smallest and the one desired by firms. This disagreement called for a compromise. As in the preceding case, the outcome depended on the 'bargaining powers' of both parties. Equation (17) summarizes the formalization proposed by Patinkin. The parameter γ indicated the firms' 'bargaining power'. The bigger it was the nearer firms got to the minimum wage. But, if an agreement was reached, γ also indicated the 'bargaining power' of workers. If γ was small the workers got a real wage near the one they desire. This key parameter determined the equilibrium real wage like a weighted average of the wages desired by the two sides of the market. This analysis was illustrated by Figure 5.2:

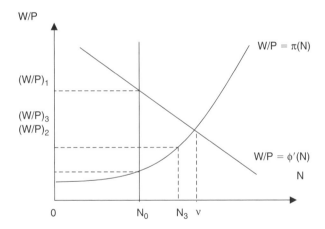

Figure 5.2   (1947a, p. 102)

The 'theory of compromise' thus determined the equilibrium value of three variables: real income, level of employment and real wage.

The members of the Cowles Commission also criticized this aspect of his work. Patinkin actually attempted to develop an alternative to the Walrasian equilibrium. He wanted to elaborate a general equilibrium concept accounting for the coexistence of involuntary unemployment and flexible prices in a perfectly competitive system and his solution was based on the 'theory of compromise'. But his colleagues at the Cowles rejected the latter. The concepts of 'coercion' or 'bargaining power' involved in the theory seemed hardly consistent with the initial assumption of perfect competition and the whole approach was deemed too ad hoc. The following quotations illustrate:

> Is not the theory of compromise and bargaining power beside the point? While bargaining power is a very important phenomenon of the real world, it does not exist in a perfectly competitive system. (J. Marschak, Comments on D. P. Unemployment in Keynesian Systems, December 1946)
>
> You introduce "institutional coefficient" α, β, which are not further reduced to behavior patterns of individuals, as the essential determinants of unemployment. This is not a theory, but a definition. . . . But it is not clear whether you think of workers and employers as individuals or as groups. In the latter case, the theory of imperfect competition would be needed to specify the choices open to each party and so explain unemployment. With such a theory the meaning of the term "coercion" is unclear.
>
> (T. Koopmans, Comments on D. P. Theory of Unemployment, March 1947)
>
> The whole idea of "bargaining power" introduced here is mystical. How and why do they bargain? The only way to bargain in a competitive system is by changing your offer.
>
> (H. Simon, Memorandum, March 1947)

One may add that Patinkin's 'compromise' models left the rate of interest and the level of money prices indeterminate. This is quite an ironic result considering that the first part of Patinkin's thesis pointed to the indetermination of the price level in the classical monetary theory, the very criticism that made him famous.[8]

Additional constraints'

Before he showed how to obtain an equilibrium with involuntary unemployment Patinkin offered his definition of this phenomenon. It was at this stage that he stated the most striking insight of the second part of his thesis, the fact that one had to modify the Walrasian budget constraint in order to make explicit the microfoundations of the Keynesian model.

As we have seen, Patinkin defined involuntary unemployment as a situation in which workers were off their supply curve. The problem is that agents' choices are the fundamental object of economic theory hence this theory has little to say about 'off the curves' points. But Patinkin noted also that the unemployed were 'coerced' 'in a relative sense only'. The fact that agents were not 'on their curve' meant that they did not achieve their Walrasian plans. This did not mean that they were off all curves and that their behaviour was no longer a subject for the theory of choice. They were still guided by a plan but this plan included 'additional constraints'. Their behaviour was then 'involuntary' as compared to the behaviour defined by Walrasian plans, plans without additional constraints, hence in a 'relative sense'. The notion of 'additional constraint' expressed with remarkable clarity the necessity of modifying the Walrasian budget constraint in order to obtain a disequilibrium model out of a Walrasian framework. In the conclusion of his thesis, Patinkin further clarified his thinking in presenting a mathematical formulation of it (Patinkin, 1947: 116–7).

Given this insight, the thesis should be considered as an anticipation of the disequilibrium theory developed in the 1970s. This theory was based on the notion of 'spillover effect' implying that an agent who could not buy or sell his desired quantity on one market would revise his demands and supplies on all other markets taking the quantity he had been allotted as a new constraint. The analysis of disequilibrium state thus implied a modification of budget constraints. The expression 'spillover effect' was borrowed from chapter 13 of Patinkin's *Money, Interest and Prices* (1956). There it described the behaviour of a firm faced with an outlet constraint. The inverse case of a household that could not sell its desired quantity of labour was analysed and formalized by Clower (1965). Both contributions were combined by Barro and Grossman to elaborate a macroeconomic model. Bénassy, Drèze and others generalized the analysis in more microeconomic frameworks (see Backhouse and Boianovsky, 2005).

But the thesis contains these latter works only in germ. All we have at this stage is the ideal-type of a theory of choice in disequilibrium. In building a microeconomic counterpart to his Keynesian macro-model, Patinkin tried to give an operational content to his general insight. He tried to apply it to the behaviour of firms and workers in disequilibrium and see if it could help him elaborate upon his model. But his results were disappointing.

The macro-model above (section 2.2) already contained a spillover effect. Yet Patinkin failed to perceive it and to theorize it. Nowhere did he apply the notion of additional constraint to the behaviour of firms in this particular instance. In order to apply the concept he built another model and formalized the decision program of firms and workers when the labour and goods markets did not clear. He then found that firms like workers had 'no room to maximize' while 'in general this need not be so' (1947: 116). In other words, Patinkin admitted explicitly that he did not obtain the results he wanted. His formalization added no depth to his analysis. Retrospectively, it appears to be a consequence of his partial equilibrium approach. Although he analysed a general equilibrium system, Patinkin focused on one market only, the market for labour, thus failing to perceive its interaction with the market for goods. This bias was worsened by the fact that he had solved in advance the problem of the introduction of income in the Keynesian consumption function. In the case of firms, Patinkin incorrectly defined the level of employment as the additional constraint. In the case of households this was correct but Patinkin failed to see the implication of this constraint for the consumption function.

4.   Putting chapters 13 and 14 of *Money, Interest and Prices* into archival perspective

The reading of his thesis shows that Patinkin changed his mind on three basic points between 1947 and 1956. First, he left the unemployment equilibrium perspective for a disequilibrium approach. Second, he went from a complete rejection of the Pigou effect to the assumption that it automatically restored full employment. Third, he abandoned the burgeoning mathematical apparatus of the thesis for the informal presentation of chapter 13. The explanation of this threefold evolution allows a better understanding of the logic and significance of the position put forward in chapters 13 and 14 of *Money, Interest and Prices*.

From equilibrium to disequilibrium

Patinkin presented his disequilibrium interpretation of the Keynesian theory for the first time in 1948 in 'Price Flexibility and Full Employment': 'what Keynesian economics claims is that the economic system may be in a position of underemployment disequilibrium' (1948: 563). Disequilibrium meant that some markets did not clear, the labour market in particular, and that some agents could not realize their desired plans (individual disequilibrium).[9] But disequilibrium also conveyed the idea that the economy was engaged in a dynamic process because prices and quantities were bound to vary in time. With Clower (1965) and Leijonhufvud (1968) this interpretation of the Keynesian theory became quite popular. In 1975, it was even endorsed by Tobin: 'The phenomena [Keynes] described are better regarded as disequilibrium dynamics' (1975: 196). But when Patinkin put it forward he was totally isolated. For the majority of economists Keynes' *General Theory* and Keynesian economics were about unemployment equilibrium. How was Patinkin led to abandon this majority viewpoint?

Mehrling (2002) contends that Patinkin's interpretation reflects the influence of the Old Chicago tradition in which he was trained during his first years at the University.[10] In this tradition, personified by the monetary economists Simons and Mints or by Knight, the economic system was considered as being in constant disequilibrium. In trying to integrate this tradition with the contributions of Keynes and Lange, Patinkin would have been naturally led to restate the 'old wisdom, using the more rigorous general equilibrium language'. This contextualization is illuminating yet only a loose explanation of Patinkin's interpretation of Keynesian economics. Mehrling suggests that Patinkin simply read Keynes 'through the lens of his training'. In other words, he confused Keynes's vision of the economy with the Simons–Mints vision. But this does not tell us why Patinkin first interpreted Keynesian economics in an equilibrium perspective and why he changed his mind. Furthermore, Patinkin always insisted on the need to read and reread a text in order to succeed in 'penetrating to its meaning, in understanding the intent of its author' (1995: 388). It is thus difficult to believe that his disequilibrium conception of the Keynesian theory was only the result of confusion. There must have been a logical reason for the evolution between his thesis and his 1948 article.

In order to understand Patinkin's final stance, one must consider the outcome of his thesis. As we have seen above, in the latter, Patinkin undertook to recast the Keynesian theory in the form of a general equilibrium model. To capture the gist of Keynes' work and to get a fair representation of a real market economy, it had to respect two key criteria: (1) absence of any assumption concerning wage and price rigidities and (2) existence of an equilibrium solution. Consequently, Patinkin set out to elaborate a 'true' Keynesian concept combining unemployment equilibrium and flexible wages (and prices), a concept that would have been on a par with the Walrasian equilibrium concept. But we have seen that the outcome, the 'theory of compromise', was hardly convincing and was rejected by the Cowles Commission members. Patinkin's failure to develop a Keynesian equilibrium led him to conclude that the Keynesian theory possessed no equilibrium concept of its own. The way out was to consider unemployment disequilibrium as the natural field of this theory, a field which, as noted by Mehrling, was familiar to Patinkin.

The Pigou effect[11]

The Pigou effect is known as the main argument used to counter Keynes' claim that a perfectly competitive monetary economy could remain trapped in a state of unemployment. Among the promoters of this anti-Keynesian argument, Patinkin is generally the first to be quoted.

Admittedly, in *Money, Interest and Prices* (1956, 1965), he asserted that the Keynesian theory should admit the existence and the efficiency of this mechanism:

> Indeed, [this interpretation] compels [Keynesian economics] to accept the classical contention that [the real balance effect] not only exists, but even succeeds eventually in raising income to the full-employment level Y_0.
>
> (Patinkin, 1956: 237)

No wonder then that Grandmont, for instance, put Patinkin among anti-Keynesians such as Pigou, Friedman and Johnson and portrayed him as an actor of the 'neoclassical counter-attack' (1983: 1).

Taking Patinkin's thesis and his correspondence into account, one is led to consider his position in a different perspective. In his thesis, Patinkin rejected Pigou's argument. Moreover, the inquiry into the genesis of his early contributions shows that Patinkin was always anxious to grasp Keynes' message and find the best way to articulate and defend it. His later works in the field of history of economic thought (Patinkin, 1976, 1982) show what a careful reader of the *General Theory* he was. So if a Keynesian is defined broadly as an economist who is both a serious reader of Keynes and a defender of what he thinks is Keynes' message, then Patinkin must be considered a Keynesian. The relevant question, therefore, is the following: how was a supporter of Keynes such as Don Patinkin led to include the Pigou effect, the arch anti-Keynesian argument, in his theory of involuntary unemployment? The combined analysis of archives and published works offers a solution to this paradox. They show that Patinkin's position stemmed from his specific interpretation of the Keynesian theory, while his incorporation of the real balance effect into the Keynesian apparatus represented his riposte to Pigou's attack.

Patinkin appears to have changed his mind about the Pigou effect over a very short period of time. This evolution happened in three stages. The first is Patinkin's PhD thesis, submitted in August 1947 at Chicago University, the second is a manuscript entitled 'Price Flexibility and Unemployment', written in November 1947, and the third is 'Price Flexibility and Full Employment', a paper published in September 1948. The arguments used in the thesis to defeat Pigou were rapidly criticized by Milton Friedman and an English economist named Alexander Henderson. The existence of controversy is revealed by a letter from Patinkin's archives:

> I am enclosing in this letter a manuscript of an article which I have just written on the whole question of the Pigou analysis. My running

controversy with you and Milton on these issues helped me formalize and rigorize my own position on these matters. For this I am greatly indebted to both of you, but now I would like to impose upon you a little bit more and ask you to read the enclosed draft and let me have your opinion on it.

(Patinkin to Henderson, 5 November 1947)

Since the 'running controversy' mentioned by Patinkin was mainly oral, it left few traces. Consequently, we do not know exactly when it happened, that is to say when Patinkin was writing his dissertation, before June 1947, or just after its submission. However, documents from Don Patinkin's Papers, held at Duke University, reveal the main points raised by Friedman and Henderson. These documents are the correspondence that followed the discussion, mostly during autumn 1947, and the manuscript to which Patinkin referred in his letter to Henderson. This manuscript, entitled 'Price Flexibility and Unemployment', a primitive version of 'Price Flexibility and Full Employment' published one year later, is annotated by Friedman and is thus evidence of the latter's viewpoint. The debate bore on the force of the Pigou effect. In his thesis, Patinkin argued that the Pigou effect might be of decreasing intensity. In this case, the augmentation of real balances would only make full employment savings converge towards a limit level below full employment investment so that equilibrium would fail to be restored. Friedman and Henderson considered that the Pigou effect was sufficiently strong to make the economic system self-adjusting. Both pointed out to Patinkin that he offered no economic justification for his counter-argument.[12] In reaction to this criticism, Patinkin developed a new line of argumentation in 'Price Flexibility and Unemployment'. Using the work of Lange (1944), he claimed that the real balance effect would not ensure the stability of equilibrium even if it ensured the existence of full employment. But in 'Price Flexibility and Full Employment', he abandoned this position and argued that a stable system could be called Keynesian if a return to full employment took 'more than one year' (1948: 563). Now, this last stage is not a consequence of Friedman's influence. As a matter of fact, some letters show that Patinkin still considered that instability was a real threat facing market systems and that it was a theoretically well-founded scenario. His stance did not result from a conversion to Friedman's Monetarism.[13]

In the first part of *Money, Interest and Prices*, Patinkin asserted that 'the assumption that there exists a real balance effect on the commodity markets is the *sine qua non* of monetary theory' (1956: 22). At first sight, this position seems to offer an obvious explanation of the role played by the real balance effect in Patinkin's version of the Keynesian theory: being monetary, the Keynesian system had to incorporate it. However, the chronology of Patinkin's writings shows that his integration of the real balance effect into the Keynesian theory was not a consequence of his monetary theory. Things actually happened the other way round. The mystery of Patinkin's evolution from 1947 to 1948 is thus further increased.

To assess the robustness of Patinkin's position one must bear in mind the theoretical context of the 1940s. Keynes' supporters were actually in a difficult situation faced with Pigou's attack. Firstly, they could but assume the existence of a real balance effect on the goods market. Secondly, they believed that this mechanism made their general version of the Keynesian model self-adjusting. Therefore, to show that the economy was not self-adjusting and to thwart Pigou, economists such as Hicks (1946), Kalecki (1944), Klein (1947) and Lange (1944) had to weaken the Keynesian model by adopting restricting assumptions. If, initially, Patinkin used their argumentation in answer to Friedman's and Henderson's criticisms, he rapidly understood the limits of this strategy.

It was in order to break this deadlock and to find a better defense of the Keynesian theory that Patinkin elaborated his own position. In turning the anti-Keynesian argument of Pigou into a necessary ingredient of the Keynesian theory, Patinkin actually offered a solution that he hoped might end the debate. This solution had its roots in chapter 19 of the *General Theory*. In this chapter, Keynes recognized the existence of stabilizing mechanisms with the very aim of revealing their inefficiency in solving the problem of involuntary unemployment. But, above all, Patinkin's solution stemmed from the internal logic of his reconstruction of the Keynesian theory. On the one hand, the Keynesian theory was deprived of any specific equilibrium concept, it was a disequilibrium theory. On the other hand, a general model had to contain a stable equilibrium solution. The Keynesian theory thus needed a stabilizing mechanism to justify the existence and the stability of a Walrasian equilibrium. Since, for Patinkin, the Pigou effect was the sole mechanism capable of doing the job, it conditioned the degree of generality of the Keynesian theory.

Disequilibrium analysis

Since Keynesian economics was about unemployment disequilibrium, Patinkin had to explain how to analyse this phenomenon. This was the aim of chapters 13 and 14 of *Money, Interest and Prices*. There, Patinkin conducted an experiment on the basis of a macroeconomic model of the IS-LM type.[14] He assumed that the economy was disturbed by an increase in the demand for bonds financed by a decrease in aggregate demand. Patinkin then assumed that prices adjusted slowly and that the elasticity of aggregate demand with respect to prices and interest was small. This implied that the goods market would remain in excess supply for a long time so that firms were forced to reduce their production until it matched aggregate demand. This outlet constraint led firms to cut down their labour demand. This was the 'spillover effect'. Patinkin assumed that prices and wages fell at the same speed so that the real wage kept its full employment value. Labour supply did not change but labour demand did. The difficulties on the goods market spilt over onto the labour market where involuntary unemployment appeared. Patinkin went on analysing how the economy returned to full employment depending on the relative adjustment speeds of prices and wages. Since this adjustment process was slow, stabilization policies were needed.

In contrast with the thesis, this presentation of the Keynesian position was largely informal. Patinkin used geometrical figures but he did not present an explicit mathematical model (except in the 'extreme case' where prices were fixed). Therefore, the development of the disequilibrium interpretation of Keynes had to await the contribution of Clower (1965), which presented explicit microeconomic foundations. So much so that the significance of Patinkin's contribution has remained a matter of controversy. In their seminal article, Barro and Grossman (1971) put Patinkin and Clower on the same footing. But others, like d'Autume (1985), underlined how rudimentary chapter 13 was: 'The symmetry of the homage paid by Barro and Grossman to Clower and Patinkin seems unduly generous to the latter' (d'Autume, 1985: 104). Once again, insights from the archives offer a clearer understanding of this episode.

If Patinkin's thesis and chapter 13 of *Money, Interest and Prices* are added together, all the ingredients are there to develop something like the Barro and Grossman disequilibrium model. In chapter 13, Patinkin pondered upon the microeconomic foundations of the labour demand function in the context of a Keynesian scenario. His answer was the spillover effect. This meant that labour demand became a function of aggregate demand, the latter becoming an additional constraint on firms' decisions. At this stage, he had discovered what his thesis lacked: a practical and fruitful application of his concept of 'additional constraint'. But, if the concept was still present in chapter 13 in the definition of involuntary unemployment, Patinkin failed to stress the fact that the spillover effect was its application to the behaviour of firms. Furthermore, Patinkin no longer tried to write down the firm's maximization program in disequilibrium. Last but not least, he failed to see that there was also a spillover effect running from the labour to the goods market because the level of employment was an additional constraint on households' maximization programs. In the thesis Patinkin failed to give operational content to his general insight, while in chapter 13 he failed to generalize his account of firms' behaviour. Chapter 13 was not a direct outgrowth of the thesis. As shown by Boianovsky (2006), in between, Patinkin tried a very different approach. In a draft of chapter 13 he developed a Wicksellian version of the theory of involuntary unemployment in which firms remained on the standard labour demand curve. At this stage, it seems as if Patinkin had abandoned the idea of a general theory of agent behaviour in disequilibrium and looked for a more modest account of the behaviour of the market system. In chapter 13 he went halfway back to the thesis but he was stopped by an important question. It was not enough to say that firms took aggregate demand as an additional constraint ($Y \leqslant Y^D$). In a perfectly competitive context firms were supposed to assume that demand for their products was unlimited. The theory of involuntary unemployment thus had to explain how firms changed their behaviour within the framework of perfect competition. Boianovsky (2006) points to the fact that Patinkin still considered this issue as unresolved in 1987.

In a letter to Leijonhufvud written in 1974, Patinkin admitted that he 'had not succeeded in achieving in [chapter 13] an integration of [his] economic intuition with [his] formal economic analysis'. Yet most ingredients needed for the kind of integration developed by his followers in the 1970s were already there. And together with a 1958 paper, they represent the basic source of Clower's contribution. This fact has remained hidden to most readers because, in his paper, Clower presented Patinkin as an enemy. Using a series of oppositions of the type heterodoxy/orthodoxy, revolution/counterrevolution or Keynes/Walras, Clower suggested that his interpretation of the Keynesian theory was radically at odds with the one defended by Patinkin.

In fact, a close analytical comparison of Clower's paper with Patinkin's works, combined with a study of their correspondence, shows that Clower's article is a sequel to chapter 13.[15] Both economists developed the same conception of the Keynesian theory as disequilibrium economics. Both pondered upon the validity of Walras' Law in a Keynesian framework. The question was raised for the first time by Patinkin in a 1958 paper. He concluded that Walras' Law was always valid. Clower arrived at the opposite conclusion. But he was just stressing the implications of chapter 13. On this point, Patinkin was in contradiction with his own analysis. Clower developed the 'dual decision hypothesis', stating that when workers suffered from unemployment they had to revise their demand for goods according to the effective level of employment. Writing down the workers' decision program he clarified the microeconomic underpinning of the Keynesian consumption function. This analysis was actually the application of the 'spillover effect' to the case of households. Besides, the modified budget constraint used by Clower appeared in Patinkin's 1958 paper. The correspondence between the two economists proves that these analytical similarities are not the outcome of independent discoveries. Clower wrote the first letter in 1958. He commented on Patinkin's paper of the same year and concluded:

> While I am at it, I should like to thank you for many pleasant and profitable hours, the result of your having written *Money, Interest and Prices*. It is a remarkable book in more respects than it is possible to mention, and should do much to make our science a better field in which to work.
> (Clower to Patinkin, 6 December 1958)

The following correspondence first demonstrates that Clower and Patinkin interacted actively during the period preceding the first presentation of Clower's 'Keynesian Counter-Revolution' at the Royaumont Conference in 1962. The economists met for the first time during summer 1959. In 1960 Patinkin accepted an invitation from Clower to stay for a month at Northwestern University as a visiting Professor. In the letters, Clower appears to be an active supporter of Patinkin in his discussion with Archibald and Lipsey on the dichotomy issue. Patinkin asked Clower to check the corrections for the second edition of *Money, Interest and Prices* (1965). He even asked him to present his article for the Royaumont Conference (where the latter would present his seminal contribution) in absentia (Letter to Clower, 19 March 1962). Finally, a letter from March 1962 seems to prove that Clower developed the Royaumont paper on the basis of Patinkin's work. In this letter, Clower announced that he had obtained some interesting results in the field of disequilibrium economics. But he did this by pointing to the weaknesses of Patinkin's study of 'disequilibrium systems'. In fact, he seemed to be disappointed by the fact that Patinkin preferred to work on his monetary theory, his 'hobby horse', instead of trying to develop the work begun in chapter 13 of *Money, Interest and Prices*:

> I think we probably have methodological differences, for I am unconvinced of the importance of this detailed discussion of the utility theory foundations of monetary theory. We all have our hobby horses, to be sure, but this one does not really fit too well with some of your other ideas, particularly the ideas adumbrated in the second half of your book on disequilibrium systems. That is still the weakest part of

your entire structure, and the weakness arises from undue concentration on the equilibrium properties of household models in part I. I will say no more on that here, since your concentration on consumer equilibrium saves me all kinds of time to concentrate on consumer disequilibrium, an area in which I am currently specializing with what I think are interesting results.

(Clower to Patinkin, 3 March 1962)

This letter shows that Clower did not break with Patinkin's approach. On the basis of an internal criticism he tried to push further the work initiated in chapter 13. If he attacked Patinkin it was because they understood differently the significance of the disequilibrium theory. Patinkin liked consensus and tried to integrate all schools of thought in a single framework. Therefore, he tended to minimize the gap between his theory of involuntary unemployment and the original Walrasian framework. Inversely, Clower's iconoclastic temper led him to overemphasize the heterodox nature of the disequilibrium interpretation of Keynes.

5.   Conclusion

Patinkin's thesis, his correspondence and the drafts he left put his work in a new light. This material shows that, from the start, Patinkin tried hard to ground Keynes' contention that involuntary unemployment was not due to nominal wage rigidity. Yet he was confronted by the absence of a purely Keynesian equilibrium concept. This difficulty led him to consider Keynesian economics as a disequilibrium theory. Paradoxically, it was again in order to reinforce the Keynesian position that he incorporated the Pigou effect in his version of Keynesian economics. The informal character of chapter 13's presentation should not induce the reader to underestimate its importance. The lack of formalization was probably due to Patinkin being very cautious after the failure of his 'theory of compromise'. It was also due to the fact that Patinkin was looking for something more complex than the solution offered later by Barro and Grossman. Finally, chapter 13 and Patinkin's works in general were a decisive source of inspiration for Clower.

References

d'Autume, A. (1985) *Monnaie, croissance et déséquilibre* (Paris: Economica).
Backhouse, R., and M. Boianovsky (2005) 'Whatever Happened to Microfoundations?', working paper.
Barro, H., and I. Grossman (1971) 'A General Disequilibrium Model of Income and Employment, *American Economic Review*, vol. 61: 82–93.

Boianovsky, M. (2006) 'The Making of Chapters 13 and 14 of Patinkin's *Money, Interest and Prices*', *History of Political Economy*, vol. 38, no. 2 (2006).

Clower, R. (1965) 'The Keynesian Counter-Revolution: A Theoretical Appraisal', in F.H. Hahn and F.P.R. Brechling (eds), *The Theory of Interest Rates* (London: Macmillan).

De Vroey, M. (1996) 'Keynes and the Marshall-Walras Divide', *Journal of the History of Economic Thought*, vol. 21: 117–36.

De Vroey, M. (1999a) 'The Marshallian Market and the Walrasian Economy. Two Incompatible Bedfellows', *Scottish Journal of Political Economy*, vol. 46: 319–38.

De Vroey, M. (2002) 'Can Slowly Adjusting Wages Explain Involuntary Unemployment? A Critical Reexamination of Patinkin's Theory of Involuntary Unemployment', *European Journal of History of Economic Thought*, vol. 9, no. 2: 293–307.

De Vroey, M. (2004) *Involuntary Unemployment: The Elusive Quest for a Theory* (London, New York: Routledge).

Grandmont, J.M. (1974) 'On the Short Run Equilibrium in a Monetary Economy', in J. Drèze (ed.), *Allocation Under Uncertainty, Equilibrium and Optimality* (New York: Macmillan), 165–80.

Grandmont, J.-M. (1983) *Money and Value: A Reconsideration of Classical and Neo-Classical Monetary Theories* (Cambridge University Press).

Hicks, J. (1937) 'Mr. Keynes and the Classics: A Suggested Interpretation', *Econometrica*, vol. V, no. 2: 147–59.

Hicks, J. (1946[1959]) *Value and Capital. An Inquiry into Some Fundamental Principles of Economic Theory*, 2nd ed. (Oxford: The Clarendon Press).

Hicks, J. (1957) 'A Rehabilitation of "Classical" Economics?', *Economic Journal*, vol. LXVII: 278–89.

Kalecki, M. (1944) 'Professor Pigou on the "Classical Stationary State": A Comment', *Economic Journal*, vol. LIV, no. 1: 131–2.

Keynes, J.M. (1991[1936]) *The General Theory of Employment, Interest and Money* (San Diego, New York, London: Harvest/Harcourt Brace).

Klein, L. (1966[1947]) *The Keynesian Revolution*, 2nd ed. (New York, London: Macmillan).

Lange, O. (1938) 'The Rate of Interest and the Optimum Propensity to Consume', *Economica*, vol. V: 12–32.

Lange, O. (1942) 'Say's Law: A Restatement and Criticism', in O. Lange et al. (eds), *Studies in Mathematical Economics and Econometrics* (Chicago).

Lange, O. (1944) *Price Flexibility and Employment*, Cowles Commission for Research in Economics Monograph No. 8 (San Antonio: Principia Press of Trinity University).

Leeson, R. (1998) 'The Early Patinkin–Friedman Correspondence', *Journal of History of Economic Thought*, vol. 20, no. 4: 433–48.

Leeson, R. (2000) 'Patinkin, Johnson and the Shadow of Friedman', *History of Political Economy*, vol. 32, no. 4: 733–63.

Leijonhufvud, A. (1968) *On Keynesian Economics and the Economics of Keynes. A Study in Monetary Theory* (Oxford University Press).

Lucas, R.E. (1981) 'Methods and Problems in Business Cycle Theory', in *Studies in Business Cycle Theory* (Cambridge: The MIT Press), 271–96.

Mehrling, P. (2002) 'Don Patinkin and the Origins of Postwar Monetary Orthodoxy', *European Journal of History of Economic Thought*, vol. 9, no. 2: 161–85.

Modigliani, F. (1944) 'Liquidity Preference and the Theory of Interest and Money', *Econometrica*, vol. XII, no. 1: (1944) 45–88.

Patinkin, D. (1947) *On the Consistency of Economic Models: A Theory of Involuntary Unemployment*, Doctoral dissertion submitted to the University of Chicago (August).

Patinkin, D. (1947a) Social Sciences Research Council Pre-doctoral Field Fellowship – Final Report, DPP4.

Patinkin, D. (1947b) Correspondence with Henderson, A. M. DPP27.

Patinkin, D. (1947c) 'Price Flexibility and Unemployment' (November) DPP27.

Patinkin, D. (1947d) 'Inconsistent Systems and Involuntary Unemployment', manuscript, DPP4.

Patinkin, D. (1948–59) Correspondence with Friedman, M. DPP27.

Patinkin, D. (1948) 'Price Flexibility and Full Employment', *American Economic Review*, vol. 38: 543–64.

Patinkin, D. (1949) 'Involuntary Unemployment and the Keynesian Supply Function', *Economic Journal*, vol. 59: 361–83.

Patinkin, D. (1951[1948]) 'Price Flexibility and Full Employment', Revised version in F.A. Lutz and L.W. Mints (eds), *Readings in Monetary Theory* (Philadelphia).

Patinkin, D. (1956) *Money, Interest and prices* (Evanston, Illinois: Row, Peterson and Company).

Patinkin, D. (1958) 'Liquidity Preference and Loanable Funds: Stocks and Flow Analysis', *Economica*, vol. XXV: 300–18.

Patinkin, D. (1976) *Keynes' Monetary Thought. A Study of Its Development*, Durham, North Carolina: Duke University Press.

Patinkin, D. (1982), *Anticipations of the* General Theory? *And Other Essays on Keynes* (University of Chicago Press).

Patinkin, D. (1987) 'Real Balances', in *The New Palgrave: A Dictionary of Economics*, vol. 3, edited by J. Eatwell, M. Milgate and P. Newman (London: Macmillan), 98–101.

Patinkin, D. (1991) 'Keynes, John Maynard', in *The New Palgrave: A Dictionary of Economics*, vol. 3, edited by J. Eatwell, M. Milgate and P. Newman (London: Macmillan), 19–41.

Patinkin, D. (1995) 'The Training of an Economist', *BNL Quarterly Review*, 195: 359–95.

Pigou, A.C. (1943) 'The Classical Stationary State', *The Economic Journal*, vol. LIII: 343–51.

Rubin, G. (2002a) 'From Equilibrium to Disequilibrium: the Genesis of Don Patinkin's Interpretation of the Keynesian Theory', *European Journal of History of Economic Thought*, vol. 9, no. 2: 205–25.

Rubin, G. (2002b) *La contribution de Don Patinkin à la 'synthèse néoclassique': genèse et portée*, PhD Dissertation, University of Paris X-Nanterre.

Rubin, G. (2004) 'Patinkin on IS-LM: An Alternative to Modigliani', *History of Political Economy*, Annual Supplement to vol. 36: 190–216.

Rubin, G. (2005a) 'La controverse entre Clower et Patinkin au sujet de la loi de Walras', *Revue économique*, vol. 56, no. 1: 5–24.

Rubin, G. (2005b) 'Patinkin and the Pigou Effect: Or How a Keynesian Came to Accept an Anti-Keynesian Argument', *European Journal of History of Economic Thought*, vol. 12, no. 1: 47–72.

Tobin, J. (1975) 'Keynesian Models of Recession and Depression', *American Economic Review Papers and Proceedings*, 65: 195–202.

Notes

1 On this see Patinkin (1995: 378–9) and Mehrling (2002).
2 Quoted by Merhling (2002). See his paper for a complete quotation.
3 One can find an echo of Lange's interpretation in Patinkin's article on Keynes in the New Palgrave. There he contends that 'a basic contribution of the *General Theory* is that it is in effect the first practical application of the Walrasian theory of general equilibrium' (1991: 27).
4 The need for microfoundations was also one of the basic tenets of the Cowles programme under the head of Marschak: 'The presentation of these reports was followed (or rather, constantly interrupted) by critical comments, a recurrent theme of which was the necessity (emphasized especially by Marschak) for basing the analysis – and the resulting empirical equations – on the principle of profit or utility maximization' (1995: 385).
5 For a complete demonstration of the following points see Rubin (2002a and 2002b).
6 'My interest is in moving from the semi-microequations to the macroequations which play so prominent a role in current economic discussion' (Patinkin, 1947: 57).
7 This amounted to assuming that expected inflation was nil, an assumption that restricted the scope of Patinkin's theory.
8 In the dissertation Patinkin did not assume that prices were fixed and no equation could be used to find their value. But in an unpublished manuscript probably written after the submission of his PhD he noted that: 'The crude Keynesian model of §2 [the Keynesian macro-model of his thesis] retains value even after consideration of Pigou's argument. For the crude model indicates what levels of national income will be generated if, say, the current interest rate and price level are maintained' (inconsistent systems and involuntary unemployment). In other words, the Keynesian model could be interpreted as a fixed-price equilibrium model. Yet this indication did not tell the reader how prices were determined in a system regulated by Patinkin's 'compromise' mechanism. This critical issue remained unsettled.
9 On this point see De Vroey (2004: 15).
10 '*MIP* can therefore be read as Patinkin's attempt to integrate not only monetary theory with value theory, but also (and closer to Patinkin's heart) to integrate the new critical perspective of Lange and Keynes with the older Chicago tradition' (Mehrling, 2002: 171).
11 This section outlines the results of Rubin (2005b).
12 Henderson actually showed that Patinkin's argument was inconsistent with his microeconomic assumptions concerning households' choices.
13 On the correspondence between Friedman and Patinkin see Leeson (1998, 2000).
14 On the relation between the macroeconomic model of *Money, Interest and Prices* and IS-LM see Rubin (2004).
15 A detailed argumentation is presented in Rubin (2005a).

6
Is IS-LM a Static or Dynamic 'Keynesian' Model?

Warren Young

Introduction

In my book (Young, 1987), I outlined the history of IS-LM, and based my approach upon 'recollections and documents', as Hicks put it (1973). About a decade later, this time with William Darity (Darity and Young, 1995), we surveyed the early mathematical models of Keynes' *General Theory*. In both cases, the focus was on the original IS-LM approach and subsequent models based upon it. In this chapter, I focus upon some overlooked aspects of the interrelationships between these various interpretations and representations, *that is, between the early models themselves*, over the decade after the original IS-LM approach of Roy Harrod, James Meade and John Hicks, and deal with the impact of what Paul Samuelson called the 'Keynes–Lange' system. I then turn to the somewhat overlooked development of the *dynamic* approach to IS-LM, as manifest in the work of Samuelson (1941) and Franco Modigliani (1944), and the relationship between them and the approach of Lawrence Klein (1947). Suggestions as to the possibility of utilizing archival resources to investigate these issues will be put forward.

From Keynes–Lange to Clower–Leijonhufvud

Oskar Lange's 1938 paper 'The Rate of Interest and the Optimum Propensity to Consume' attempted to solve what can be termed the *Malthus–Ramsey problem*. Lange noted that Malthus posed the problem as early as 1820 in his *Principles of Political Economy* with 'unsurpassed clarity' when he wrote (Malthus, 1820: 8–9, 369–70):

> If consumption exceeds production, the capital of the country must
> be diminished, and its wealth must be gradually destroyed from its

want of power to produce; if production be in great excess above consumption, the motive to accumulate must cease from the want of will to consume. The two extremes are obvious; and it follows that there must be some intermediate point, though the resources of political economy may not be able to ascertain it, where taking into consideration both the power to produce and the will to consume, the encouragement to the increase of wealth is greatest.

In his 1938 paper, Lange termed this point the '*optimum* propensity to save which maximizes investment' (1938: 24, italics in original), and went on to say that 'the general theory of interest outlined' in his 'paper enables us to solve this problem and to determine the *optimum* propensity to save which maximizes investment' accordingly. He continued (1938: 24):

> Since investment per unit of time is a function of both the rate of interest and expenditure on consumption a decrease of the propensity to consume (increase in the propensity to save) has a twofold effect. On the one hand the decrease of expenditure on consumption discourages investment, but the decrease in the propensity to consume also causes . . . a fall of the rate of interest which encourages investment on the other hand. The optimum propensity to consume is that at which the encouraging and the discouraging effect of a change are in balance.

A decade earlier, in his classic *EJ* paper 'A Mathematical Theory of Savings' (1928), Frank Ramsey had re-stated Malthus's problem as 'How much of its income should a nation save?' (1928: 543). Ramsey went on to define the 'maximum obtainable rate of enjoyment or utility' as 'Bliss' (1928: 545). The notion of the optimum propensity to save and *balance* is implicit in Ramsey's assertion that (1928: 545)

> in all cases we can see that the community *must save enough* [our emphasis] either to reach bliss after a finite time, or at least to approximate to it indefinitely . . . Enough must therefore be saved to reach or approach bliss some time, but this does not mean that our whole income should be saved. The more we save the sooner we shall reach bliss, but the less enjoyment we shall have now, and *we have to set the one against the other* [my emphasis].

While Lange's 1938 paper was reprinted in Gottfried Haberler's volume *Readings in Business Cycle Theory* (1944), it received detailed attention only a decade after its publication, in Klein's book *The Keynesian Revolution* (1947) and especially in Samuelson's *Foundations of Economic Analysis* (1947). Klein asserted that Lange's notion of the 'optimum propensity to consume' was similar to that of the earlier underconsumptionist [Malthusian] idea of 'the proper balance' of 'consumption out of income' (1947: 135). Klein, however, took the view that (1947: 135)

> [a]s far as we are concerned, the optimum propensity to consume (*in the schedule sense*) [italics in original] is that propensity which interacts with the investment schedule to give a full-employment level of national income, and there are an infinite number of consumption functions which will do this.

Samuelson, in *Foundations of Economic Analysis* (1947), went much further in his treatment of what he termed the 'Keynes–Lange' system (1947: 354) not only providing it with a specific 'mathematical form' but describing it as an 'equilibrium system' (1947: 276–7). Samuelson went on to say, however, that '[i]f we are to derive meaningful theorems, we must clearly proceed to a consideration of a more general dynamic system which includes the stationary Keynesian analysis as a special case'. He then proceeded to develop a 'differential system' of 'dynamical' equations leading to an 'equilibrium' which is stable under conditions which hold 'unambiguously'. On this basis Samuelson 'establishes . . . theorems' which are not only 'useful' but 'important' that are derived directly from the equilibrium conditions of the dynamized 'Keynes-Lange' system, that is, 'if the equilibrium is stable' (1947: 278–9). We will discuss this in detail below, in the context of our discussion of Samuelson (1941), which is the source of the presentation in his 1947 volume. In his conclusion to *Foundations* (1947), Samuelson further developed the question in the 'comparative dynamics' of the Keynes–Lange system he earlier analysed in terms of 'comparative statical analysis' regarding the influence on investment of 'a change in thriftiness' (1947: 353). As he put it (1947: 353), the wider problem was 'what happens to capital *in the long run* [italics in original] as a result of a change in thriftiness'. In Samuelson's view (1947: 353–4).

> Thus, if instead of simply asking what level of consumption maximizes current investment, we widen Professor Lange's question and seek the levels of consumption leading to the most capital *at each instant of time* [italics in original], we shall find that capital formation in a run of any length is only maximized if at each instant the Lange criteria are met.

Now, in their 1947 books, neither Klein nor Samuelson took notice of the *extension* of the *Keynes–Lange* system by Timlin (1942) – whose work *was*, however, noted by Modigliani in his seminal 1944 *Econometrica* paper (1944: 45). Her extension of the *Keynes–Lange* system proceeded in a number of ways. First, she reemphasized the simultaneous and interdependent nature of the system. Secondly, she stressed the interest rate as the key to the solution of the simultaneous and interdependent system; this emanating from its *dual role* as *both* independent and dependent variable. Thirdly, and most importantly, she developed a diagrammatic representation of Lange's *Walrasian* system which *did not* reflect the static equations of the IS-LM interpretations of the Keynesian system à la Hicks, Harrod and Meade (Young, 1987; Darity and Young, 1995). Rather, it emphasized the 'system of the *shifting* equilibrium [my emphasis] which lies at the heart' of the *Keynes–Lange* General Equilibrium system according to Timlin (1942: 7). This being said, and in light of the *original* aspects of Mabel Timlin's extension of the *Keynes–Lange* system, we called it the *Lange–Timlin* system accordingly (Young, 1987).

At this point, however, we must briefly recount the reinvention, some two decades later, of the forgotten *Lange–Timlin* system by Robert Clower and Axel Leijonhufvud in their works in the 1960s (Clower, 1965; Leijonhufvud, 1967, 1968, 1969; also see Clower and Leijonhufvud, 1975; Leijonhufvud, 1983; Young, 1987). In his well-known 1965 article 'The Keynesian Counter-Revolution', for example, Clower made no mention of either Lange's 1938 paper or Timlin's 1942 book, the importance of which we have seen above. This is difficult to understand because Clower's general approach is foreshadowed in Lange's 1938 paper, and in the 1965 paper, he presents Keynes's system in a very similar way to Lange's and Timlin's further development of it.

In outlining his interpretation of what he considered the cardinal element underlying Keynes' *General Theory*, which he called the 'dual-decision hypothesis' of household (consumption-saving) behaviour, Clower attempted to reconcile Keynes' with Walras' Law, which, as he said, was formally equivalent to Say's Law (Clower, 1965: 275, 279, 289). Clower's justification for his approach will not be discussed here. Suffice to say, however, that according to Clower, 'Keynes either had a dual-decision hypothesis [of household behaviour] at the back of his mind, or most of the *General Theory* is theoretical nonsense' (Clower, 1965: 287–90).

Interestingly, Lange, in his 1938 paper, introduced the income identity $Y = C + I$, as 'the sum of the budget equations of the individuals', and noted 'investment or saving decisions can be different'. He then distinguished between Walras' approach – 'the equality of the value of the *capitaux neufs* and the excess of income over consumption', i.e. saving – and that of his own system which, in Lange's view, is 'as in the theory of Mr. Keynes' because it 'is an identity'. According to Lange, 'whatever the investment and savings decisions are, the volume of total income always adjusts itself so as to equalize saving and investment actually performed. This is a simple budget relationship, for the individual's incomes are equal to the sum of expenditure on consumption and investment'. Lange claims that his identity 'corresponds to the sum of the budget equations in the Walrasian system' and shows 'how expenditure on consumption and investment determine the total income. When this budget relationship is taken account of, there is no need any more for a separate equation indicating the equilibrium of saving and investment decisions based on some given income, however defined'.

Clower's 1965 attempt to link Keynes' system with that of Walras by the dual-decision hypothesis would seem, then, to originate in Lange's 1938 paper and Timlin's subsequent development of the *Keynes–Lange* system (Lange, 1938: 14, 22–3; Timlin, 1942). In his works published between 1967 and 1969, Leijonhufvud was even more explicit than Clower in his attempt to base his views of Keynes' theory upon a Walras-type system (Leijonhufvud, 1967, 1968, 1969). Again, however, there is no mention of Lange's 1938 paper or Timlin's 1942 book. Taking his lead from Clower, Leijonhufvud asserted in his 1967 paper, for example, that the Clower approach was the most suitable 'interpretation' of Keynes's *General Theory* (1967: 402–4). In an article published a decade after Clower's 'rediscovery' – albeit unattributed – of Lange's approach and Timlin's extension of it, Clower and Leijonhufvud took what they called a 'Keynesian perspective' on 'the coordination of economic activities' (Clower and Leijonhufvud, 1975). To be brief, they simply restated the link that Lange had made between Keynes and Walras some 30 years earlier, which was subsequently developed by Timlin more than two decades prior to Clower's 1965 paper. In essence, Clower and Leijonhufvud simply turned the *Keynes–Lange* and *Lange–Timlin* systems into one variant of the '*neo-Walrasian* synthesis' (Clower and Leijonhufvud, 1975: 184).

Samuelson, Modigliani and Klein: from statics to dynamics, 1941–7

In the April 1941 issue of *Econometrica*, Samuelson published a paper entitled 'The Stability of Equilibrium: Comparative Statics and Dynamics', which was to become Chapter IX of *Foundations of Economic Analysis* (1947). In this paper, he developed 'techniques . . . of . . . fruitful applicability' in order to analyse what he called 'the Keynesian system' (1941: 113). As he put it (1941: 113), 'I shall analyse in some detail the simple Keynesian model as outlined in the *General Theory*. Various writers, such as Meade, Hicks, and Lange, have developed explicitly in mathematical form the meaning of the Keynesian system'. He went on to outline an equational system of the form:

$$C(i, Y) - Y + I = -\alpha$$
$$F(i, Y) - I = -\beta$$
$$L(i, Y) = M$$

(1941: 114, equations 56–8)

Samuelson then provided 'three relations to determine the three unknowns [i, Y, I] in terms of three parameters [α, β, M]' (1941: 114, equation 59), going on to call this '*the Keynesian equilibrium system*' (my emphasis).

He then proceeded to devise a 'more general dynamic system', encompassing 'the stationary Keynesian analysis as a special case', and considered two distinct cases, the first of which was 'based upon a differential system' (1941: 115). In order to do this, he replaced the static equations (1941: 114, equations 56–8) with 'dynamical ones' (1941: 116, equations 63–5), and provided a solution set for them (1941: 116, equation 66). He then established the conditions for the unambiguous stability of the dynamic equations (1941: 116, equations 68 and 69).

The second case Samuelson considered was that of a 'dynamic system' based upon a difference equation set which, if 'none of the variables are taken as given' (1941: 119) was specified by him as (1941: 120, equation 85)

$$C(i_t, Y_{t-1}) - Y_t + I_t = 0,$$
$$F(i_t, Y_t) - I_t = 0,$$
$$L(i_t, Y_t) - M = 0$$

He then went on to present the conditions that assured stability of equilibrium (1941: 120).

There are a number of important things to notice in Samuelson's representation of what he called 'the Keynesian system'. First, he utilized a consumption function, rather than a savings function. Second, he specified consumption as being a function of both income and the interest rate, as did Lange (Young, 1987: 80). And this, in contrast to the approaches of Hicks, Harrod and Meade before him (Young 1987; Darity and Young 1995: 23) and Modigliani (1944: 46) and Klein (1947: 199ff) subsequently, all of whom utilized savings rather than consumption functions in their respective models of 'the Keynesian system', as they interpreted it. However, 'Samuelson's innovative step', as we put it over a decade ago (Darity and Young, 1995: 29) 'was to introduce an income lag in the consumption function, and to push the analytics into the realm of solutions of difference equations'. Moreover, as we noted (1995: 29, note 19) 'while the mathematics of difference equations . . . [was] alien to Keynes' mode of presentation, Samuelson (1988) contends they were very much present in the conceptual structure of his argument, if not in the *General Theory*, then in Keynes's Galton Lecture, published in the *Eugenics Review* in 1937'.

Less than three years later, in the January 1944 issue of *Econometrica*, Modigliani published a paper entitled 'Liquidity Preference and the Theory of Interest and Money'. This has been widely recognized as the apex of the neoclassical synthesis (Young, 1987: 121–5; Darity and Young, 1995: 24–6). What has received less attention is the *dynamic model* in Modigliani's paper (1944: 62–4), and *no comparison, as far as I know, has ever been made between Modigliani's dynamic model of 1944 vintage and Samuelson's dynamic model of 1941 vintage*. Moreover, Modigliani *did not mention* Samuelson's dynamic model in his 1944 paper, although he did cite Lange and Timlin respectively (1944: 46, note 4, 50, note 9, 52, note 11).

In Section 10 of his 1944 paper, which he called 'A dynamic model of the Keynesian theory and the stability of equilibrium', Modigliani developed a 'system of difference equations' which he 'considered as the simplest dynamic model' of the 'theory' he presented (1944: 62). Modigliani specified a system of difference equations (1944: 63, equations 2.1–2.6), and went on to develop stability conditions (1944: 63–4), going on to say that if these conditions 'are satisfied, the variables approach their equilibrium values, which are the same as those obtained by solving the static system' he presented in this section on 'Macrostatic systems' (1944, Section 2: 46–48). It is important to note here that Modigliani's stability condition for the system of difference equations (1944: 64) and that of Samuelson's 'Case 2' system of difference equations (1941: 119, equation 83) are *parallel*; and this, while Modigliani did not cite Samuelson (1941) at all.

In his 1947 book *The Keynesian Revolution*, Klein mentioned Samuelson's 1941 paper (1947: 112, note 25), but Modigliani's 1944 paper is not cited by Klein at all. In addition, Klein did not include Modigliani as a supporter of Keynesian economics amongst economists working in the US in the list he provided (1947: 184), which included Hansen, Samuelson, Smithies, Mosak, Metzler, Hagen, Lerner and even Lange, although he added a caveat to the effect that 'some individuals in this group would not call themselves Keynesians' (1947: 184, note 6). On the other hand, he cited Lange's 1938 paper in his book (1947: 135, note 13). Moreover, in the 'technical appendix' to his book, Klein made a specific reference to the stability conditions in Samuelson's 1941 dynamic model when he wrote 'Professor Samuelson has shown that if a dynamic model for which our static system is the stationary solution, is to be stable then the denominator must be negative' (1941: 205). This directly follows from the equilibrium condition Samuelson set out for his 'dynamical' system of equations as described above (1941: 116, equations 63–9).

Suggested questions for archival research

The following questions arise, that can be answered only by means of studying the papers of Clower, Leijonhufvud, Samuelson, Modigliani and Klein respectively:

(1) Why are Lange's 1938 paper and Timlin's 1942 book not mentioned by Clower and Leijonhufvud in any of their works?
(2) Why is Samuelson's 1941 paper not mentioned by Modigliani in his 1944 paper?
(3) Why is Modigliani's 1944 paper not mentioned by Klein in his 1947 book?

The papers of Clower, Leijonhufvud and Modigliani are accessible at Duke University. Samuelson's papers are at MIT Special Collections (MC 403), while only those of Klein remain to be deposited in archives; however, some of the individuals involved can be directly approached with the questions listed above and others, relating to the relationship between their respective works. Answers to these questions should throw new light on the *interrelationship* between some of the '*second generation*' of interpreters of Keynes's *General Theory*, and provide at least a partial answer to the question: is IS-LM a static *and* dynamic 'Keynesian' model?

References

Clower, R. (1965) 'The Keynesian Counter-Revolution: A Theoretical Appraisal', in F. Hahn and F. Brechling (eds), *The Theory of Interest Rates* (London: Macmillan); reprinted in R. Clower (ed.) (1969), *Monetary Theory* (Harmondsworth: Penguin).
——, and A. Leijonhufvud (1975) 'The Coordination of Economic Activities: A Keynesian Perspective', *American Economic Review: Papers and Proceedings* vol. 65: 182–8.

Darity, W., and W. Young (1995) 'IS-LM: an Inquest', *History of Political Economy*, vol. 27: 1–41.

Haberler, G. (ed.) (1944) *Readings in Business Cycle Theory* (Philadelphia: Blakiston).

Hicks, J. (1973) 'Recollections and Documents', *Economica* (n.s.) vol. 40: 2–11.

Klein, L. (1947) *The Keynesian Revolution* (New York: Macmillan).

Lange, O. (1938) 'The Rate of Interest and the Optimum Propensity to Consume', *Economica* (n.s.) vol. 5: 12–32.

Leijonhufvud, A. (1967) 'Keynes and the Keynesians: A Suggested Interpretation', *American Economic Review Papers and Proceedings*, vol. 57: 401–10.

—— (1968) *On Keynesian Economics and the Economics of Keynes* (Oxford University Press).

—— (1969) *Keynes and the Classics* (London: Institute of Economic Affairs).

—— (1983) 'What Was the Matter with IS-LM', in J. Fitoussi, (ed.), *Modern Macroeconomic Theory* (Oxford: Blackwell).

Malthus, T. (1820) *Principles of Political Economy* (London: J. Murray).

Modigliani, F. (1944) 'Liquidity Preference and the Theory of Interest and Money', *Econometrica*, vol. 12: 45–88.

Ramsey, F. (1928) 'A Mathematical Theory of Saving', *Economic Journal*, vol. 38: 543–59.

Samuelson, P. (1941) 'The Stability of Equilibrium: Comparative Statics and Dynamics', *Econometrica*, vol. 9: 97–120.

—— (1947) *Foundations of Economic Analysis* (Cambridge, MA: Harvard University Press).

—— (1988) 'The Keynes-Hansen-Samuelson Multiplier-Accelerator Model', *Japan and the World Economy*, vol. 1: 3–19.

Timlin, M. (1942) *Keynesian Economics* (University of Toronto Press).

Young, W. (1987) *Interpreting Mr Keynes: The IS-LM Enigma* (Oxford: Polity-Blackwell).

7
The Post Keynesian Assault on Orthodoxy: Insights from the Weintraub Archive

*J.E. King**

Introduction

Before the emergence of New Classical Economics in the late 1970s, and New Keynesian Economics in the following decade, there were three competing schools of thought in postwar macroeconomics. One, Monetarism, was avowedly anti-Keynesian. Based at the University of Chicago and led by the 1976 Nobel laureate Milton Friedman, Monetarism dovetailed neatly with the free-market microeconomics of his colleagues George Stigler (Nobel laureate 1982) and Gary Becker (Nobel laureate 1992). As the name suggests, the Monetarists defended the Quantity Theory of Money, which Keynes had dismissed. They warned of the inflationary dangers of any attempt to hold unemployment below its 'natural' rate, and advocated small government, balanced budgets and strict rules limiting the rate of growth of the money supply.

The mainstream Keynesian opponents of the Monetarists included Paul Samuelson and Robert Solow (of the Massachusetts Institute of Technology) and James Tobin (of Yale University), each of them Nobel laureates (in 1970, 1987 and 1981, respectively). Subsequently often described as 'Old Keynesians', these proponents of the Keynesian-Neoclassical Synthesis rejected the Quantity Theory in favour of the IS-LM model, with the inflation rate linked to the unemployment rate via a Phillips Curve that was supposed, at least in the short run, to be downward-sloping and relatively stable. The Old Keynesians were, like the Monetarists, neoclassical in both their microeconomics and their treatment of long-run questions (in the 1956 Solow growth model unemployment is eliminated through capital–labour substitution in response to relative price changes). In the short run, however, they argued that discretionary fiscal and monetary policy was necessary to increase (or, where appropriate, to decrease) aggregate demand so that non-inflationary full employment could be achieved.

The third school emerged in the 1960s out of a growing sense of dissatisfaction with the Keynesian-Neoclassical Synthesis; by the mid-1970s it was describing itself as Post Keynesian. In Cambridge (UK) the first generation of Post Keynesians included Joan Robinson and Nicholas Kaldor. They cooperated (somewhat uneasily, as will be seen below) with Americans such as John Kenneth Galbraith (Harvard) and Sidney Weintraub (University of Pennsylvania). It was always an oppositional current, and none of the leading Post Keynesians was ever awarded the Nobel Prize. They claimed to take Keynes's *General Theory* seriously, unlike the Old Keynesians, who had – as Robinson once wrote – 'put Keynes to sleep'.

John Maynard Keynes' *General Theory of Employment, Interest and Money* (Keynes, 1936) is an enigmatic book, open to a variety of interpretations both at the time of publication and ever since. Bare references to 'Keynesian' macroeconomics are not uncommon, but they are almost always confusing. A little more information is contained in the frequently used qualifiers, 'Old', 'New' and 'Post' Keynesian, though even here considerable scope remains for controversy. Stripped down to the bare essentials, Post Keynesian economics rests on the principle of effective demand: in capitalist economies, output and employment are normally constrained by aggregate demand, not by individual supply behaviour. Since a decision not to have lunch today – as Keynes famously put it – does not entail a decision to have lunch tomorrow, investment drives saving and not the other way round. Moreover, there exists no automatic or even minimally reliable mechanism that will eliminate excess capacity and involuntary unemployment. Interest rates depend on monetary considerations, not on the so-called 'real' forces of productivity and thrift. There is no 'natural rate of interest' to equilibrate investment and saving, so that a *ceteris paribus* increase in the propensity to save will prove self-defeating, resulting in lower output and reduced employment but not in higher levels of saving.

Thus far Post Keynesians agree with Samuelson, Solow and Tobin, but strongly disagree with many (if not all) 'New' Keynesians, who rely upon *ad hoc* market imperfections to support conclusions that Keynes derived without them. Post Keynesians part company with the Old Keynesians, however, in denying the validity of the Keynesian-Neoclassical Synthesis and in rejecting both the IS-LM model in the short run and the notion of the long run as a sort of magic kingdom where the future is knowable (at least probabilistically), expectations are always fulfilled, money has no real significance and all resources are fully employed. On their interpretation of the *General Theory*, uncertainty is inescapable, expectations are tentative and unreliable, money affects output as well as prices, and demand-deficient unemployment is the central macroeconomic problem. This led the Post Keynesians to criticize the neoclassical theories of capital, growth and distribution and to insist on the importance of cost inflation and the role of incomes policy as an indispensable weapon with which to fight it (King, 2002).

Sidney Weintraub (1914–83) was born in New York and attended New York University as both an undergraduate and a graduate student, also spending a year at the London School of Economics (1938–9). His first academic position was at St John's University in Jamaica, NY. In 1950 he moved to the University of Pennsylvania where, with the exception of a two-year spell at the University of Waterloo (1969–71), he spent the rest of his career. From the mid-1950s Weintraub, a prolific writer on all aspects of economic theory and policy, concentrated on macroeconomics, and in particular on the defects of mainstream Keynesianism. In the stagfla-tionary 1970s his proposals for a tax-based incomes policy attracted con-siderable attention, although they were never implemented. In 1978 Weintraub and Paul Davidson founded the *Journal of Post Keynesian Economics*, which is probably his most important legacy. Biographical sketches can be found in Bloomfield (1981–2), Bloomfield and Davidson (1984), King (1995b) and E.R. Weintraub (2002, chapters 7–8); Weintraub (1983) is an engaging memoir.

The Weintraub papers, held at the Manuscript Department, William R. Perkins Library, Duke University, offer a rich variety of insights into his life and career, and into the early development of Post Keynesian economics in the United States – and elsewhere. They have yet to be fully catalogued, but were grouped by staff at the Perkins Library, since the files arrived with no established order. There are 24 boxes, each containing several folders; the location of items cited below is identified by box number, followed by a diagonal slash, followed by the folder number (for example, 1/5 refers to box 1, folder 5). The bulk of Weintraub's correspondence is in boxes 1–6, with the period 1970–83 most strongly represented; further letters to and from Weintraub are scattered throughout the collection. Other boxes are organized by subject, the most interesting dealing with the Trieste Summer School (box 7) and the establishment of the *Journal of Post Keynesian Economics* (box 8). A detailed description of the Weintraub archive is provided by Hoaas (1985).[1] Thus far, relatively little use has been made of the archive by scholars, though there are a handful of specialist studies of Weintraub and his work (Lodewijks, 1990, 1991; King, 1995a).

This chapter is in seven parts. The first section outlines the archival evi-dence on Weintraub's (deteriorating) relationship with the mainstream of the economics profession in the US, chiefly through his correspondence with journal editors over article rejections and unfavourable reviews of his books. The second section describes his contacts with the Cambridge Post Keynesians, including Joan Robinson, Richard Kahn and Nicholas Kaldor, from 1957 until his death in 1983. Section 3 deals with his friendship with George Shackle, and the fourth section is devoted to his relations with US Post Keynesians, including Paul Davidson, Hyman Minsky and Alfred Eichner. In the fifth section, archival evidence on the establishment of the *Journal of Post Keynesian Economics* is presented. Section 6 deals with some of Weintraub's less successful ventures, including his temporary move to Canada, the upheavals at Rutgers University, abortive efforts to establish a Post Keynesian think tank and the Trieste Summer School. The chapter concludes with an assessment of what the Weintraub papers tell us about the personality of this original, important but also very difficult figure.

1.   Weintraub and the American mainstream

At the outset of his academic career, Sidney Weintraub had every reason to believe that he would enjoy considerable success in the mainstream of the economics profession. In 1942, at the tender age of 28, he published articles almost simultaneously in the *American Economic Review*, the *Quarterly Journal of Economics* and the *Journal of Political Economy*, 'an uncommon feat I suspect' (Weintraub, 1983, p. 224, referring to Weintraub, 1942a, 1942b, 1942c). Two decades later he was both deeply disaffected with conventional economics and increasingly marginalized within the profession. This was partly the result of theoretical and policy differences, but it also reflected a profound shift in economic methodology that had left him behind.

   At first he seems to have regarded himself as an innovative mainstream macroeconomist, attempting to explore the mysteries of Keynes' aggregate supply function (Weintraub, 1957) and to develop a genuinely Keynesian theory of functional income distribution (Weintraub, 1958). But he grew more and more dissatisfied with what he came to dismiss as 'Classical Keynesianism', typified by the income–expenditure (or 'Keynesian cross') and IS-LM models used in introductory and intermediate teaching, where all the crucial variables were defined in real terms and no account was taken of changes in the price level. When inflation did come under discussion, it was explained purely in terms of excess aggregate demand, and measures to reduce consumption, investment or government expenditure were seen as the only possible remedy. The simultaneous rise in inflation and unemployment in 1958–9 – a first glimpse of the stagflation of the 1970s – made this seem highly questionable.

As Weintraub came to realize, it ignored the role of cost inflation (especially wage inflation) and rendered meaningless any attempt to bring inflation under control by acting directly on the determinants of the money wage level. Weintraub was certainly not the only economist in the US to voice these objections, but, along with Gardiner Means and John Kenneth Galbraith, he was among the most consistent and unyielding of critics. Some of his arguments did eventually find acceptance among more orthodox theorists, but this amounted (or so he believed) to only a belated and grudging recognition of his work.

There was another factor, in some ways even more fundamental, which served to estrange Weintraub from the majority of the profession. This was a question of methodology. After 1945 there was a dramatic increase in the level of mathematical sophistication of economic theory, and corresponding changes in the statistical techniques that were used in empirical research. Weintraub had very little sympathy for this radical transformation of his discipline, and as his son relates he was in any case a very poor mathematician (E.R. Weintraub, 2002, chapter 7). He neither wished to participate in the formalist revolution in economics, nor would he have been capable of doing so. Mainstream theorists, for their part, came to view him as an anachronism. More and more their journals were closed to him, not through personal animus – though there was some of that, too – but because his work simply did not aspire to the new scientific standards that had been set.

Other Post Keynesians suffered similar rejection by an increasingly intolerant orthodoxy. Hyman Minsky (1919–96), only five years Weintraub's junior, announced the start of his academic career in 1957 with two long articles in the *Quarterly Journal of Economics* and the *American Economic Review* (Minsky, 1957a, 1957b), but before long was reduced to publishing his work in what were generally regarded as second- or third-rate publications. Paul Davidson (born 1930), who represented the best of the next generation, crept into *Econometrica* and the *Journal of Political Economy* but was soon himself excluded from all the leading journals. Younger Post Keynesians had simply no chance. Arguably, expulsion from the mainstream affected Weintraub more deeply than anyone, given his high ambitions and prickly personality.

On the other side of the Atlantic there were, of course, Post Keynesians with analogous personalities: neither Nicholas Kaldor nor Joan Robinson, for example, could be described as unambitious or unassertive. But the Americanization of economics was a gradual process, and the principal British journals – above all the *Economic Journal* – remained open to the first generation of Cambridge Post Keynesians pretty well until the end

(Robinson died in 1983 and Kaldor in 1986). Indeed, Robinson was able to publish in the *Quarterly Journal of Economics* as late as 1975 (Robinson, 1975). At all events, in Europe the alienation from the mainstream came rather later, and was perhaps felt less deeply, than Weintraub's.

The Weintraub archive contains a wealth of correspondence relevant to these themes. Many letters illustrate his early friendly relations with some of the leaders of the economics profession in the US, and his subsequent alienation from it is reflected in rejection letters from journals and hostile (or, even worse, indifferent) reviews of his books. (Some of the latter are reserved until section 7, due to the light that they shed on Weintraub's personality). In 1957, for example, we find Robert Clower writing to Weintraub to praise his recent *Economic Journal* paper on the aggregate supply curve:

> The spate of recent articles on the topic, each of which has served to muddy more water than it has cleared, should be choked off at this stage. Herewith my personal thanks for providing a reference to which I may refer future students of aggregate economics for a beautifully clear statement of what Keynes 'should have meant' if we could suppose that he was a rational being.[2]

Two years later Dennis Robertson commented very favourably on Weintraub's *American Economic Review* article on the macroeconomic theory of wages: 'I have lately been reading your article again with great appreciation of its clarity and thoroughness'.[3] Although Robertson was an Englishman, his somewhat pre-Keynesian approach to macroeconomics closely resembled the majority opinion in the United States.

Some years later Weintraub proudly recalled these accolades from Clower and Robertson, though he got them mixed up.[4] As late as 1969 he remained on friendly terms with another mainstream stalwart, Robert Solow:

> Dear Bob:
> Enclosed. After you read it I hope you will agree that it is not even remotely a personal attack. I have too much respect for you and your work – even if you forget my book....
> I am sending a copy of the paper on to Stiglitz, with a short note.[5]

Solow replied in friendly terms:

> [T]here are some ideas for which you claim credit that I regard as part of the furniture of economics. We gave no reference for them

not because we claimed originality, but for the same reason that one would not footnote Marshall on referring to the price-elasticity of demand. . . .

I don't think any harm could come from your sending your Comment to the QJE. I'd have to consult Stiglitz, of course, but my inclination would be to reply in a sentence or two agreeing that you are one of the furniture-makers.[6]

Weintraub's comment was eventually published in the *Quarterly Journal of Economics* (Weintraub, 1970). But there was by now a growing tendency for his work to be rejected by the leading US journals, sometimes quite rudely. In 1962 he had already run into trouble with the *QJE*, his paper 'Towards a Theory of the Constancy in the Wage Share' being rejected by the acting editor, Robert Dorfman, on the grounds that it lacked theoretical depth.[7] A decade later, he had two papers rejected simultaneously by the *American Economic Review*. One referee concluded his report on 'Income Distribution in Macroeconomics: A Simplified Approach' in the following words:

I have discussed this paper formally above as though it were a potential contribution to the literature. In fact, there is nothing in this paper that can possibly be construed as contributing anything. Frankly, I am amazed that anyone would submit something like this to a professional journal – let alone to the *AER*. It would be fortunate to receive a passing grade in a principles course.[8]

He had no greater success with the *Western Economic Journal* or (its new title) *Economic Inquiry*, with Robert Clower rejecting one paper on the grounds that it contained 'serious and wrong-headed implicit theorizing',[9] and a second as 'a mishmash of material that you have been writing about over the years and publishing in various papers over and over again'.[10] Clower later responded, to a letter from Weintraub that has not survived: 'To tell the truth Sidney, I think the problem with some of your writing is that you simply get too impatient with your audience. I know I have the same trouble, and as a result neither write nor publish very much. You seem to write a lot, but it is often very irritable in tone, indicating the kind of impatience that I have just referred to'.[11] Even the *Economic Journal* was starting to prove unsympathetic, a 1971 letter from Roy Harrod beginning: 'My dear Sid, I am horrified to hear that you have been submitted to having to read the jejune comments of a foolish referee. I wish that I were still Editor of the Journal'.[12]

The reviews of Weintraub's books gave him no greater cause for satisfaction. He probably did not help his cause by publishing with Chilton, a Philadelphia company previously known only for its automobile repair manuals, for which he became in effect unnamed academic editor. This was perilously close to self-publishing, and must have served to discredit his work somewhat in the minds of reviewers. The archive contains some rather tense correspondence with Robert Solow, who had reviewed *An Approach to the Theory of Income Distribution* (Weintraub, 1958) for the *Journal of Political Economy*: 'can't you say anything at all nice about any of the first seven chapters?', Weintraub asked. 'I'm not really mad, just disappointed. I had not expected a very sympathetic treatment from nonKeynesians but had thought there would be a little more welcome from neutrals or those who don't get mad at the mere mention of his name'.[13] In the following year Weintraub wrote to Bernard F. Haley, then editor of the *American Economic Review*, asking (unsuccessfully) for the right of reply to Abba Lerner's review of his *A General Theory of the Price Level, Output, Income Distribution and Economic Growth*.[14] Subsequent complaints concerned the critical reception of his books *Some Aspects of Wage Theory and Policy* (Weintraub, 1963) and *A Keynesian Theory of Employment, Growth and Income Distribution* (Weintraub, 1966), the former complaint eliciting an angry response from John Gurley, then editor of the *AER*.[15] (These two cases will be re-examined in section 7.) In sum, the archive leaves no doubt that by the mid-1960s Weintraub saw himself, and was increasingly seen by his fellow economists, as unorthodox, if not downright heretical.

2.   Weintraub and Cambridge

By the early 1970s Post Keynesianism had become an international phenomenon, with strong connections between its US, British and Italian streams (Lee, 2000b). It was not always so. In the 1950s and early 1960s international contacts between Post Keynesians were limited and often quite fraught. From a twenty-first century perspective it may be difficult to comprehend an era in which there was no email, air travel was a luxury and long-distance telephone calls were so expensive that they were restricted to dire emergencies. Transatlantic mail was also expensive and took the best part of a week each way, so that correspondence occurred with a time lag of at least a fortnight. The result was, more often than not, mutual ignorance and – occasionally – unnecessary ill-feeling.

From October 1938 to May 1939 Sidney Weintraub had been a graduate student at the London School of Economics, where he was part of a lively and talented group of young economists that included Arthur Lewis,

Paul Rosenstein-Rodan and Tibor Scitovsky (Weintraub, 1983). That he failed to keep in touch with many of them is suggested by the first reference in Weintraub's papers to his English experiences. Writing to Lionel Robbins in 1955, in a (vain) attempt to promote his textbook on *Price Theory*, Weintraub regretted this loss of contact with his old friends. 'Of those about LSE or its environs, I suppose I know only [Alfred] Stonier, D.H. Robertson, Nick Kaldor and [John Keith] Horsefield. Perhaps when you see them you will convey my regards'.[16] As Kaldor was universally known as Nicky (and never as Nick), we have to suppose that Weintraub was drawing on sixteen-year-old memories rather than on any more recent contact. Two years later he visited the UK and lunched with Kaldor and (separately) with Joan Robinson. Kaldor's invitation, although addressed to 'Dear Sidney', was signed 'N. Kaldor', which again indicates a somewhat distant relationship between the two men.[17] Ironically in view of subsequent events, Joan Robinson was rather more welcoming.[18]

The next reference to Cambridge economics came three years later, when Martin Bronfenbrenner wrote to Weintraub from the University of Minnesota, telling him that he had recently outlined Weintraub's ideas at a seminar there. 'Nicholas Kaldor was through here shortly thereafter and gave two talks devoted largely to his 'distribution' theory of growth. He did not however mention your work; I can't say this surprised me, in view of the insularity of British economists generally and the Cambridge variety in particular'.[19] Further evidence of this insularity came at the end of the year in the form of a rather patronising letter from Richard Kahn. It is likely that Weintraub had sent Kahn an offprint of his *International Economic Review* article, 'The Keynesian theory of inflation: the two faces of Janus' (Weintraub, 1960),[20] in which he argued that both the income-expenditure and IS-LM models were useless for policy purposes, since they ignored inflation, and needed to be replaced by an aggregate demand and supply analysis in which variations in the money wage level occupied centre stage. The response was not what Weintraub must have intended:

I feel somewhat surprised by the line taken by your article in the May number of the International Economic Review. To my mind Keynes was the first economist to put on a firm and clear basis the role of the wage bargain. When I say 'clear and firm' I mean also realistic – in contradistinction to those who, rather remarkably, even today conduct analysis on the assumption of perfectly flexible money wages.

As to his followers, I wonder whether in the first place I might draw your attention to paras. 30–56 of my evidence to the Radcliffe Committee, of which I am sending you a copy under separate cover.

Kahn concluded by recommending that Weintraub consult three articles by Joan Robinson, dating from 1937, 1943 and 1958. The message was brutally clear. Cambridge had (of course) got there first. Weintraub was nothing more than a colonial interloper.[21]

Understandably stung by this dismissal, Weintraub dashed off an immediate three-page typed reply:

> To quote from your letter, I, too, 'feel somewhat surprised by the line taken by you' in writing me when you say 'Keynes was the first economist to put on a firm and clear basis the role of the wage bargain'.
>
> Is there anything in my article to dispute this? Am I not careful to say that the trouble is with Keynesians, rather than Keynes? I did not think I would have to underline the distinction for someone like yourself.

Weintraub had repeatedly proclaimed his debt to Keynes, both in his book (Weintraub, 1958) and in articles in the *American Economic Review* and the *Economic Journal* (Weintraub, 1956, 1957):

> How much impression has all this . . . made? As I look at the assembly-line of 'Keynesian' books and articles I would say practically none. And yet, your letter suggests the wage-unit is the customary approach to these problems. I hope it is – in Cambridge. I wish it were outside too. I just don't believe you have shown the necessary willingness to examine and call in question the 'Keynesian' theory that is taught by prominent 'Keynesians'.

As for his alleged deficiencies in scholarship:

> I don't suppose you are really serious in thinking that I should have had your Radcliffe Committee testimony before me at the time I was writing. Likewise, it is possible that some injustice was done Mrs. Robinson in omitting her from the final footnote references. . . .
>
> . . . I have used her *Accumulation* in two classes. Over a twenty year writing period of my own, can she find a single critical footnote? On two occasions I have invited her here as a guest lecturer and, on the last occasion, her brusqueness was really something to behold. Still, I have the highest respect for her, if this assurance is required. In my opinion her *Accumulation*-volume has been unfairly dealt with in the profession – hardly the first case of such treatment.

Weintraub ended on a conciliatory note, offering to arrange a visiting lectureship for Kahn at the University of Pennsylvania in 1961 or 1962:

> An invitation in the midst of a storm – maybe this makes it all a tempest in a teapot – and reflects better my own good thoughts of you and of Mrs. Robinson. Someday, someway, someone will invent a device which will distinguish intellectual friends from foes. A chilling prospect.[22]

This encounter must have rankled with Weintraub, for he referred to it in correspondence with both Geoff Harcourt and Jan Kregel sixteen years later.[23] Kahn seems to have passed his letter on to Robinson for a reply. She eventually came up with a rare, if somewhat backhanded, apology:

> I am sorry you should be so much offended with Kahn and myself. If I wrote discourteously it must be because I was in a frantic rush. Please accept my apologies.
>
> On the main question this is evidently a 'semantic misunderstanding'. To you 'Keynes' theory' means some latter-day nonsense, while to us, the old guard, it is a coherent system of analysis in which the wage-price relation is an essential part.[24]

This was enough to mollify Weintraub, who responded by return of post to thank Robinson for her 'gracious note; I trust it ends an incident which may have caused some anguish on both sides. Surely you must sense my feelings of esteem that go back more years than either of us should care to have mentioned'. The unpleasantness between them was indeed the result of 'a 'semantic' misunderstanding':

> I have never doubted Keynes' position on the wage and price level, nor your own. . . .
>
> So, I salute the 'old guard' on this issue; I did not need any convincing though I am happy to have the new evidences of the renewed faith. But it is hardly the same, I assure you, on this side of the ocean. Here [a] Keynesian is one who lives with the 45-degree diagram, who writes of the consumption function in real terms in an age of inflation without once mentioning the price level, who argues a liquidity preference theory, also in real terms despite the relation of the price level to transactions balances, whose investment function is independent of price-level phenomena, and who teaches his students, from his blasted diagram, that inflation is due to 'excess demand' so that tighter monetary policy, higher tax measures, and reduced government programs

must be used to achieve stability. Also, and so sadly and so alien to Keynes, that inflation and deflation are 'symmetrical' phenomena.

This reflected poorly on the quality of scholarship in the US:

> What nonsense we have been teaching, and all by and descendant from the 'eminent' American Keynesians. . . .
>
> The appalling thing is that our teaching tradition is so designed that no one reads the original, and everyone reads the insipid, and watered, text-books. Including our most 'eminent' over here, I have rarely encountered anyone who reads Keynes's Book V, or pays any attention to the chapter on the 'Choice of Units'. And yet, all this is so crucial to the particular price level issues of the post-war world.

Weintraub signed off as 'A very unreconstructed Keynesian'.[25]

Nothing came of Weintraub's offer to Kahn, but Robinson was eventually to take up his offer and visit him at the University of Waterloo, in Ontario, where Weintraub spent two years (1969–71); she had grandchildren nearby. He visited Cambridge again in 1963, apparently giving a talk to Kaldor's research students and meeting up with Robinson. There was a noticeable change in the tone of Kaldor's letters, the first one again being signed 'N. Kaldor' and the second 'Nicky'.[26] For her part Robinson remained formal, addressing him as 'Professor Weintraub' and signing herself 'Joan Robinson'.[27] The formality remained as late as 1968, when Weintraub next wrote to Robinson with praise for her *Economic Philosophy* (Robinson, 1962): 'I find it one of the most meaningful items I've read; it is also a delight to go through'. Weintraub's letter was still addressed to 'Mrs. Robinson', and signed 'Sidney Weintraub'. It ended on a slightly acid note: 'All this is an effort to be complimentary, and say well-done. What price will I have to pay for my pains?'[28] Robinson did not rise to the bait, replying briefly (by return of post) to thank him, and taking up his reference to 'the recent 'switching' controversy': 'The neo-neoclassics seem to have survived the shock of double-switching but I cannot help feeling that the younger generation will begin to see through them. Do not despair – truth will prevail'.[29]

Some of Weintraub's American friends remained deeply suspicious of Cambridge and all its works. Later in the same year Abba Lerner wrote dismissively of Post Keynesian distribution theory:

> More generally, my feeling is that you and I have been taken for a ride by Kaldor, Joan Robinson and Company, that Kalecki went as far as it is

sensible to go with the assumption the workers consume everything and capitalists consume nothing, and that Pasinetti's most ingenious rectification of this by daring re-definition, constitutes a waste of valuable resources. . . .

During my stay in Cambridge what disturbed me most, and I never could get to the bottom of it, was the continuous fulmination against 'marginalism'. I understand you to say that we have to turn to marginalism to make any coherent and complete statement, including the explanation of what makes k what it is, and with this I am in *vehement* agreement. I would like to see a diatribe against the fulmination rather than the gentle way in which you put it.[30]

Although Weintraub never broke completely with marginal productivity theory, he was increasingly favourably disposed to what he would later describe as the 'Kaldor-Kalecki-Robinson revolution' in economics. As he told Lerner, 'I think the macro relations do illuminate distribution aggregates . . . I don't think 'marginal productivity' concepts are quite so useful in our less than competitive economy, and in so many non-profit service sectors'.[31]

Weintraub continued to correspond with Robinson, arranging her 1971 visit to Waterloo and sending her offprints of his papers. They were now on first-name terms, and in a December 1970 letter she made her opinion of Harrod very clear:

Harrod completely misunderstood what I was trying to do. My question was: Assuming that we have a steady rate of growth actually going on, what determines the rate of profit? Samuelson once tried to maintain that with Harrod saving, that is saving independent of the distribution of net income between wages and profits, the Pasinetti formula does not work and so the marginal productivity theory has to be true. This was obviously nonsense. I brought in the degree of monopoly to show that even with Harrod saving the rate of profit is determinate.

A rise in the degree of monopoly taking place as an event at a point in time would be likely to precipitate a Keynesian slump, and a fall a Keynesian boom.

I think I understand Harrod's theory much better than he does. I had some correspondence with him after his comments on my article and I think we finally reached agreement, though I am not sure that he really understands the point.[32]

This marks the end of the Weintraub–Robinson correspondence, at least so far as the Weintraub archives are concerned. He remained on friendly terms with Kaldor right up to his death (on 19 June 1983). They shared a deep contempt for Friedman and the monetarists, and a common concern that the 1983 Keynes centenary conference in Cambridge had been hijacked by anti-Keynesians.[33] Weintraub's rather ambivalent attitude towards Robinson is apparent from an unpublished 'Comment on Professor Johnson's "Cambridge in the 1950s" ' that he submitted to *Encounter* in 1974. In a highly jaundiced description of his experiences, Harry Johnson (1974) had written 'a cogent ex cathedra assault on 'unscientific' economics, meaning any ideas which disturb his conservative temperament'. While he was right to complain about the unfavourable Cambridge obituaries of Dennis Robertson, there was much to object to in his article:

> Obviously, Johnson's pontifical peroration stands as a sore thumb to the eye-witness professional history. For myself, I welcome the association with Joan Robinson. Alas, while I seem generally to agree with the analysis of that great lady, I often demur on her policy prescriptions – probably reflecting error on my part. Controversy has enlivened our dinner hours which have been too few because of the spatial facts.
>
> I regret that I did not meet the luminous Joan until 1957. Insofar as our work overlapped (and mine also with [the] now Lord Kaldor), I trace it mainly to common roots in the *General Theory* on which our interpretations often clash with the more numerous American Keynesians. So much for direct influence!'[34]

In 1976, in a long letter to Geoff Harcourt, Weintraub went much further: 'I think I saw the problem [with IS-LM] earliest, with Joan seeing where it was going only after she got into capital theory. If we ever meet again I'll tell you of a battle with her way back, when she and Richard Kahn thought I was 'attacking' her, rather than the Hicks-Samuelson Bastards'.[35] He had made the same point in a letter to Jan Kregel a month earlier:

> I'm interested in Kahn and [*Lloyds Bank Review*]; I haven't seen it yet. I can tell you sometime of an early dispute with him, and Joan who required a long time before realizing that what was taught here in the name of Keynes was not their conception and yet they did not appreciate what it was all leading to until a late stage, after my Classical Keynesianism. It seemed that [it was not] until the price level literally exploded and until the Capital dispute waxed hot that she realized that Keynesians were of different breeds. So I think that at that time I was clearer on where the American variety was heading. When we meet, if you are interested, I can fill in the details; I think we became

friends after that imbroglio. Recalling some of this I may again be a bit sensitive to the suggestion that the awakening came only from the U.K. Mind, I take little credit for my own thoughts came from Keynes, and hence the overlap. But I did not always have Cambridge support – or even awareness of the separate camps.[36]

In his letter to Harcourt, Weintraub had expressed an additional criticism of Robinson:

> I think Joan can be faulted in not being clear on a 'historical' process. You know, our mechanical dolls, the econometrician big model-men, also have 'history' in their coefficients (tho they never seem aware of it). What I think Joan should be saying is that history plays some unpredictable tricks because of unpredictable humans – animal spirits. From one standpoint, all history is 'endogenous', yet much is so unpredictable – this is the 'exogenous aspect'.

But there were no hard feelings: 'Joan will be here soon', he noted in a postscript, 'and I will see her in NY, and perhaps at Rutgers with Paul [Davidson]. I have missed her'.[37]

3.   An English gentleman

In the final years of his life Weintraub renewed contact with another old friend from his LSE days, George Shackle (1903–92). Brunner Professor of Economics at Liverpool University from 1951 to 1969, Shackle is unusually hard to classify. He was a thoroughgoing subjectivist, but kept his distance from Austrian economics and is perhaps best characterized as an idiosyncratic fundamentalist Keynesian, whose emphasis on the importance of uncertainty and ignorance – 'unknowledge', as he preferred to describe it – marked him out very clearly from the vulgar Keynesian mainstream. Shackle wrote many books on these themes, and also a well-respected account of theoretical developments between the wars, *The Years of High Theory* (Shackle, 1967).[38] By 1975 he had been retired from Liverpool for six years, but was still publishing prolifically. Shackle was also a great letter-writer. His long correspondence with his former student Stephen Frowen shows him to be a very reserved and formal person, but also a caring and compassionate friend and colleague (Frowen, 2004).

The Frowen correspondence is devoted largely to personal matters and reveals relatively little about Shackle's ideas, but his exchanges with Weintraub are much more illuminating. The Weintraub archive contains ten letters from Shackle,[39] all of them carefully composed and handwritten in his distinctive and rather elegant script. The first is dated 28 July 1975 and is a response to an invitation for Shackle to contribute a chapter to an edited book on modern economic thought:

> I am greatly honoured by your invitation to write chapter 2 of your book, and shall be very happy if I can be of use to you in this way. May I refer to one or two matters?
>
> You will know that over very many years I have increasingly taken a line of my own far from the beaten track. In writing about Keynes, I should give a radically different account from that outlined in the synopsis of Part II. However, that is titled 'Keynesianism'. In any case, I wholly agree with you that such oppositions of view are a good thing. The student should be encouraged from the beginning to think for himself, and what better stimulus to this than finding that writers disagree among themselves? I do appreciate very warmly indeed your undertaking 'not to make stylistic changes or alter content or meaning'. Please forgive my saying, I could not agree to write the chapter except on the understanding that *no* changes would be made in my manuscript, not even by 'the grammarians of the Press'. I take extreme pains to get my thoughts and their expression clear, and after an intense effort involving many long-haul copyings, it seems to me reasonable to make such a condition. You have nobly anticipated it, and I hope what I write will cause you no misgivings.
>
> May I retain copyright of my piece? I have five commitments for the months ahead, to address conferences and give lectures and seminars, [and] it would be a help for me to have the chapter in hand as ammunition.
>
> I am distressed we have never met since LSE. What a time and place that was! The cross-roads of everyone and everything in economics.[40]

Five months later Shackle had written his chapter.[41]

> I now enclose the chapter which I have written for your book *Some Trends in Modern Economic Thought*. In writing it I felt that sort of happiness which I think augurs well. I have taken my best pains over its detail, but the main current flowed swiftly of its own accord. May I refer to one or two matters? In seeking to express intricate and subtle matters, I feel it necessary to provide myself with as many of the oral speaker's arts and advantages as possible. My use of italic is deliberate and very carefully considered. I have been exact with presentation.

I have tried to give the reader the *background* of the great theoretic expansion of the thirties, as well as an account of the new developments themselves. The chapter is thus in some sense self-contained.

I hope, very much indeed, that it will please you. May I beg that you will accept or reject it as it stands? I think we agreed upon this.[42]

The formalities of English academic life had by now been sufficiently relaxed for Shackle to address his letters to 'Dear Sidney' instead of the previous 'Dear Professor Weintraub', and to sign himself 'George Shackle' rather than 'G.L.S. Shackle'.[43] With his usual great modesty, he had 'screwed up [his] courage' and enclosed a copy of his Keynes Lecture, delivered to the British Academy in November 1976 (Shackle, 1976): 'I fear that in this piece the buzzing of the bees in my bonnet will be heard loud and clear. But it was to that end that I wrote it . . . I fear the effect on treasured friendships but you are an understanding critic'.[44]

And so it proved. Two months later Shackle wrote in a state of excitement:

Your letter has just this moment come. It will go into my special archive of most treasured letters, because of your words about *Time and Choice*. They have intensely delighted me. Theory of Games has so immense a fertility that I cannot doubt it would provide illustrations of many of my themes. My basic feeling about Theory of Games is that it assumes (no matter with how much intervening complexity) that each player's knowledge is fundamentally complete. How else could there be a calculus of strategy? And if so, where is there room for the supreme battle-winning ploy, *surprise*?[45]

The letter concluded with strong encouragement for Weintraub: 'Your *Journal*: I eagerly look forward to news of this exciting enterprise'.

Appropriately enough, late in 1977 Shackle became one of the (many) eminent economists invited to join the editorial board of the new *Journal of Post Keynesian Economics*.[46] He accepted with alacrity:

I am extremely excited about your planned new journal. It will be a great honour and a marvellous incentive for me to have some association with this venture. It will, in my judgement, be perfectly timed. Economics needs to change direction and ideals. Humanity and History must come into it afresh. Your journal could be the vehicle. It is presumptuous of me to offer suggestions, but I am truly thrilled at the possibilities. There are young men (in their thirties) in England, Scotland and Ireland, already occupying Chairs, who will I believe set both the direction and the pace of economic theory in these Islands in the coming years. I can name four men of true brilliance.[47]

Unfortunately there is no way of identifying the brilliant young professors to whom Shackle was referring. He took out a ten-year subscription[48] to the *Journal*, and promised to do a little refereeing and to write the occasional article:

> I will try to be of some use on the Board. My domestic circumstances are difficult nowadays on account of illness, and I would ask the Editors not to expect a great deal from me. The manifesto has great drive and spirit, and it will be intensely interesting to see both the response to your initiative and the reaction to it.
>
> '[E]conomics is essentially a moral science and not a natural science'. Your quotation from Keynes puts the whole theme in a sentence.
>
> I think the first thing to be done is to re-establish the notion of a *moral science*. This is the theme I would like to attempt if I accepted your invitation to prepare a paper for the first issue. Would this be acceptable?[49]

Weintraub wrote to Shackle early in 1978 to inform him of the encouraging sales for *Modern Economic Thought* and to promote his latest book, *Capitalism's Inflation and Unemployment Crisis* (Weintraub, 1978). He also described the problems encountered by the Post Keynesian theorist Douglas Vickers in publishing his new book on financial markets. Shackle's reply was especially revealing:

> I am extremely intrigued by what you tell me of Professor Vickers' new book, and one reason for rejection by a commercial publisher. I have long suspected that I am a Jonah, and that those who, for example, put my name down as a referee when applying for appointments are sadly misguided. Praise from me is likely to be fatal to their chances. I feel a little sad that you will not allow Professor Vickers to set out the full philosophical (or 'theological') foundation of his views. The properties and powers of money are elusive beyond words, I think that insight into them calls for a penetration into the heart of our feelings, fears and ambitions. The nature of money, I would say, is at the opposite pole to the old hydraulic ideas, where money had no effect on anything except by turning up on the spot 'in the flesh' as a solid roll of banknotes or equivalent. If Professor Vickers' deeper thoughts are too difficult for the text, could they not go in an Appendix? But I dare not make suggestions.[50]

Shackle read each issue of the *Journal* attentively, writing to Weintraub in March 1979:

> I have just read with extreme delight your note on Samuel Johnson: a closet post-Keynesian? The quotations show him to be a profound searcher of the human heart, such as economic theory needs. When economic theory had made so splendid a start in the eighteenth century, with Cantillon, Adam Smith and, as you have now shown, Samuel Johnson, why did it eventually lose the memory of their inspirations ('Moral Sentiments' for example) and turn itself into a calculus?
>
> I do hope things are better for you, that you are not oppressed with anxiety or deeply troubled feelings.[51]

The final three letters all date from spring 1983, just before Weintraub's death. They deal with the American's health and with Shackle's continuing involvement with the *Journal*, which included brief published comments on two articles by Randall Bausor (Bausor, 1982–3, 1984; Shackle, 1982–3, 1984). He took a special interest in a new, posthumously published book by Alan Coddington, of which he wrote:

> I have secured a copy of Alan Coddington's book *Keynesian Economics* and have read the first two chapters. If the whole book is of the quality of these chapters it will represent Coddington's brilliant, deep, incisive mind at the height of its powers, and make more painful than ever the terrible loss our field of thought has suffered [from his early death]. Your last letter suggested that you would like me to write a review article for the JPKE. I will most gladly do so. His first book, on *The Theory of Bargaining*, was his DPhil thesis at York, for which I was the external examiner, and for which I wrote a foreword when it was published by Allen and Unwin.[52]

Shackle soon finished the book, which lived up to his initial expectations, and seven weeks later he wrote again to Weintraub, enclosing a review article:

> In writing this piece, my central hope has been to give you pleasure. I have been fascinated in many unexpected ways by Coddington's book. I have studied and thought about it intensively, and done my utmost to make the fine blade of his thought flash as it ought and dazzle his readers. The change of mind which this book shows, in relation to his papers of earlier years, is one question of great interest,

but the change itself has greatly illuminated for me the *nature* of the contrast between the two camps into which our profession seems to be settling. Using the word 'classical' in its general cultural sense, as in speaking of architecture, I would call the two camps classical and romantic, or science-seeking and rhetorical. Here by 'rhetoric' I mean the exploitation of the riches of language to suggest and develop meanings and involvement of meaning, in a way that transcends the bare and arid imaginations of logic, though founded on reason. I suspect that the word 'romantic' occurs in Coddington's book, but the index gives no help in finding it again.[53]

Weintraub must have accepted almost by return of post, for Shackle's next (and final) letter was written within a fortnight:

> Your enchanting letter has given me a new zest for things. I am deeply gratified by your exceeding kind words. Of course you are right about 'bootstraps', this is a typical Robertsonian flourish and one that would not have come readily to Nicky's pen 45–50 years ago. Would you kindly substitute Robertson for Kaldor in my manuscript?[54]

Sadly, Weintraub's recovery proved only temporary; his death a month later terminated the correspondence.

4.   The American Post Keynesians

Inevitably the Weintraub papers contain a substantial volume of correspondence with North American Post Keynesians. In this section I concentrate on his relationship with Paul Davidson, Hyman Minsky, John Kenneth Galbraith and Jan Kregel.[55]

Davidson began as Weintraub's student and disciple, soon graduating to the status of colleague, collaborator and, eventually, co-editor of the *Journal of Post Keynesian Economics*. The tensions that were generated by the latter role can be inferred from a 1978 dispute between them, which is discussed in section 7 below. However, the first letter from Davidson to 'Dear Professor Weintraub', signed 'Paul', in July 1959, testified to his junior status:

> I have just finished reading your new book.
>   Let me be one of many to enthusiastically congratulate you on 1 the beauty of the exposition and argument, and 2 on sounding the death knell for the equation of exchange. In a few simple statistical

comparisons you have probably stirred up a 'hornet's nest', but I am sure that when the dust settles, the Chicago school will have retired to lick its mortal wounds.[56]

Three and a half years later a significant change in their relationship became apparent, with Davidson, now writing to 'Dear Sid', describing the critical reactions of his publisher's readers to the manuscript of his new textbook, *Aggregate Supply and Demand Analysis* (Davidson and Smolensky, 1964). Three of them (including Thomas Mayer) had liked the book, while a fourth, R.A. Gordon, 'was not very much impressed'; the publisher had discounted Gordon, and

> [t]he only major deletion that we are making from the book is our discussion of the finance motive. I have found it impossible to communicate with Miles Fleming or Tom Mayer on this point. After having read the *EJ* for 1937 and 1938 (by the way, is there any other literature on the finance motive besides the Ohlin-Robertson-Keynes writings in these two EJ issues?), I am convinced that we are correct, *but* that to include it in the text would merely obfuscate our main message.[57]

Davidson's influential article on Keynes' 'finance motive' subsequently provoked a considerable controversy in Post Keynesian circles, especially in Europe (Davidson, 1965; Graziani, 1984). This letter shows him to have been interested in the topic at an early stage in his career.

Davidson spent the academic year 1970–1 in Cambridge, from which he wrote to Weintraub frequently and at some length. These letters add both substance and detail to his later recollections of a fruitful but often frustrating visit (King, 1994). In September 1970 he attended a conference on money at Sheffield University:

> I have had two encounters with Friedman this week and he is retreating. He has an addendum to his March 1970 JPE paper which he presented at Sheffield. He gave me credit in a footnote for pointing out to him . . . that the 'Keynesian' model in his JPE paper is not compatible with Keynes. Nevertheless, Milton refuses to discuss Keynes.
>
> Roy Harrod was Milton's discussant at Sheffield and also pointed out that Friedman was using Keynes's name in vain.

Davidson was getting on well with Joan Robinson, but found another US visitor, Robert Solow, 'emotionally unbalanced – insisting that he had always argued that there was no such thing as an Aggregate Production

Function or an Aggregate Stock of Capital. Thus the 'controversy' never existed anywhere but within Joan's mind, according to Solow'.[58]

A month later, Davidson reported that he was on good terms with Richard Kahn, whose office he shared, but was beginning to encounter difficulties with Robinson:

> My meetings with Joan R. varies [*sic*] from lukewarm to sizzling hot. She is obviously interested in brain-washing me. Her office is right across from mine and she pops in once or twice a day with either a question or an explanation. We had a very big go round on internal rate of return vs. present value calculation for investment decision[s]. She is obviously less open minded than most and has just about abandoned Keynes for Kalecki.[59]

By December he was describing Robinson as 'harder to communicate with in person than in writing', and most unhappy with his reformulation of her analysis in terms of his preferred aggregate supply–aggregate demand model.[60] Three months later he told Weintraub that his sense of isolation had deepened, despite new contact with Austin Robinson, who had discussed Keynes with him. Davidson found the new editors of the *Economic Journal* (Brian Reddaway and David Champernowne) very unimpressive: 'What a fall for the E.J. from the days of Keynes and Harrod'. There remained large intellectual differences with Joan Robinson:

> My falling out with Joan R – was not serious – only she refused to discuss growth paths in which financial aspects would create disappointed expectations. In fact, she refuses to discuss the possibility of 'errors' at all – saying that 1 the analysis is too difficult + 2 first let's get 'tranquil' or correct expectations paths down pat. When I point out to her that if expectations were never disappointed there would be no role for money – she hears but refuses to listen.[61]

Evidently Davidson was already coming to regard himself, rather than the Cambridge Post Keynesians, as Keynes' legitimate heir and only reliable interpreter.

This proprietorial attitude must have contributed to the very cool relationship between Davidson and Hyman Minsky, who reviewed his *Money and the Real World* in noticeably unenthusiastic terms (Davidson, 1972; Minsky, 1974). Minsky's own book, *John Maynard Keynes*, took a very different line. 'I saw the Minsky book in draft for a UK publisher', Jan Kregel wrote to Weintraub,

> and while I quite liked having him finally write down what he'd been saying privately for all these years, I did think he took liberties with the title! (Better title *Hyman Minsky* than John Maynard K, or 'what K would have written if Minsky had had his ear)'. And his leg certainly derserves [*sic*] to be pulled, and sharply for there is just no excuse for his review of Paul's book (and I know a number of people who wrote to him and said so, and I wasn't even one of them).[62]

Minsky had already responded to these criticisms in a November 1974 letter to Weintraub:

> I really am sorry that Paul took umbrage at my review. I thought I commended Paul highly in the review article and I thought I was very favourable to his book, commending it to all and arguing that students must be made aware of the serious issues it raises. However I do have a serious substantive quarrel with his approach, which is the approach adopted by Joan Robinson and Kreigal [*sic*] among others. They insist upon defining as a base for their argument a steady growth process and elucidating the circumstances under which this process can be maintained. They also conclude more or less in passing that the maintenance of steady growth is difficult if not impossible under capitalist processes.
>
> My perspective is that once you define the financial institutions of capitalism in any precise form then the normal path of the economy is intractably cyclical and the problems of macroeconomic theory is [*sic*] to spell out the properties of the cyclical process. Thus much of what is valid in Paul's analysis is diminished in significance because of his basic approach . . . without a cyclical perspective uncertainty is more or less of an empty bag.
>
> We should expect that more of us who are close in spirit if not in substance would engage in quite sharp disputation both in private and in public, for it is only in our insiders discussion that we can hammer out a precise statement of the alternative to standard theory. We have to be able to take it from each other.[63]

Weintraub and Minsky were good friends ('Hy' and 'Sid' are used in their correspondence), and the former was inclined to take the latter's side in his dispute with Davidson:

> Needless to say I regret what appears to be an irate letter by Paul. . . .
> On re-reading your review I would conclude that it is not damaging at all. Moreover, the tone was not at all harsh; he could interpret it as

favorable while critical. New serious books, as you adjudged this, come off better. So I think he was overly sensitive. . . .

On quarrels within the 'fraternity', I would also agree with you – especially if we had our own journal. As I see it, this is our major lack. Standard versions of Hicksian Keynesianism, and Monetarism, are dead even though they still dominate our journal space. Editors are still facing backwards.[64]

The intriguing possibility that the Post Keynesians might establish 'our own journal' was premature; another four years would elapse before the first issue of the *Journal of Post Keynesian Economics* appeared.

Minsky's theoretical differences with Davidson persisted, as he informed Weintraub a little more than a year later: 'I am not sure about Paul's views on finance. His insistence on working in a growth rather than a cyclical context and his difference [deference?] to *The Treatise* muddies the message from my point of view'.[65]

Weintraub's response (if any) cannot be located, but it seems that he was anxious to paper over the cracks. He told Geoff Harcourt, a few days later, that Davidson's *Money and the Real World*, together with Minsky's 'excellent book on Keynes', provided 'the modern foundation for a 'proper' monetary theory . . . in contrast to the silly Friedmanites and the equally silly portfolio people who almost forget the medium [of exchange] aspects of money'.[66] For his part Minsky was never fully reconciled with Davidson, although the two men seem to have agreed not to attack each other in print. Minsky came to realize that he had significant analytical differences also with Weintraub, whose insistence on the central role of 'the wage/price nexus' was misguided:

> The money wage reactions in the recent inflations reflect a transitory mode of operation of a capitalist economy – a mode that ruled for a brief interval during which trade unions had sufficient political support so that they could protect their own and other workers from inflation, even as the government used expansionary finance to support business profits.[67]

With the benefit of hindsight, it can be seen that this 1982 assessment was spot on.

Weintraub's dealings with John Kenneth Galbraith were less troubled. A letter from Galbraith in September 1963 indicates a friendly, if rather distant, relationship. 'Dear Weintraub', Galbraith began. 'I have just been reading your 'Wage Theory and Policy'. It is very good, and your chapter on 'Toward a National Policy' is the first consequence of good theory and good sense I have seen. You have – this depends a little on the accessibility of the audience – performed an important and rare service'. He signed himself 'J.K. Galbraith'.[68] By 1974, however, they were on first-name terms, with 'Sid' sending 'Dear Ken' an appreciative three-page response (single-spaced) to his *Economics and the Public Purpose* (Galbraith, 1973).[69] Weintraub and Galbraith were in much more frequent contact in 1977–8, as plans were finalized for the new *Journal*. This stage of their correspondence is discussed in the following section.

Jan Kregel was a frequent and enthusiastic correspondent, first in 1975–6 from the University of Southampton and then in 1979–80 from the Confederazione Generale dell'Industria Italiana in Rome and the University of Groningen in the Netherlands. He commented acidly on the deflationary policies of the British government:

> The [L]abour government is selling its support of an honest to goodness Kalecki-style political trade cycle as good socialist policy. Unemployment is the price that must be paid to get the country back on its feet so unemployment there must be (for how long or to what effect is not stated). Meanwhile while the Govt is imposing a fixed wage rise and making noises about encouraging investment the CBI (equivalent to NUM in the US) has stated that there will be no investment until there has been enough unemployment to bring wage rises to zero and they are battening down the hatches to ride out the storm for as long as it lasts. It's as if everyone has agreed that a good bout of self-flagellation through a good slump will miraculously bring down the price level. Excess capacity is running anywhere up to 50% in some sectors yet the Chancellor warns against reflation causing excess demand to feed price rises while at the same time praying that the world boom will come in time to restore investment.

Kregel was unsettled at Southampton, and interested in returning to the United States:

> Thanks for your efforts concerning the place at Penn. I think I'm slowly becoming resigned to the fact that there are very few places with a lot of discussion and interaction (aside from Cambridge and possibly one or two places in Italy) and vested interests are always present although the high priests may change. Southampton is certainly no winner in this respect, aside from Ivor [Pearce] who is always ready and willing to listen on most any subject (and with whom, despite

very different lines of thought, I can almost always find agreement – save on the question of capital where I've finally succeeded, I hope, in convincing him that what he dislikes is how the questions are posed rather than the answers to them which he dislikes because he would prefer other questions!).[70]

Nothing came of the position at Penn, and four months later Kregel described his continuing job search:

> For the moment I'm in for a couple of places here – I've just been short-listed for the Chair in Manchester, but getting much further than that is not very likely. Indeed, it's quite something having made it that far.[71]

The correspondence also sheds light on Kregel's evolving ideas on the treatment of expectations in macroeconomic theory. Evidently Weintraub had criticized the forthcoming *Economic Journal* paper in which Kregel described Keynes's procedure in analysing uncertainty through models of static, stationary and shifting equilibria, each depicting different assumptions about uncertainty and disappointment:

> Your comments on the last paper are probably right, but it seems funny to write down a Z function or even to draw it – sort of like talking about a circle and then drawing one, it seems so obvious that everyone knows, but perhaps not.
>
> I can't remember the point about Agg[regate] S[upply] in the paper, but what I was trying to stress was that the inclusion of user costs which are themselves a function of expectations about costs and prices makes it just as dependent on expectations as [Aggregate] D[emand] and thus just as likely to shift. . . .
>
> The suggestion of using periods where things are 'settled' I have to take exception [to]. The trick behind the whole idea of the three models is that one does not have to make such assumptions in order to treat the problem. Instead one makes assumptions about the real world in order to treat the problem. Keynes presumably thought that the stationary model was the analytical equivalent of a period of time that was 'settled', but it could be done without having either to (a) wait until such a period occurred (unlikely – cf. his comments concerning comparisons of quantities and prices over time – for how do we know what a settled period is) or (b) assume that the world is somehow in a 'settled' condition (which is patently irrealistic [*sic*] as anyone will freely volunteer if you try to make such an assumption). Thus, as he

says (I paraphrase) it's not the economy that is stationary in one case and moving in the other, but the effect that expectations have on the system. This allows us to analyse using the stationary and static models and to use the results of these two to advise using the shifting model for it is here that the knowledge (kept always at the back of our minds) of all the changes and interactions and shifts will be required to try and gauge the probable movement of the system where indeed 'anything can happen'.[72]

Four years later, writing from Rome, Kregel told Weintraub that

Karl Brunner has just been through again, this time talking about the determinants of foreign exchange prices. I may now be more interested in looking at rational expectations. He started out by noting a number of empirical 'properties' of exchange rates, the most important of which he considered to be their 'random walk' behaviour. He then proceeded to show how traditional 'models' could not square these results. The flow model is inadequate because the major demand factor is the commercial balance which is determined by income – no random walk here. Capital flows are added on an *ad hoc* basis or in relation to interest rate differentials, but again, either imposed random or stable behaviour. The solution is to give up on the 'flow' model and look at 'rational expectations' in the context of an asset adjustment model. Here we have rational decisions based on accumulated experience, but since it is not based on complete or perfect information there are errors, which are randomly distributed. Thus the change in foreign exchange prices ΔS has a rational component, g (this is in fact little more than a trend!) and an error term u: $\Delta S = g + u$. He then proceeds to give a 'scientific' explanation to g and u. g is the difference between expected future price and the current price while u represents the actual divergence of the future price and the expectation or $\Delta S = (E_t S_{t-1} - S_t) + (S_{t-1} - E_t S_{t-1})$. The first term is the 'Expected Component' [and] the second is the 'Unexpected Component'. When he was finished I congratulated him for finally having looked at Sraffa and Keynes, for the first term is simply the difference between the future and the spot price which Sraffa in 1932, applying the interest parity theorem, turned into the concept of the 'own rate of own return' which was valid for *any* durable asset. Keynes then adopted this framework in his investment analysis calling the own rate of return the MEC and noting that the curve could shift bodily thus adding the second term of the equation. This was then applied in Chapter 16 and 17 to produce a theory of a monetary economy. Thus, the very same factors Bunner [*sic*] had outlined as the 'scientific' explanation of exchange rates Keynes had used to produce a general theory of asset holding identifying money's crucial position within the range of assets.

The only response I got to this objective contribution to Brunner's knowledge of history was that he 'explained' expectations and the 'Keynesians' did not, but he was clearly perturbed at being taken for a Keynesian! If this is all rational expectations is, then I don't see what all the excitement is about.[73]

A year later, having moved to the University of Groningen, Kregel returned to the matter:

You should, by this time, have received the second draft of my effort on Rational Expectations . . . Since I finished that draft I've come across some of A.G. Hart's work, which was done at Chicago and LSE in the 30s, and has almost all the relevant RE points and then dismisses it as trivial. He mentions in a preface to the reprint of his Ph.D. thesis that he went to London to work with Hayek and I wondered if you mighn't know something about him and his activities in London at that period.

There is no record of Weintraub's reply.[74]

5.   A journal is born

As mainstream journals were increasingly closed to Post Keynesian contributors, the question of alternative outlets could hardly be avoided. There were in the mid-1970s a number of heterodox journals specializing in economics, or ranging more widely over the social sciences, but Weintraub regarded none of them as suitable. The two long-standing Marxist publications, *Science and Society* and *Monthly Review*, were clearly beyond the pale, and even the more eclectic *Review of Radical Political Economics*, established in 1969, was far too radical for Weintraub's taste. As Davidson wrote, in a 1977 manifesto for their new *Journal*:

an outlet [will] be provided for encouragement to young aspiring and talented economists who do not fit the conventional pigeon-holes and who are averse to the succor offered by the Radical Economists who have organized in utter rejection of the conventional sects. The QJPKE would provide a less categorical, more rational and reasonable alternative, in the humanistic spirit of Keynes.[75]

The *Review of Social Economics* was certainly responsive to Post Keynesian ideas, but its Catholic associations would have discouraged people like Davidson, Minsky and Weintraub, all (secular) Jews.[76]

Weintraub explained his attitude towards the principal heterodox journals in an important 1978 letter to Martin Bronfenbrenner:

> Anyway, on the JPKE. If the Evol. Econ. journal was adequate, why need another? But their interest seems to be Ayres, Veblen and such cats to the exclusion of the modern scene. On *Challenge*, Mike Sharpe has different, and lighter, objectives. No, I share your doubts entirely about the Cambridge Journal. Likewise, tho the JPKE arose out of interest in Sraffa, when I started to count heads I suspected about 35 people might be involved – we could mimeo the stuff. Yet for a long time I have felt that there is need for something more topical, on problems, and for theory connected with policy.[77]

The 'Evol. Econ. journal' was of course the *Journal of Economic Issues*, set up in 1967 as the organ of the Association for Evolutionary Economics and therefore as the voice of institutionalism; as Weintraub explained to Bronfenbrenner, he regarded it as stranded in the past. *Challenge*, re-established in 1973 by the radical commercial publisher Myron (Mike) Sharpe after a six-year hiatus, was (and remains) an excellent popular forum for policy debate, aimed at the educated layperson rather than the economics profession. The *Cambridge Journal of Economics*, which commenced publication in 1977 under the auspices of the Political Economy Society in Cambridge, was too tightly controlled by 'the Srafia' to have much appeal to Weintraub.[78] 'So', he continued, 'this would be my attitude':

> I feel the AER has become rigid and closed to points of view not reflected on its editorial board, on money, the price level, and distribution. Too, its concern is not with this world. I would go down the list of other journals, and their inadequacy for controversy. . . .
>
> So I'll remain, I think as I have been, my own man, publishing items with which I agree, and disagree, trying to move things on especially in areas where I think policy papers ought to be encouraged. Save the world? No, but try to keep thought honest, with more openings for dissent from the competitive, certain and stationary models.[79]

The new journal would be aimed at academic economists (and their more alert colleagues in business and government) who were dissatisfied with orthodox macroeconomics, hostile to monetarism, and interested in developing theoretical and policy alternatives.

The Weintraub archive has two categories of material relating to the establishment of the *Journal of Post Keynesian Economics*: correspondence between Weintraub, Davidson and potential sympathisers, and some of the documents that they produced to publicize the venture and attract support. Since there is very little in print on the origins of the *Journal*,[80] the archive sheds considerable new light on a very important episode in the history of Post Keynesian economics. Although John Kenneth Galbraith does not mention the *Journal* in either of his published memoirs, it could not have succeeded without his encouragement and (especially) his financial contribution. Weintraub first wrote to Galbraith in May 1977 suggesting the need for 'a new journal established here that could make some dent [in], if not break, the Establishment stranglehold'. He reported on the recent successful 'Post-Keynesian' conference at Rutgers University (the inverted commas and the hyphen are Weintraub's), attended by some 80 people, among them Davidson, Minsky, Harcourt and Lorie Tarshis (see below). 'I think there is an audience for something different . . . I think what would be required would be about $3 to $5 thousand per year for about 3 years. Any thoughts? It seems a pity that these small sums remain the immediate stumbling block'.[81]

In his reply Galbraith declared his support and offered a cash contribution:

> On the question of a journal which I suppose might be called 'A Journal of Post-Keynesian Economics', I would be very much attracted. There should be a place where young scholars with a strong policy orientation can find an outlet for their work. . . . If this could be given practical form and there is enough enthusiasm, I would be willing to raise half of the amount needed up to, say, $5,000, matching in effect contributions large and small from other sources.[82]

A delighted Weintraub replied by return of post:

> Your wonderful letter was just what I required. Since picking it up a few hours ago I have been on the phone to Davidson who is 'super-chairman' of all social 'science' at Rutgers and he has seen the graduate dean and the provost. They talk of even going further than I thought necessary, speaking of a 10,000 sum as feed money.

Weintraub himself would serve as Managing Editor, 'perhaps with Paul D.', unless Galbraith wanted the job: 'If you indicated an interest I assure you I would gladly hand over all or part, as you wish, of the editorial chores to you'. He noted that the *Cambridge Journal of Economics* had an association with Academic Press. Support from a commercial enterprise would also be necessary for the new *Journal of Post Keynesian Economics* – either Weintraub's own publisher (Addison-Wesley) or perhaps Galbraith's (Houghton Mifflin of Boston). 'Why not do this at Penn?' (This was the University of Pennsylvania, Weintraub's employer since 1950.) 'I am not enamored of the administration. I have never had a day's secretarial assistance and I refuse to chase grants for them to do what I don't want to do'.[83]

As he told Galbraith, Weintraub had a very broad and non-sectarian conception of the *Journal*. 'I do have in mind a journal of policy, and theory for policy, in much the same way Adam Smith, Keynes, etc., yourself, Joan, myself have conceived our subject. I would restore the literary tradition, accept math where it is a clarification, relegate proofs and econometric processing to a small print appendix'. His provisional list of 55 potential Board members was correspondingly expansive:

> On the Board of Directors, the list could be imposing enough to guarantee a serious publication. Yourself, Joan, myself, Paul D., perhaps Leontief, Kaldor, Kahn – m'lords – Lerner, Minsky, Tarshis, Harcourt, Kregel, Wiles, Ritter, Pearce, Katzner, Eichner, Alice Vandermeulen, Maris [*sic*], Passinetti [*sic*], Dillard, Hamberg, etc. Paul Davidson tells me he is sure that Hicks, seeing the sour turn of the subject, would be interested. Maybe Tinbergen and even Patinkin.[84]

Many, but by no means all, of these luminaries became members of the founding Editorial Board; Kahn, Lerner, Patinkin and Tinbergen were among the absentees.

The tireless Weintraub now fired off a salvo of letters, soliciting subscriptions and contributions for the *Journal*. The enthusiastic response of George Shackle (see section 3) was not always matched elsewhere. Joan Robinson, for example, was less than encouraging:

> I am very glad for your sake that the new project has got going but I am rather dubious about bringing out journals to be read by people who agree already. I hope you will succeed in breaking through the crust of orthodoxy. I fear I cannot accept the invitation to be on your board as I cannot guarantee to be available for refereeing.[85]

This must have pained Weintraub, for Robinson wrote again to mollify him:

> You quite mistake everything I said. Of course I am strongly in favour of your views being published. The only trouble is to get people from the opposite camp to read them.

> As for having my name on your Board, I really would prefer not to. I hate being a 'name' unless I am actually engaged in the work. This is a point of view which is little understood nowadays but I am old-fashioned.[86]

Courteous as ever, Piero Sraffa also declined to become involved: 'I was delighted to hear of your new journal and I wish you all the success which I am sure it deserves. As you know I am a very slow contributor to journals and at my extreme old age slower than ever. I therefore feel I had better not undertake to make a contribution'.[87] This at least was entirely true. John Hicks also expressed support but refused to join the Editorial Board,[88] while Kenneth Boulding declared himself

> very much interested in your proposal for a journal of 'Post-Keynesian Economics'. I am very sympathetic to the objectives of the proposed journal and I agree that the more standard journals have a distressingly narrow editorial policy. I am a little worried, however, about the potential market, particularly as it seems to me that the objectives of your proposed journal overlap to a considerable extent with those of the *Journal of Economic Issues* . . . I would hate to see the two journals try to occupy a niche which can really only support one, and this might be fatal to both of them.

Boulding urged Weintraub to contact Warren Samuels, the editor of the *Journal of Economic Issues*, to discuss an appropriate division of labour. 'I confess I am a little unhappy with the proposed name of the journal. I appreciate its subtlety, as Keynes in many ways was a post-Keynesian himself, but I think tying it to a single name like Keynes is a little unfortunate'. But Boulding's own suggestions were not particularly felicitous, as he himself recognized.[89]

Fortunately the majority of Weintraub's correspondents reacted more positively. An early (but undated) flyer has an impressive series of lists of names, with Davidson and Weintraub as Editors and Galbraith as chairman of the 'Honorary Board of Editors'. This august body comprised a ten-man 'Academic Board'[90] and (listed separately) nine representatives of 'Banking, Business, and Public Affairs'. In addition there was a 52-member 'Managing Board of Editors', three of whom were women.[91] This closely resembles the organizational structure reported in the first (Fall 1978) issue of the *Journal*. An earlier typewritten list, with handwritten additions, had proposed a rather simpler structure, with an 'Honorary (Executive)

Board' including academic and business members, alongside a 'Managing Board of Editors'; the latter had only 32 typed names, with another six written in.

Other relevant documents in the Weintraub archive include a mimeo-graphed programme for the April 1977 Rutgers conference referred to above, on 'Post-Keynesian Theory and Inflation Policy'. The conference was 'intended to serve as a forum for the exchange of ideas and scholarship by those economists whose work falls within the tradition established by Keynes, Kalecki, Robinson, Kaldor and Sraffa'. There were to be four sessions, chaired respectively by Davidson, Arthur Bloomfield, Weintraub and Edward Nell. In the first session, Minksy and Basil Moore spoke on 'The Monetary Aspect of Inflation'; then John Burbidge and Eichner spoke on 'The International Dimension'; Melville J. Ulner and Lawrence Seidman discussed 'Incomes Policy as a Stabilizing Device'; and in the final session Luigi Pasinetti and Stephen Rousseas spoke on 'Beyond Post-Keynesian Theory: the Unexplored Issues', with Harcourt as discussant. The projected publication of the Conference Proceedings did not take place, but the participants were subsequently all invited to support the *Journal*, all but one of them (John Burbidge) becoming foundation Board members.[92]

There are also three (undated) drafts of a manifesto in the joint names of Davidson and Weintraub setting out the case for a new journal. What appears to be the first[93] is a nine-page 'Proposal for The Post-Keynesian Economic Journal (PKEJ)'; a 'statement of Purpose' is followed by a set of organizational suggestions, a provisional budget and a four-page 'Rationale'. This seems to have been drafted by Davidson and revised in the light of comments from Galbraith and Weintraub.[94] In the second draft the title has changed to the *Quarterly Journal of Post-Keynesian Economics*, and a much longer statement is provided of the case for a new journal, preceded by a one-page summary of the case against:

It should be noted that 1977 has also witnessed the founding and first issues of a similarly conceived publication in the U.K., namely, the Cambridge Journal of Political Economy [*sic*] having more or less parallel objectives. The founding of the Cambridge journal indicates that our own perceptions have much basis in the prevailing facts, of a real need to be satidified [*sic*] which conventional journals have all but ignored and spurned.[95]

The third draft, headed '*The Journal of Post-Keynesian Economics* (JPKE)', is a much punchier document, purged of the organizational and financial detail and now citing Keynes on economics as 'essentially a moral science' rather than 'a 'positive science' without ideology'.[96] This version is closest to the published 'Statement of Purposes' that appeared in volume I, number 1 of the *Journal* in Fall 1978.

One mystery on which the Weintraub papers are largely silent is the circumstances under which the *Journal* acquired its commercial publisher, M.E. Sharpe of White Plains, New York. Evidently neither Addison-Wesley nor Houghton Mifflin were interested in the venture. At first it was expected that Rutgers would act as sponsor. Thus Davidson wrote to Weintraub in late July 1977 informing him that 'the President of Rutgers University has given his blessing to the establishing of the *Journal of Post Keynesian Economics* at Rutgers in New Brunswick . . . I am currently negotiating with University officials to obtain a few thousand dollars a year for the next three years as additional seed money'.[97] This was not forthcoming, although the previously mentioned typed list of Board Members, dated 18 October 1977, is on a joint *JPKE*/Rutgers letterhead. 'Myron E. Sharpe, Challenge Magazine', is already listed among the 'Managing Board of Editors'. The move from Rutgers to Sharpe must have been related to the major upheavals that were going on in the Economics department at Rutgers (see section 6), but the details remain obscure.

Returning to intellectual matters, there are at least five statements of the intentions of the *Journal*'s founders, in the three typescript proposals, the printed invitation to become a Charter Subscriber, and the first published issue. They differ only in emphasis, and Davidson's statement of 'Purpose' that opened the first draft proposal is as good as any:

> To publish a scholarly journal of economics stressing major innovations in theoretical constructions for dealing with contemporary economic problems and policy. Many of these developments have been so neglected in existing U.S. journals that a vast range of exciting ideas are currently unattended and unknown by U.S. economists. The omission of this analysis from major U.S. journals appears to be due, in large part, because [sic] it conflicts with the vested interest embodied in the conventional orthodoxy. . . .
>
> Accordingly, the PKEJ will provide a forum for all economists who are committed to the cumulative growth and development of a body of economic theory suitable for analyzing the real world and for providing an intelligent guide to public policy. Specifically, the journal will be devoted to the development, elaboration, refinement, empirical testing, and distillation of the policy implications of a body of theory most appropriate to modern real-world economic systems where production

occurs primarily by market-oriented firms (often large multinational corporations) operating in a monetary system with its associated market institutions and arrangements in the face of an uncertain future.

The PKEJ will be committed to the principle that the cumulative development of economic theory is possible only when the theory is viewed as being continuously open to challenge, both in terms of its underlying assumptions and in terms of its ability to explain the real world and provide a reliable guide to the future.[98]

This promise has been proudly kept (O'Hara, 2003).

6.   Difficulties, failures and misfortunes

Things did not always work out so well for Weintraub. The archive contains information on four episodes which were less successful than the establishment of the *Journal*: his temporary move to the University of Waterloo, the upheavals at Rutgers, the abortive Research Institute and Center for Economic Studies (RICES), and the failure of the Trieste Summer School.

Weintraub's Waterloo

In 1969–71, on leave from the University of Pennsylvania, Weintraub was chair of the economics department at the University of Waterloo in Ontario. A two-page article from (presumably) the University's staff newsletter reveals Weintraub's high hopes for the Canadian venture. He had 'set a formidable new goal for himself . . . to set up a top notch graduate program in Economics at Waterloo', helping to halt or even reverse the brain drain that had seen so many fine Canadian graduates move to the US. This would involve aggressive recruiting of high-quality staff and PhD students, with many of the students coming from outside the discipline: 'Prof. Weintraub feels graduate Economics students shouldn't necessarily do undergraduate work in the Economics department. 'The best entry into Economics today is through Mathematics. Undergraduates interested in Economics should major in Mathematics with a minor in Economics', he advises'. The feature ends – inevitably, perhaps – on a very upbeat note: 'Though he appears soft spoken and mild mannered, Prof. Weintraub is a man brimming with formidable energy, enthusiasm and ideas. His advice to others: "Everyone should be an optimist!" '.[99]

In all probability the article was designed to counter adverse publicity, for a seven-page memorandum from Weintraub to the Vice-President

Academic, J.S. Minas, paints a much darker picture of his early days at Waterloo:

> I entered Canada on July 25. Our home furnishings arrived on July 30. On August 1, I saw the newspaper version of the Mathews report, and an editorial in the Toronto Daily Star, listing the Economics Department as one in danger of being de-Canadianized, through my being chairman and a U.S. citizen.[100]

Weintraub was understandably aggrieved at the need to defend himself against unwarranted allegations of discrimination against Canadian nationals in appointments to the department and in the selection of graduate students. In any case, he argued, science was essentially international in character:

> Speaking for the economics department, there is not, I can assure Mathews and his cronies, a Canadian Price Theory, or Employment Theory, or Growth Theory, or International Trade Theory, or Income Distribution Theory. Certainly there is not a U.S., or English, or German, or French Theory. Differences in facts, in institutions, in policies, in problems, exist, of course. Whether I am at this university, or not, I suspect that the Economics Department will devote its energies to sorting out theoretical ideas, as is done in all countries, while it seeks to illuminate the special aspects pertinent to Canadian experience and development. It will not be de-Canadianized, it will not be U.S. oriented, it will not be Soviet inspired, it will not be Maoist. *It will be simply Economics*, as the subject and science has evolved and descended to us, hopefully for new advances in the hands of some gifted individuals who, if we are fortunate, may be added to our faculty at Waterloo. They will not come if Mathews' views prevail.[101]

Waterloo did not develop – and still does not have – a PhD programme in economics, and Weintraub returned to Philadelphia in 1971 at the end of his two-year leave of absence, as he was required to do by the terms of the taxation agreement between the United States and Canada to avoid being taxed on his Canadian salary.[102]

The Rutgers debacle

By the mid-1970s it seemed that Rutgers University in New Brunswick, New Jersey might form a solid base for Post Keynesian economics in the United States in much the same way that Chicago was the acknowledged home of Monetarism and conservative microeconomics. Paul Davidson was chair of the Department of Economics and Allied Sciences, and numbered among his colleagues other Post Keynesians such as Alfred Eichner and Nina Shapiro, with visitors who included Jan Kregel, Alessandro Roncaglia and Sergio Parrinello. The administration at Rutgers had offered moral support for the establishment of the *Journal*, and initially also held out the prospect of a significant financial contribution. By 1986 all this was in ruins. Davidson had left for the University of Tennessee at Knoxville, Shapiro had been forced out, and the few remaining dissidents at Rutgers were an embattled minority. Two years later, Alfred Eichner was dead.

Again the published record is rather sparse (but see Lee, 2000a: 32–5 on the neoclassical counter-attack that soon eliminated Post Keynesian teaching from much of the Rutgers programme). There are only four letters in the Weintraub archive with a bearing on the Rutgers debacle. The first indication of problems for the Post Keynesians there comes in a May 1979 letter from Kregel, then working temporarily in Rome for the Confederazione Generale dell'Industria Italiana:

> We are tentatively planning to return to New Brunswick for the autumn term and then to come back here or to go to the Netherlands where I have received what appears to be a very attractive offer (80 teaching hours per year). A combination of a desire to be a bit closer to my father and an attachment to Paul has brought this about. The whole situation at Rutgers is really unfortunate, but more so because of the potential that is there. I have run into no less than 25 to 30 students and young professors who are looking for a University in the U.S. to attend which will give them an opportunity to study something other than the mainline approach. If Rutgers could be brought under control it could be turned into an international centre in no time. So I'm turning out to be the eternal optimist and will give it one more try (much to Paul's surprise I guess) although with much lower expectations than previously.[103]

As late as June 1980 Davidson was still hoping that the central administration at Rutgers would 'go ahead with establishing either an institute or a Center for Post Keynesian Economics', to commence operations in September.[104] Although the *Journal of Post Keynesian Economics* letterhead used in early 1981 by both Weintraub and Davidson gives the latter's address as 'Bureau of Economic Research' at Rutgers, the Bureau was effectively a shell organization.

The Post Keynesians' failure to bring Rutgers 'under control' is high-lighted by Weintraub's letter to the President of the University, written in the same year in defence of Davidson, whose position was becoming untenable:

Just a few hours ago I returned from what I thought was a very effect-ive program on Post Keynesian Economics organized at Rutgers largely by Alfred Eichner. The session chaired by Paul Davidson was easily the highlight, perhaps the best of such things I have ever attended. And my own experience goes back to Jacob Viner in our country, and Dennis Robertson and Friedrich Hayek who were Keynes' contemporaries.

At the close of the session, in general personal discussion, Hy Minsky, an outstanding man in our country presently, were [*sic*] appalled to learn that Davidson does not teach in your graduate program. This is simply scandalous.

Davidson is the *only* 'world class' economist on your faculty. Davidson has already made significant *original* contributions to monetary theory. His positions, not so long ago unfashionable against the Friedman juggernaut, are now perceived to have been pertinent and most astute.

I think this assessment of Davidson's caliber would be shared by any panel of front rank people you queried, and put on a list alongside the other department members.

Yet for his originality and creativity Professor Davidson has been assigned to teach elementary economics. A not too far-fetched analogy would be to exile Einstein to innocuous subjects just because he was different.

What seems to have happened is that Paul simply refused to teach the content of a monetary theory course that would be dictated by the supposed Graduate governing group. It seems to be a case of democracy running wild, even to thinking that academic freedom confers a license – to incompetents substantially – to decide what someone else should do in his classroom.

In my 31 years here on the graduate faculty no one would have the effrontery to tell me what to teach; my answer would be stronger than Paul's. I served as graduate chairman longer than anyone here; not once did I presume to tell others how to conduct their course.

An injustice is being done to an outstanding, brave and creative man by others who believe that votes convey power regardless of equity and responsibility. I write because I feel such things keenly and that you should be apprised of the situation. Faculties simply have no right to tyrannize over the attitudes of their colleagues and decide 'correct' economics by majority vote. I have in my time, overturned 'majority' economics.[105]

There is no record of a reply.[106]

The think tank that never was

For several decades conservative economists in the US and Western Europe had successfully propagated their ideas through non-University research institutes, publishing houses and societies, drawing heavily on funds supplied by wealthy sympathisers and corporations (Cockett, 1994). There was nothing comparable on the centre-left, despite the liberal (in European parlance, social democratic) proclivities of a small but significant minority of Wall Street financiers who found the Post Keynesian message more appealing than the monetarist or Old Keynesian alternatives. Eventually the Post Keynesians would be able to offer a limited challenge to the right-wing think tanks through the Levy Institute at Bard College, in upstate New York, set up with the support of Leon Levy in 1986, and the Centres of Full Employment and Equity at the University of Missouri (Kansas City), the University of Newcastle (New South Wales) and the University of Maastricht, all supported by the investment banker Warren Mosler at the end of the millennium. In 1978, however, there was nothing.

With the *Journal* successfully launched, Weintraub turned his mind to filling this gap. The archive contains correspondence and documents on his proposal for a Research Institute and Center for Economic Studies (RICES), beginning in the summer of 1979 and fizzling out early in 1982. He turned first to Galbraith:

> Is it not time to undertake a deeper and broader venture to focus on our national malaise of inflation, stagflation and slumpflation? It seems to me that only a political oriented venture will do. As I see it there are a few possibilities: (1) a center for studies, such as the National Bureau [of Economic Research] with much less emphasis on an elegant and luxurious set of facilities, merely sponsoring longish pamphlets; (2) a Center, affiliated with a university that will have Ph.D. purposes; there are already enquiries from prospective students: where do you send them? (3) a public campaign into the political arena perhaps affiliated with [Ralph] Nader or some other group. All sorts of diverse opinion can be drawn in. . . .
>
> I would be willing to devote my energies to it but clearly it requires someone of your stature and reknown [*sic*], with contacts and judgement of the art of the possible.[107]

Galbraith replied favourably:

> I've been turning over in my mind a similar thought. Should there be in the next few weeks or months some cohesive action to urge the indispensability of:
>
> 1) limits on money wages as part of an anti-inflation strategy;
> 2) if people are really worried about productivity, a shift from high interest rates which inhibit investment to greater budget restraint which inhibits consumption;
> 3) companion steps to produce greater equity in income distribution;
> 4) effective limits on oil imports as an elementary step toward greater international stability?
>
> Let me give some further thought as to how we might assemble a consensus on this and who would be influential. Meanwhile, will you do your best?[108]

Little seems to have been done for almost a year, until Davidson wrote to Galbraith in connection with 'our 'continuing conference' concept':

> After some deliberation I have decided that I think I should be the one that should get to see people like Stewart Mott and others who would be willing to finance such a relationship. I think with the draft proposal that Sidney has already sent to you and with some ideas of my own following our fruitful discussion on May 16, I can sell the idea.[109]

At the same time, Davidson wrote to Eric Roll and Stuart Speiser in similar vein.[110] The inside front cover of early issues reveals that both men were members of the *Journal*'s Honorary Board of Editors, representing 'Banking, Business and Public Affairs'. Formerly a distinguished academic economist, Roll was now a merchant banker in London, and a member of the House of Lords. Speiser was a prominent New York tort lawyer and partner in the law firm of Speiser and Krause; he was co-author of a paper in an early issue of the *Journal* (Beltran-del-Rio, Hamrin and Speiser 1979; see also Speiser, 1985.). Roll did not reply until January of the following year, by which time Davidson was able to report only limited progress. Everything had been put on hold until after the US presidential elections (in November 1979), though in the meantime Speiser had been contacting 'wealthy individuals in the United States' to solicit their support.[111]

Davidson now sent Speiser and Roll a nine-page proposal for a Research Institute. In opposition to the conservative perspective of the incoming Reagan administration, RICES would promote liberal policies on inflation, unemployment, monetary policy and energy conservation. In all, 26 areas of policy concern were identified, with the Institute providing '[p]rofessional studies, frequently updated', that 'could serve as position papers for liberal presidential and Congressional candidates.'[112] But neither Galbraith's nor Speiser's efforts to promote the RICES concept proved successful, despite much work on Speiser's part.[113] A year later Weintraub wrote to another potential business supporter, William C. Musham of the New York company Gear Inc., enclosing 'a copy of a proposal I put together about 2 years ago'.[114] This is the final reference to RICES in the Weintraub papers.

Conflict in Trieste

Post Keynesian ideas had long been influential in Italy, which sent its brightest graduate students to Cambridge, at least in the 1950s and early 1960s, and published a number of heterodox journals, including the influential *Metroeconomica*. For a time Joan Robinson used the term 'Anglo-Italian school' as a synonym for 'Post Keynesian' (King, 2002: 10). The Italians were able to use their political contacts to obtain support from the regional government of Friuli–Venezia Giulia and the local University administrations to run a series of international conferences and summer schools, beginning in 1981 and ending, amid some acrimony, in 1987 or 1988. There are good published accounts of the Trieste Summer School in French (Arena, 1987) and Italian (Parrinello, 1988), but little or nothing in English. The Weintraub archive, however, is a useful source of information on this sad but instructive episode.

In March 1980 Weintraub was invited to attend an eight-day 'round-table meeting' in Udine in the following September to discuss the establishment of an international summer school.[115] The invitation was confirmed in June, with the offer of a 450,000 lire travel grant from the Italian National Research Council.[116] The round-table had now been shortened to five days, with the organization of the summer school to occupy two half-day sessions; the remaining six sessions would be devoted to theoretical debate. The strong influence of Pierangelo Garegnani is apparent in the choice of topics for discussion, but the 'partial list of possible participants' suggests a commitment to pluralism.[117] A third letter, in early July, confirmed the programme and listed 34 participants. The meetings would be divided between Udine, where theoretical discussions would take up three and a half days, and Trieste, where details of the summer school would occupy most of the remaining day and a half. The theme of the round-table was to be 'A Critical Appraisal of the Present State of Economics', with individual sessions devoted to 'An Evaluation of the Theory of Value and Distribution from the Marginalists to the Revival of the Classic[al] Approach'; 'The Principle of Effective Demand in the Short and Long Period'; 'Monetary Theory and Modern Economics'; 'Modern Economic Theory as a Basis for Economic Policy?'; 'Economic Growth and Development'; and 'Theory of International Exchange and Natural Resources'.

Of the participants nine were Italian (Garegnani, Angelo Marzollo, Ignazio Musu, Parinello, Pasinetti, Massimo Pivetti, Alberto Quadro Curzio, Alessandro Roncaglia, Fausto Vicarelli), five came from the United States (Davidson, Donald Harris, Minsky, Nell, Weintraub), two from the UK (John Eatwell, Ian Steedman), and others from France (Claude Berthomieu), India (Krishna Bharadwaj, Gautam Mathur), Brazil (Antonio Castro), Australia (Harcourt), Poland (Cesary Jozefiak, Wiktor Herer), the Netherlands (Kregel), Germany (Heinz Kurz, Bertram Schefold, Steiger), Mexico (Nora Lustig, Jaime Ros), Spain (Francisco Perez Garcia, Josep Vegara Carrjo), Argentina (Hugo Scolnik), Austria (Josef Steindl) and Yugoslavia (Radmila Stojanovic). They constituted a diverse set of dissident economists, though some of the more interesting of the original invitees declined to attend.[118]

The proposed summer school would cater for 'advanced students in those areas which are in the forefront of modern political economy'. Four broad areas were specified: 'a) value and distribution, b) money and effective demand, c) theory and policy of development and international economics, d) fact and experience in economic policy'. Teaching would be by means of lectures, seminars and plenary discussions, with the occasional address by invited speakers. It would be an intensive learning experience:

> It is envisaged that above five hours per day should be devoted to formal activity with five students per instructor in courses. The initial Summer's programme should be from two to four weeks. A proposal of two weeks of formal activity followed by three or four days of concluding discussion and student assessments would fit this time frame.[119]

In December 1980 Weintraub learned that a Center of Advanced Economic Studies had been set up under the auspices of the University of Trieste, and grants had been obtained from the Italian National Research Council and the Education Committee of the regional government. A two-week summer school was planned for the last week in August and the first week of September 1981, with about 50 participants (20–25 teachers and 25–30 students), and a two-day conference to open the school. Geographical quotas were proposed for students: six from Italy, seven from other western European countries, six from the US, four from Latin America, four from India and 'other Afro-Asian countries', two from eastern Europe and one each from Australasia and Canada.[120] The conference proceedings were eventually published as a book (Kregel, 1983).

   In August 1982 the conference themes were 'Theories of Accumulation and The Control of the Economy', with one day devoted to each at the end of the summer school. The provisional programme lists Garegnani and Weintraub as presenting the two 'basic papers' on these themes, which were to be discussed by Kregel, Nell, Parrinello and Vianello (Garegnani) and by Bharadwaj, Davidson, Harris and Pasinetti (Weintraub).[121] The mounting tension between the different theoretical tendencies represented at the conference can be inferred from Kregel's letter to Weintraub in April 1982:

> We have just completed one of our planning meetings for the summer school. Sergio [Parrinello] presented your response to our request for a contribution to the Udine Conference on the Theory of Accumulation and I've got the job of sounding you out on your willingness to proceed. I can well understand your hesitance, especially if you have a book in the works and given your frequent travels this past year. On the other hand, Pier[angel]o [Garegnani] is quite keen to see what the post Keynesian side can 'produce' by way of a substantive theory of accumulation (he is, of course, convinced that there is none to be produced, and has never gone very deeply into the Kaldor-Robinson attempts, much less your own 'black' book on employment and growth. Thinking that he might come off better this year than last, he is eager to have the topic done by a clearly identifiable pK man).[122]

Evidently Kregel at least was already beginning to think in terms of two 'sides', one describing itself as 'Post Keynesian' and the other as 'classical' or 'Sraffian'. In the 'Provisional Programme' of the Summer School, lectures on 'Effective Demand in the Short Period' were to be given by Nell, Kregel and Weintraub, while Garegnani, Kurz and Vianello were to lecture on 'Effective Demand in the Long Period'.[123]

   Weintraub had discussed some of the relevant theoretical issues in correspondence with Garegnani in the previous year. His original letter has not survived, but Garegnani's reply indicates the nature of the American's worries about the analysis of long-period positions, the concept of equilibrium, the role of the stationary state and the theory of supply and demand in the history of economic thought. (This letter is reproduced as an Appendix to the present chapter.)[124] The different positions adopted on these issues soon came to split the staff of the Trieste Summer School into competing, not to say antagonistic, factions. In 1982 the organizing committee agreed upon 'a division within the competence of the Committee into three sections to which three different Advisory Boards are associated. Each of the three Sections covers a different area of economic theory and is assisted by its own Advisory Board'. This was not quite accurate: the 'areas of competence' of Sections A and B really represented different schools of thought, not 'different areas of economic theory'. Garegnani was the coordinator of Section A, whose 'Area of Competence' was 'The Surplus Approach. Criticism of Marginalism. The Theory of Effective Demand and the Long Period'; Kregel coordinated Section B, with responsibility for 'The Post Keynesian Approach. Criticism of Marginalism. Money and Finance'.[125] The Advisory Board for Section B consisted of Davidson, Harris, Minsky, Nell, Pasinetti, Otto Steiger, Vicarelli, Weintraub and Paolo Sylos Labini. The intention was, Parinello told Weintraub in January 1983, that all this would provide 'the opportunity of a more agile organisation of the School'.[126]

Had he lived, Weintraub would presumably have attended the third Summer School in August 1983. He was scheduled to speak at sessions on 'Interpretations of Keynes' [T]heory of Effective Demand' and 'Economic Policy Issues from an Effective Demand Perspective', while Garegnani was to lecture on 'The Classical Theory of Value and Distribution'. In the 'Tentative Programme' the two Sections had now become 'Projects', which more accurately reflected what was going on. The two-day conference at the end of the Summer School was arranged – perhaps with conciliation in mind – to reflect the work of Section (now Project) C, its tentative title being 'The Economic Dynamics of Resources, Technology and Employment – theories and policies for open economies'. The 'First List of invited lecturers and rapporteurs' included some interesting newcomers, among them Amartya Sen and Weintraub's colleague from Penn, Oliver Williamson, who is not generally thought of as a Post Keynesian. It is not clear who proposed them, or whether they actually attended.[127] The Summer School itself continued for a few more years, but the divisions between the Sraffian and Fundamentalist Keynesian camps proved too deep for any satisfactory long-term cooperation to be possible. Student accounts of Trieste differ, with Fred Lee (who attended the 1981 school) describing it as a most valuable intellectual experience – 'the supposed conflict had little impact on us students' – while Peter Kriesler (who was there only for the conference in 1981 but attended the Summer School two years later) has vivid memories of the factional rivalries. Some of the tensions at the 1981 Summer School are reflected in a paper written at the time by Geoff Harcourt, the first of his several surveys of Post Keynesianism (Harcourt, 1982).[128]

7.   A troublesome Jevonian seditionist

In reminiscences published just after his death, Weintraub described himself as a 'Jevonian seditionist', in revolt against the tyranny of estab-lished authority (Weintraub, 1983). Such individuals are few in number, quite distinctive in character and personality, and not always easy to get on with. There is ample evidence from the archive to show that Weintraub, too, was a difficult man. Warm-hearted, generous and enthusiastic, he was also prickly and pugnacious, easily offended and quick to give (often entirely unintended) offence. In a revealing passage in a long 1978 letter to Martin Bronfenbrenner, Weintraub himself admitted as much:

> Now, about the world going to the dogs; do I 'worry?' I don't think so. I notice the same in dept. 'meetings'. I go, resolved not to speak up for I can't really care about most frivolous matters that occupy the group. Yet within a few minutes, when I hear the nonsense (in my view) offered as reason, you *know* I am involved, not uncommonly stand-ing (or sitting) alone against the collectivity. So it is something deeper, competition and testing, and more [often] than not, finding it hard to listen to either illogic or words unconnected to motives. (There are harsher words to describe this). So, I am engaged. Yet despite the debate I end it all, and generally have in my life, without personal hostility. I doubt I can change – I choose generally to absent myself from the conclave, in recognition of the 'right to failure' of the younger members of the dept – a practice not shared by the other 'controlling' eldsters.[129]

The accuracy of this self-portrait is confirmed, over and over again, in the archive (though one might question the phrase 'without personal hostility'). Some of Weintraub's reactions to unfavourable reports on his papers were mentioned in section 1. Even before he came to see himself (not without justification) as a persecuted heretic, he was rarely able to retire quietly and lick his wounds. In 1951, for example, he wrote to Earl

Hamilton, the editor of the *Journal of Political Economy*, to question the competence of one of his referees:

> I would not, in the normal course, write a letter of this sort. I am accustomed, through the years, to see the acceptance of some of my writing ventures and the rejection of others. Yet a little over a year ago, again on the advice of an 'expert' – the same one? – you returned another paper of mine. To test his judgement I sent it untouched to the *Review of Economic Studies*, where it met a kindlier reception. I submit the evidence indicates that your 'expert' is not an infallible guide in economic theory.
>
> Needless to say, this is my last attempt to have an item published in your journal. I am under no illusions. I am sure the Journal of Political Economy will survive. Yet I do seriously want to protest against 'expert' humbug and complacency. It is time that these views were brought to the attention of your 'expert', whatever his accolades, student hosannahs, and press notices, he ought [to] be informed that none of us have quite been made the repository of all truth. He might sometimes give some credence to the work of others.[130]

Weintraub reacted with equal asperity to reviews of his books that he deemed inaccurate, unsympathetic or simply insufficiently favourable, whether written by friend or foe. 'I think you have neglected and maybe failed to give me credit', he complained to Abba Lerner in 1960, 'for what I think to be the most important theoretical accomplishment of my little book' (see Lerner, 1960, reviewing Weintraub, 1959).[131]

The extent of his ambitions can be gauged from a letter written in the previous year to Father John A. Flynn, the President of his former university, St. John's: 'At the moment you wrote me I was in the midst of completing a book that I think will change the future state of all economics. I know this is a strong claim, but I think events will justify it'.[132] Weintraub was here echoing Keynes's description of the *General Theory* in what is now a well-known letter to George Bernard Shaw.[133] No conceivable reviewer could possibly live up to such expectations, and Weintraub was duly disappointed once again in 1964 when the *American Economic Review*, now edited by John Gurley, failed to do justice to his book, *Some Aspects of Wage Theory and Policy*: 'You must be rather desperate for reviewers, judging by the assignment made of my book. I've read it and searched in vain for one complimentary remark, one suggestion that the book had an idea, one concession that there might even be a useful thought in it'.[134] Three years later he fired off a three-page volley of objections to a review of his *A Keynesian Theory of Employment, Growth and Income Distribution* by Rendigs Fels, who replied at similar length. This correspondence, at least, was conducted in a friendly tone.[135]

Correspondence with his son Roy reveals the strengths and weaknesses of Weintraub's character. Most of the letters are warm and supportive, but there is one astonishingly vicious response, apparently to a paper in which Roy had dared to criticize his father:

> I would have returned your 'paper' but it would not be worth the postage. So I just tore it up. It might contaminate the place.
>
> I am old fashioned: I think parricide should be performed, if at all, privately. . . .
>
> I suspect that I will survive your fresh evidence of insolence and impudence. You're hardly my most formidable antagonist. Hateful, maybe. Formidable, no. . . .
>
> Rest at peace. I will not write again. But I assure you if you do this again publicly I will not let it rest. I still write more than you.[136]

Six years later, Sidney was inviting Roy to write for the *Journal of Post Keynesian Economics* and congratulating him on the progress of his career:

> I've told you I have enjoyed, in my travels, being asked if you are my son. I can't help but think of the new fame I have! It has not been your direct intention, but you've done it for me, whether in Iceland, Australia, Sweden, Italy, or Germany – or Yugoslavia, as last year.
>
> Thanks, chum. . . .[137]

Like his family, Weintraub's closest friends and colleagues sometimes found him hard to get on with. In a long and bitter 1978 letter, Paul Davidson took issue with his former mentor's editing practices: 'When I agreed to be the co-editor of the *Journal of Post Keynesian Economics* I believed that you and I would be jointly responsible for the material that appears in the journal. However, as events have occurred I have a queasy feeling that you are, perhaps unconsciously, attempting to totally dominate the journal'. This was especially evident in the manner in which Weintraub dealt with submissions to the *Journal*:

> [T]here were any number of places where you would write comments which explicitly or otherwise stated that this particular passage was not the way I, Sidney Weintraub, would have written it or would have discussed it and, therefore, you ought to change it to the way I would

do it. I believe that if we attempt to force authors into such a tight mold we are not doing justice to our statement of purpose which you wrote and which I strongly support, namely, that we expect a diversity of views and approaches. If we force everything into the mold that you are apparently pressing for in your comments, then I think we would run dangerously close to following the same sort of editorial policy that we object to in the AER and the JPE.[138]

Weintraub had behaved in a similar way at the April 1977 conference at Rutgers:

At that time you, as Chairman of your session, did attempt to use a heavy hand by lecturing the audience for much too long at the beginning of the session; later you abruptly and somewhat discourteously cut off Robin Marris when he began to make comments on his paper which you found contrary to your own approach or view. You may remember as Convener of the conference I had to intervene in this session to restrain you; nevertheless, as many people came up to me later to tell me, you turned a sympathetic audience into a somewhat hostile one. Moreover, you created something of an enemy from someone who was an ally. I hadn't told you until now but Robin Marris phoned me after he received our invitation to join the editorial board of the JPKE and indicated he was very sympathetic to the position we had taken in the Statement of Purposes but he could not join the board because of the way you handled his talk at the April conference.

Davidson concluded with a detailed set of proposals for a more equal role in editing the *Journal*. 'I certainly did not become co-editor to be just the office manager of the JPKE and I am sure you didn't invite me to be co-editor so that you could make all the important editorial decisions'.[139] Possibly not, but three years later Weintraub was still able to describe the *Journal* as being 'like Mary's little lamb, it goes with me'.[140] He must have been a very difficult man to work with.

Appendix[141]

Dear Sidney,
I apologise for my delay in answering your letter but I am very slow at writing theory. Especially now that I have become involved in attempting to organise a Ph D course in our Faculty – to which I am very glad you agree to participate as a proponent.

First, about the relation between the notion of long period position (LPP) and that of equilibrium: I do not think they stand in a relation like that of 'pure' to 'perfect competition'. The distinction between them relates rather to a distinction between different *explanations* of the same phenomena, between alternative theories of distribution, prices and outputs: in the sense that LPP is intended as a general notion; equilibrium as [is?] its marginalist specification.

Thus I do not think that the 'equilibrium' of the marginalists referred any less to a notion of centre of gravitation than the notion of LPP used by the classics. Some exemplification is given of [at?] the beginning of my *On a Change etc.*, p. 29 but it could be easily extended.

It is true that (as I mentioned in that same paper) this meaning is now disclaimed by most (some?) marginalists. But this has been a defensive posture taken after Keynes and, partly, after the capital criticism in order to save what could be saved of the theory. Keynes had shown that the system does *not* gravitate to full employment: the marginalists (helped in this by the incompleteness of Keynes [*sic*] criticism relying on what were usually considered 'frictions' retarding the effects of the main forces) reacted by saying: *o.k.*, but this is a question of 'stability' (*i.e.* gravitation), about which it should be separated from the notion of equilibrium which in its 'purity' does not depend on the latter (and can thus continue its life somewhere in the theory). As if it had not always been evident that a notion of equilibrium only makes sense to the extent in which the economic system gravitates towards it (*i.e.* is a stable equilibrium). (e.g. Marshall, *Principles*, 8th ed., App. H, 2).

For the same reason what I understand as LPP has nothing to do with the 'ultimate' stationary state (I do not believe that this notion is particularly classical: it is that of J. S. Mill, a [illegibile word(s)] of transition, deeply influenced by such an un-classical writer as Senior. And even in Mill it played, I think, a secondary role): LPP are the two positions which Ricardo implicitly compares when he says that corn tariffs will lower the actual average profit rate in England; or the two which

Marx compares when he says that the increase in real wages in a period of fast accumulation will lower the rate of profit.

Let me now come to the questions of demand and supply you also raise in your letter. Demand and supply are words which have been used in money [*sic*] different meanings: Demand and supply (as mentioned in my *On a Change etc*, p. 29, as points and not as functions have been used by Smith and all classical writers to explain gravitations to 'natural' or 'normal' prices, and hence wage and profit rates. However today, after a century of marginalism, it is difficult to separate these words from their marginalist meaning: *i.e.* functions which *determine* the normal wage and profits and hence prices relying ultimately on the substitutability between factors. You would agree with me that Keynes [*sic*] analysis in no sense needs these notions (indeed it is hardly compatible with them). The problem is to distinguish these different meanings which is just what the marginalists are unable or unwilling to do.

Many good wishes
Piero.

PS. Thanks for the invitation to collaborate with the J. P. K. E.: as you know I am very unprolific, but I will try my best.

References

Arena, R. (1987) 'L'école internationale d'été de Trieste (1981–1985): vers une synthèse classico-keynesienne?', *Oeconomica* 7 (March): 205–38.

Bausor, R. (1982–3) 'Time and the structure of economic analysis', *Journal of Post Keynesian Economics* 4 (3) (Spring): 413–24.

Bausor, R. (1984) 'Towards a historically dynamic economics: examples and illustrations', *Journal of Post Keynesian Economics* 6 (3) (Spring): 360–76.

Beltran-del-Rio, A., R.D. Hamrin and S.M. Speiser (1979) 'Increasing capitalism's capitalists – a challenge for economists', *Journal of Post Keynesian Economics* 1 (3) (Spring): 41–54.

Bloomfield, A.I. (1981–2) 'Sidney Weintraub: a profile', *Journal of Post Keynesian Economics,* 4 (2) (Winter): 291–300.

Bloomfield, A.I., and P. Davidson (1984) 'Bloomfield and Davidson on Weintraub', in H. W. Spiegel and W.J. Samuels (eds), *Contemporary Economists in Perspective*, Greenwich, CT: JAI Press, pp. 201–13.

Cain, G.C. (1964) Review of S. Weintraub, *Some Aspects of Wage Theory and Policy* (1963), *American Economic Review* 54 (4:1) (June): 516–18.

Chick, V. (1987) 'Coddington, Alan (1941–1982), in J. Eatwell, M. Milgate and P. Newman (eds), *The New Palgrave: A Dictionary of Economics*, London: Macmillan, Volume 1, p. 465.

Cockett, R. (1994) *Thinking the Unthinkable: Think-Tanks and the Economic Counter-Revolution, 1931–1983,* London: Harper Collins.

Coddington, A. (1983) *Keynesian Economics: The Search for First Principles,* London: Allen & Unwin.

Davidson, P. (1965) 'Keynes's finance motive', *Economic Notes* 17 (1) (March): 47–65.

Davidson, P. (1972) *Money and the Real World,* London: Macmillan.

Davidson, P. (1998) 'Twenty years old and growing stronger every day', *Journal of Post Keynesian Economics* 21 (1) (Fall): 1–10.

Davidson, P., and E. Smolensky (1964) *Aggregate Supply and Demand Analysis*, New York: Harper and Row.

Dixon, R.J. (1981) 'A model of distribution', *Journal of Post Keynesian Economics* 3 (3) (Spring): 383–402.

Ford, J.L. (1994) *G.L.S. Shackle: The Dissenting Economist's Economist*, Cheltenham: Edward Elgar.

Frowen, S.F. (ed.) (1990) *Unknowledge and Choice in Economics* (Proceedings of a Conference in Honour of George Shackle), London: Macmillan.

Frowen, S.F. (2004) *Economists in Discussion: The Correspondence between G.L.S. Shackle and Stephen F. Frowen, 1951–1992*, Basingstoke: Palgrave Macmillan.

Galbraith, J.K. (1973) *Economics and the Public Purpose*, Boston: Houghton Mifflin.

Garegnani, P. (1976) 'On a change in the notion of equilibrium in recent work on value and distribution: a comment on Samuelson', in M. Brown, K. Sato and P. Zarembka (eds), *Essays in Modern Capital Theory*, Amsterdam: North-Holland, pp. 25–45.

Garegnani, P. (1978) 'Notes on consumption, investment and effective demand: I', *Cambridge Journal of Economics* 2 (4) (December): 335–53.

Garegnani, P. (1979a) 'Notes on consumption, investment and effective demand: II', *Cambridge Journal of Economics* 3 (1) (March): 63–82.

Garegnani, P. (1979b) 'Reply', *Cambridge Journal of Economics* 3 (1) (March): 181–7.

Graziani, A. (1984) 'The debate on Keynes' finance motive', *Economic Notes* (March): 5–34.

Harcourt, G.C. (1982) 'Post Keynesianism: quite wrong and/or nothing new', *Thames Papers in Political Economy* (Summer): 19; reprinted in P. Arestis and T. Skouras (eds), *Post Keynesian Theory: A Challenge to Neo-classical Economics*, Brighton: Wheatsheaf (1985), pp. 125–45.

Harrod, R.F. (1951) *The Life of John Maynard Keynes*, London: Macmillan.

Hart, A.G. (1937a) 'Anticipations, business planning, and the cycle', *Quarterly Journal of Economics* 51 (2) (February): 273–97.

Hart, A.G. (1937b) 'Failure and fulfillment of expectations in business fluctuations', *Review of Economics and Statistics* 19 (1) (May): 69–78.

Hoaas, D.J. (1985) 'The personal and professional papers of Sidney Weintraub', *Journal of Post Keynesian Economics* 7 (4) (Summer): 603–6.

Johnson, H.G. (1974) 'Cambridge in the 1950s', *Encounter* 17 (1) (January): 28–39.

Kahn, R.F. (1976) 'Thoughts on the behaviour of wages and monetarism', *Lloyds Bank Review* 119 (January): 1–11.

Keynes, J.M. (1936) *The General Theory of Employment, Interest and Money*, London: Macmillan.

Keynes, J.M. (1973) *The Collected Writings of John Maynard Keynes. Volume XIII. The General Theory and After. Part I: Preparation*, London: Macmillan and Cambridge University Press for the Royal Economic Society.

Keynes, J.M. (1982a) *The Collected Writings of John Maynard Keynes, Volume XXIX*, London: Macmillan and Cambridge: Cambridge University Press for the Royal Economic Society.

King, J.E. (1994) 'A conversation with Paul Davidson', *Review of Political Economy* 6 (3) (July): 357–79.

King, J.E. (1995a) *Conversations with Post Keynesians*. London: Macmillan.

King, J.E. (1995b) 'Sidney Weintraub: the genesis of an economic heretic', *Journal of Post Keynesian Economics*, 18 (1) (Fall): 65–88.

King, J.E. (2002) *A History of Post Keynesian Economics since 1936*, Cheltenham: Edward Elgar.

King, J.E., and A. Millmow (2003) 'Death of a revolutionary textbook', *History of Political Economy* 35 (1) (Spring): 105–34.

Kregel, J.A. (1976) 'Economic methodology in the face of uncertainty: the modelling methods of Keynes and the Post Keynesians', *Economic Journal* 86 (342) (June): 209–25.

Kregel, J.A. (ed.) (1983) *Distribution, Effective Demand and International Relations: Proceedings of a Conference Held by the Centro di Studi Economici Avanzati, Triestse, at Villa Manin di Passariano, Udine*, London: Macmillan.

Kregel, J.A. (1984) 'Rational expectations: radical assumptions and conservative conclusions', in E.J. Nell (ed.), *Free Market Conservatism: A Critique of Theory and Practice*, London: Allen & Unwin, pp. 98–118.

Lee, F.S. (2000a) 'On the genesis of Post Keynesian economics: Alfred S. Eichner, Joan Robinson and the founding of Post Keynesian economics', *Research in the History of Economic Thought and Methodology*, Volume 18C, pp. 1–258.

Lee, F.S. (2000b) 'The organizational history of Post Keynesian economics in America, 1971–1995', *Journal of Post Keynesian Economics* 23 (1) (Fall): 141–62.

Lee, F.S. (2002) 'Mutual aid and the making of heterodox economics in postwar America: a Post Keynesian view', *History of Economics Review* 35 (Winter): 45–62.

Lerner, A.P. (1960) 'On generalizing the general theory' [Review article of S. Weintraub *A General Theory of the Price Level, Output, Income Distribution and Economic Growth*, 1959], *American Economic Review* 50 (1) (March): 121–43.

Lodewijks, J. (1990) 'Sidney Weintraub, the English dons, and an unpublished obituary of Harrod', *History of Economic Thought Society of Australia Bulletin*, 13 (Winter): 8–17.

Lodewijks, J. (1991) 'Sidney Weintraub and the "noxious influence of authority" ', *History of Economics Review* 16 (Summer): 112–18.

Minsky, H.P. (1957a) 'Central banking and money market changes', *Quarterly Journal of Economics* 71 (2) (May): 171–87.

Minsky, H.P. (1957b) 'Monetary systems and accelerator models', *American Economic Review* 47 (5) (December): 859–83.

Minsky, H.P. (1974) 'Money and the real world: a review article', *Quarterly Review of Economics and Business* 14 (2) (Summer): 7–17.

Minsky, H.P. (1975) *John Maynard Keynes*, New York: Columbia University Press.

O'Hara, P.A. (2003) '*Journal of Post Keynesian Economics*', in J.E. King (ed.), *The Elgar Companion to Post Keynesian Economics*, Cheltenham: Edward Elgar, pp. 315–20.

Parrinello, S. (1988) 'Il ruolo di una scuola estiva di economia', *Economia Politica* 5 (3) (December): 335–41.

Robinson, J. (1962): *Economic Philosophy*, London: Watts.

Robinson, J. (1975) 'The unimportance of reswitching', *Quarterly Journal of Economics* 89 (1) (February): 32–9.
Robinson, J. (1979) 'Garegnani on effective demand', *Cambridge Journal of Economics* 3 (2) (June): 178–9.
Roncaglia, A. (1991) 'The Sraffian schools', *Review of Political Economy* 3 (2) (April): 187–219.
Shackle, G.L.S. (1967) *The Years of High Theory: Invention and Tradition in Economic Thought 1926–1939,* Cambridge University Press.
Shackle, G.L.S. (1976) 'Time and choice, Keynes lecture in economics', *Proceedings of the British Academy* 57: 309–29.
Shackle, G.L.S. (1977) 'New tracks for economic theory, 1926–1939', in S. Weintraub (ed.), *Modern Economic Thought*, Oxford: Blackwell, pp. 23–37.
Shackle, G.L.S. (1982–3) 'Comment', *Journal of Post Keynesian Economics* 5 (2) (Winter): 180–1.
Shackle, G.L.S. (1983–4). 'The romantic mountain and the classic lake: Alan Coddington's Keynesian economics', *Journal of Post Keynesian Economics* 6 (2) (Winter): 241–51.
Shackle, G.L.S. (1984) 'Comment', *Journal of Post Keynesian Economics* 6 (3) (Spring): 388–93.
Solow, R.M. (1959) Review of S. Weintraub, *An Approach to the Theory of Income Distribution* (1958), *Journal of Political Economy* 67 (4) (August): 420–1.
Solow, R.M., and J.E. Stiglitz (1968) 'Output, employment, and wages in the short run', *Quarterly Journal of Economics* 82 (4) (November): 537–60.
Sraffa, P. (1932) 'Dr. Hayek on money and capital', *Economic Journal* 42 (165) (March): 42–53.
Speiser, S. (1985) 'Broadened capital ownership – the solution to major domestic and international problems', *Journal of Post Keynesian Economics* 7 (3) (Spring): 426–34.
Vickers, D. (1978) *Financial Markets in the Capitalist Process*, Philadelphia: University of Pennsylvania Press.
Weintraub, E.R. (2002) *How Economics Became a Mathematical Science*, Durham, NC: Duke University Press.
Weintraub, E.R. (2005) '2004 HES presidential address: autobiographical memory and the historiography of economics', *Journal of the History of Economic Thought* 27 (1) (March): 1–11.
Weintraub, S. (1942a) 'Monopoly equilibrium and anticipated demand', *Journal of Political Economy* 50 (3) (June): 427–34.
Weintraub, S. (1942b) 'The classification of market positions: comment', *Quarterly Journal of Economics* 56 (4) (August): 666–73.
Weintraub, S. (1943c) 'The foundations of the demand curve', *American Economic Review* 32 (3) (September): 538–52.
Weintraub, S. (1950) 'The theory of consumer monopsony', *Review of Economic Studies* 17 (3): 168–78.
Weintraub, S. (1956) 'A macroeconomic approach to the theory of wages', *American Economic Review* 46 (5) (December): 835–56.
Weintraub, S. (1957) 'The micro-foundations of aggregate demand and supply', *Economic Journal* 67 (267) (September): 455–70.
Weintraub, S. (1958) *An Approach to the Theory of Income Distribution,* Philadelphia: Chilton.

Weintraub, S. (1959) *A General Theory of the Price Level, Output, Income Distribution and Economic Growth*, Philadelphia: Chilton.
Weintraub, S. (1960) 'The Keynesian theory of inflation: the two faces of Janus?', *International Economic Review* 1 (2) (May): 143–55.
Weintraub, S. (1963) *Some Aspects of Wage Theory and Policy*, Philadelphia: Chilton.
Weintraub, S. (1966). *A Keynesian Theory of Employment, Growth, and Income Distribution*, Philadelphia: Chilton.
Weintraub, S. (1970) 'Solow and Stiglitz on employment and distribution: a new romance with an old model?', *Quarterly Journal of Economics* 84 (1) (February): 144–52.
Weintraub, S. (ed.) (1977) *Modern Economic Thought*, Oxford: Blackwell.
Weintraub, S. (1978) *Capitalism's Inflation and Unemployment Crisis: Beyond Monetarism and Keynesianism*, Reading, MA: Addison-Wesley.
Weintraub, S. (1978–9) 'Samuel Johnson: a closet Post Keynesian?', *Journal of Post Keynesian Economics* 1 (2) (Winter): 170–1.
Weintraub, S. (1983) 'A Jevonian seditionist: a mutiny to enhance the economic bounty?', *Banca Nazionale del Lavoro Quarterly Review* 146 (September): 215–34, reprinted in J.A. Kregel (ed.), *Recollections of Eminent Economists, Volume 1*, London: Macmillan, 1988, pp. 37–56.
Worswick, D., and J. Trevithick (eds) (1983) *Keynes and the Modern World: Proceedings of the Keynes Centenary Conference, King's College, Cambridge,* Cambridge University Press.

Notes

* I am grateful for assistance from Geoff Harcourt, Fred Lee, Robert Leeson, John Lodewijks, Rosemary Moore, Robert Solow and E. Roy Weintraub. None of them is responsible for errors of fact or opinion.
1   On the status of the Weintraub archive in 1991 see also Linda McCurdy, Head of Public Services for Special Collections, Perkins Library, to Frederic S. Lee, 30 November 1991. Copy in author's possession. (I am very grateful to Fred Lee for this and other acts of kindness.) Since then there have been some significant additions to the archive, including correspondence between Roy Weintraub and his father. This has not yet been integrated with the rest of the collection, and the collection as a whole has not yet been fully processed. The box and folder numbers cited below may change when the collection is further processed, and material may then be most easily located by category, the principal categories being Correspondence, Subject Files, Writings, Miscellany, Clippings, Photographs and Volumes (Robert L. Byrd, Director, Rare Book, Manuscript and Special Collections Library, Duke University: personal communication, 21 September 2005). Roughly speaking, references to boxes 1–6 are to Correspondence files, and references to boxes 7 and upwards are to Subject Files (the subject should be clear from the context).
2   R.W. Clower to Weintraub, 1 November 1957 (1/8).
3   Dennis Robertson to Weintraub, 14 January 1959 (1/10).

4   Weintraub to Rendigs Fels, 6 January 1967 (1/18). For his lapse of memory, which involved a confusion of the letters from Robertson and Clower, see E.R. Weintraub (2005, pp. 1–2).
5   Weintraub to Robert Solow, 18 February 1969 (1/20). The 'enclosed' was evidently a comment on Solow and Stiglitz (1968); see Weintraub (1970).
6   Solow to Weintraub, 22 February 1969 (1/20).
7   Robert Dorfman to Weintraub, 9 October 1962 (1/13).
8   'Referee's Comments', undated two-page typescript evidently enclosed with a letter from George H. Borts to Weintraub, 17 February 1971 (2/3); see also Borts to Weintraub, 21 January 1971, on 'your inflation paper', and Weintraub to Borts, 26 January 1971 (both 2/3); Borts to Donald W. Katzner, 25 July 1972, Katzner to Weintraub, 8 August 1972 (both 2/4).
9   Clower to Weintraub, 1 August 1973; see also Weintraub to Clower, 6 August 1973, Clower to Weintraub 1973 (all 3/1).
10 Clower to Weintraub, 11 July 1974 (3/2).
11 Clower to Weintraub, 11 September 1974 (3/3).
12 Roy Harrod to Weintraub, 13 January 1971 (10/1); the 'jejune comments' have not survived. Weintraub was on very good terms with Harrod, who often taught at the University of Pennsylvania and stayed with the Weintraubs while he looked for more permanent accommodation. Roy Weintraub remembers learning how to mix martinis, at Harrod's direction, and hide the empty gin bottles (personal communication, 27 April 2005). The archive contains a letter to Leonard Silk of the *New York Times* offering an obituary tribute: Sidney Weintraub to Leonard Silk, 15 March 1978 (4/3).
13 Weintraub to Solow, 11 September 1969; there is a three-page reply: Solow to Weintraub, 29 September 1959 (both 1/10). See also Solow (1959).
14 Weintraub to Bernard F. Haley, 29 March 1960; see also Weintraub to Abba P. Lerner, 2 January 1960 (both 1/11), referring to Lerner (1960), which is a review of Weintraub (1959).
15 'In your letter of July 1 you imply that because my views differ from yours I 'have succeeded in eliciting' an unkind and unfair review of your book. This is a serious charge, which is entirely untrue, and I do not intend to let the matter drop here'. John G. Gurley to Weintraub, 8 July 1964 (1/15). There is no evidence that the matter was taken further.
16 Weintraub to Lionel Robbins, 13 October 1955 (1/6).
17 Nicholas Kaldor to Weintraub, 2 April 1957 (1/8).
18 'Delighted to see you in Cambridge. Lunch here which ever day suits you best. Let us know when to expect you'. Joan Robinson to Weintraub, 11 April 1957 (1/8).
19 Martin Bronfenbrenner to Weintraub, 21 May 1960 (1/11).
20 This is not clear from Kahn's letter, but Abba Lerner, at least, did receive an offprint from Weintraub at about this time: Lerner to Weintraub, 7 October 1960 (1/11).
21 Richard Kahn to Weintraub, 29 November 1960 (1/11).
22 Weintraub to Kahn, 5 December 1960 (1/11).
23 Weintraub to Jan Kregel, 20 January 1976 (10/16); Weintraub to Geoff Harcourt, 21 February 1976 (3/5). More details of these letters are provided in section 2 below.
24 Joan Robinson to Weintraub, 4 January 1961 (1/12).

25   Weintraub to Robinson, 11 January 1961.
26   Kaldor to Weintraub, 6 March 1963, 27 April 1963 (1/14).
27   Robinson to Weintraub, 7 May 1963 (1/15).
28   Weintraub to Robinson, 28 February 1968 (1/19).
29   Robinson to Weintraub, 7 March 1968. Misplaced faith in the younger generation was a recurrent theme in Robinson's thinking at this time (see King and Millmow, 2003).
30   Lerner to Weintraub, 20 November 1968 (1/19). (Weintraub used the symbol *k* to denote the aggregate mark-up over wage costs, and thus as a proxy for the profit share in national income.)
31   Weintraub to Lerner, 2 December 1968 (1/19).
32   Robinson to Weintraub, 18 December 1970 (2/3). Weintraub replied: 'Roy was upset with me too – as I expected. But the annoyance lasted less than a day from a following letter': Weintraub to Robinson, 5 January 1971 (2/3).
33   Kaldor to Weintraub, 3 November 1982, Weintraub to Kaldor, 1 December 1982 (6/2); Kaldor to Weintraub, 1 January 1983 (6/3). In the event, some 'Old' Keynesians were included (Worswick and Trevithick, 1983).
34   Weintraub's covering letter was characteristically truculent: 'I should like to submit the enclosed Comment for publication, provoked by the article of Professor Johnson. While I think a good portion of his article is simply outrageous, it should invite some useful controversy on the nonsense of 'true' and 'scientific' economics. I have never regarded myself as remotely 'left-wing' or 'radical'. But if such defamation be the price of understanding events and improving the quality of life, so be it': Weintraub to Melvin J. Laskey and Anthony Thwaite [Editors of *Encounter*], 21 June 1976 (12/3).
35   Weintraub to Harcourt, 21 February 1976 (3/5). 'Bastard Keynesianism' was a term coined by Joan Robinson to describe the mainstream, IS-LM, version of Keynesian macroeconomics.
36   Weintraub to Kregel, 20 January 1976 (10/16). The reference is to Richard Kahn's article in *Lloyd's Bank Review* (Kahn 1976), which, as Kregel wrote, 'is creating quite a stir here – for he accuses the Unions of missing the point to their and the country's peril. Unfortunately the point has been lost in the cacaphony [*sic*] of the unionists and business [editors] who are accusing him of 'union bashing'!'
37   Weintraub to Harcourt, 21 February 1976 (3/5).
38   For details of Shackle's life and work see Ford (1994).
39   Weintraub's letters to Shackle are not in the Weintraub archive.
40   Shackle to Weintraub, 28 July 1975 (10/16). Stephen Frowen reminds me that Shackle reminisced about his LSE days in his after-dinner speech at a University of Surrey conference in his honour (the speech is reprinted in Frowen, 1990, pp. 192–6).
41   It was published as Shackle (1977).
42   Shackle to Weintraub, 27 December 1975 (10/16).
43   The significance of this should not be underestimated; it took Shackle 28 years, and the insistence of his second wife Catherine, before he was able to move to first-name terms in his correspondence with Stephen Frowen (see Frowen, 2004: pp. xiii, 206–7).
44   Shackle to Weintraub, 16 July 1977 (8/6).
45   Shackle to Weintraub, 17 September 1977 (9/1). Shackle's Keynes' lecture was entitled 'Time and Choice' (Shackle, 1976).

46 See section 5 below.
47 Shackle to Weintraub, 16 July 1977 (8/6).
48 He enclosed a cheque for $175; a contemporary (but undated) flyer offered individual subscriptions at an annual rate of $17 ('An Invitation', 9/1).
49 Shackle to Weintraub, 21 January 1978 (9/2). (The letter is incorrectly dated 1977). The illness referred to was that of Shackle's first wife Susan, who died later that year.
50 Shackle to Weintraub, 24 January 1977 (4/1). The reference is to Vickers (1978). Shackle's support as a referee for the academic career of Stephen Frowen had indeed brought Frowen no success whatever: he was held at the top of the lecturer scale at the University of Surrey for no less than twelve years (Frowen, 2004: 206).
51 Shackle to Weintraub, 20 March 1979 (5/1). The references are to Weintraub (1978–9) and – presumably – to Adam Smith's *Theory of Moral Sentiments*. It is unclear what exactly was troubling Weintraub at this time.
52 Shackle to Weintraub, 3 March 1983 (6/3); the book referred to is Coddington (1983).
53 Shackle to Weintraub, 20 March 1983 (6/3). Coddington had killed himself shortly after completing his manuscript (see Chick, 1987).
54 Shackle to Weintraub, 4 May 1983 (6/3). Shackle's review article appeared in the Winter 1983–4 issue of the *Journal of Post Keynesian Economics*.
55 There is also some correspondence with Alfred S. Eichner and Paul Wells: Eichner to Weintraub, 17 January 1977, Weintraub to Eichner, 23 January 1977 (both 4/1), Davidson to Eichner, 2 October 1978 (4/5); Wells to Weintraub, 15 January 1979, 3 May 1979 (5/1).
56 Paul Davidson to Weintraub, 17 July 1959 (1/10); the reference is to Weintraub (1958).
57 Davidson to Weintraub, 21 February 1963 (1/14).
58 Davidson to Weintraub, 19 September 1970 (2/1).
59 Davidson to Weintraub, 21 October 1970 (2/1).
60 Davidson to Weintraub, 3 December 1970 (2/2).
61 Davidson to Weintraub, 29 March 1971 (10/5).
62 Kregel to Weintraub, 24 February 1976 (3/5).
63 Hyman Minsky to Weintraub, 19 November 1974 (3/3); the final sentence is a handwritten insertion to the typed letter. Geoff Harcourt remembers Minsky taking strong exception to a minor criticism in his own review of *John Maynard Keynes* (personal communication, 10 May 2005).
64 Weintraub to Minsky, 29 November 1974 (3/3).
65 Minsky to Davidson, 13 February 1976 (10/16).
66 Weintraub to Harcourt, 21 February 1976 (3/5). The reference is presumably to the medium of exchange function of money, and the 'silly portfolio people' would have been epitomised by James Tobin.
67 Minsky to Weintraub, 20 April 1982 (6/1).
68 J.K. Galbraith to Weintraub, 30 September 1963 (1/14). The reference is to Weintraub (1963).
69 Weintraub to Galbraith, 1 April 1974 (3/2).
70 Kregel to Weintraub, 4 October 1975 (3/4). The CBI is the Confederation of British Industry and the NUM the National Union of Manufacturers, a US employers' peak body not to be confused with the (British) National Union of Mineworkers.

71   Kregel to Weintraub, 5 February 1976 (3/5).
72   Kregel to Weintraub, 27 October 1975; the reference is to Kregel (1976). Weintraub's reply has not survived.
73   Kregel to Weintraub, 20 July 1979 (8/5). The reference is to Sraffa (1932).
74   Kregel to Weintraub, 31 August 1980 (5/4). The references are presumably to Hart (1937a, 1937b) and to Kregel (1984), where he argues that the chief differences between Keynes and the rational expectations theorists stem from their contrasting analyses of the real factors in the economy, not from their (substantially similar) models of expectations.
75   Paul Davidson and Sidney Weintraub, 'Proposal for the *Quarterly Journal of Post-Keynesian Economics*', undated typescript, p. 8 (9/1).
76   On the Association for Social Economics, publisher of the *Review of Social Economy*, see Lee (2002, pp. 51–2).
77   Weintraub to Martin Bronfenbrenner, 23 January 1978 (4/3).
78   The term seems to have been coined by Peter Wiles, who had also declined to join the Board of the *Journal of Post Keynesian Economics* (*ibid.*). In practice the Sraffians were already themselves deeply divided on fundamental issues, as would soon become apparent in acrimonious exchanges between Joan Robinson and Pierangelo Garegnani in the *Cambridge Journal* itself (Robinson, 1979; Garegnani, 1978, 1979a, 1979b; see also Roncaglia, 1991).
79   *Ibid.*
80   Celebrating the twentieth anniversary of the *Journal of Post Keynesian Economics*, Davidson (1998) has less than three pages of text, and several pages of – quite delightful – photographs of early contributors. See also Lee (2000a, 2000b, 2002).
81   Weintraub to Galbraith, 4 May 1977 (9/1).
82   Galbraith to Weintraub, 23 May 1977 (9/1).
83   Weintraub to Galbraith, 27 May 1977 (9/3).
84   *Ibid.*
85   Robinson to Weintraub, 23 September 1977 (9/1).
86   Robinson to Weintraub, 5 October 1977 (9/2).
87   Piero Sraffa to Weintraub, 4 October 1977 (9/1).
88   John Hicks to Davidson, 30 September 1977 (9/1).
89   Kenneth Boulding to Weintraub, 27 July 1977 (9/1). They included *Journal of Critical Economics* (which Boulding described as 'too subtle'), *Journal of Normative Economics* ('a bit too specific) and *Journal of Innovative Economics* ('might date too rapidly'). Sadly the Weintraub archive fails to support Davidson's later claim that *Journal of Keynesian Economics* was under serious consideration, but was rejected owing to the unfortunate acronym (King, 1994: 376).
90   'JPKE Editorial Boards', printed but undated (9/1). The Academic Board consisted of Boulding, Lawrence Fouraker, Harcourt, Albert Hirschman, Walter Isard, Kaldor, Lerner, Gunnar Myrdal, Shackle and Herman Wold. All but Harcourt were aged over 70.
91   Eileen Appelbaum (mis-spelled, as usual, 'Applebaum'), Barbara Bergmann and Alice Vandermeulen.
92   'Post-Keynesian Theory and Inflation Policy', mimeographed two-page leaflet and registration form, c. April 1977 (9/1); PD and SW, draft of a two-page letter to all those who attended the Rutgers conference appealing for Charter subscriptions to the *Journal of Post Keynesian Economics* (9/2).

93   Only one has the finally-agreed title (*Journal of Post Keynesian Economics*), and
     it is reasonable to suppose that this was the final draft. I assume that the shorter
     of the other two versions was the original, and that it was lengthened – as
     is invariably the case with jointly-authored documents – in the course of
     discussion between Davidson, Galbraith and Weintraub (all 9/1).
94   On Davidson's authorship of (presumably) the first draft, see Galbraith to
     Weintraub, 17 August 1977 (9/2).
95   Paul Davidson and Sidney Weintraub, 'Proposal for the *Quarterly Journal of
     Post-Keynesian Economics*', 16-page typescript, undated (9/1).
96   PD and SW, '*The Journal of Post-Keynesian Economics* (JPKE). A Statement of
     Purpose', p. 5 (9/1).
97   Davidson to Weintraub and Galbraith, 29 July 1977 (9/2).
98   'Proposal for the Post-Keynesian Economic Journal (PKEJ)', p. 1 (9/1).
99   'He has empty chairs to fill. . .', undated press cutting (11/7).
100 Memorandum, Weintraub to J.S. Minas, 7 August 1969 (1/20).
101 Memorandum, Weintraub to Minas, 7 August 1969 (1/20). Original stress.
102 There were also personal issues associated with Weintraub's move to Waterloo
     and his return to Philadelphia (personal communication from E. Roy
     Weintraub, 27 April 2005).
103 Kregel to Weintraub, 21 May 1979 (5/1). In fact, Kregel did accept the offer
     from Groningen.
104 Davidson to Galbraith, 3 June 1980 (11/4).
105 Weintraub to Edward Bloustein, 12 April 1981 (5/5).
106 There is evidence that Weintraub himself was unsettled around this time.
     When E. Ray Canterbery held out the prospect of a vacancy at Florida State
     University, in Tallahassee, he expressed some interest; nothing came of the
     offer. E. Ray Canterbery to Weintraub, 3 August 1981; Weintraub to Canterbery,
     4 September 1981 (both 5/5).
107 Weintraub to Galbraith, 11 August 1979 (5/2).
108 Galbraith to Weintraub, 24 August 1979 (5/2).
109 Davidson to Galbraith, 3 June 1980 (11/4). Stewart Mott was described by
     Stuart Speiser as an 'obvious fat cat' and potential supporter of RICES: Stuart
     Speiser to Davidson and Weintraub, 7 April 1981 (11/4).
110 Davidson to Speiser, 3 June 1980; Davidson to Eric Roll, 4 June 1980
     (both 11/4).
111 Davidson to Roll, 12 February 1981 (11/4).
112 Davidson and Weintraub, 'A Liberal Program From RICES', undated;
     Davidson to Speiser, 24 February 1981 (both 11/4).
113 Speiser to Davidson and Weintraub, 13 January 1981, 18 February 1981,
     7 April 1981 (all 11/4).
114 Weintraub to William C. Musham, 21 January 1982; 'The RICES functions',
     two-page typescript, unsigned and undated (both 11/4).
115 Organising Committee to Weintraub, 11 March 1980 (7/4). The Committee
     consisted of three economists (Garegnani, Kregel and Sergio Parrinello) and
     the mathematician Angelo Marzollo from the University of Udine. Parrinello
     was secretary. Kregel added a handwritten note to Weintraub: 'Dear Sid.
     Hope you can see your way clear to an Italian junket in the autumn to try
     and get the European wing off the ground. Best wishes, Jan'.
116 Sergio Parrinello to Weintraub, 3 June 1980 (7/4).

117   'A Critical Appraisal of the Present State of Economics', undated one-page typescript, presumably enclosed with the letter cited in note 96.

118   'Programme and Suggested Contributors for the Udine Round Table', undated and unsigned one-page typescript, presumably enclosed with the letter from Parrinello to Weintraub, 4 July 1980 (7/4). Those missing from the previous list included the Marxists George Catephores and Michel Aglietta, and the radical development economists Celso Furtado, Albert Hirschman and Lance Taylor.

119   'Tentative Proposals for the Organization of the Summer School', one-page undated typescript of the same provenance (7/4).

120   Parrinello to Weintraub, 6 December 1980 (7/5); cf. Davidson to Roll, 12 February 1981 (11/4).

121   Centre for Advanced Economic Studies, 'International Summer School of Economics' and 'Conference on Theories of Accumulation and the Control of the Economy' (printed cover and five-page typescript, undated but almost certainly early 1982) (7/6).

122   Kregel to Weintraub, 26 April 1982 (7/6).

123   As note 101.

124   Garegnani to Weintraub, 15 April 1981 (7/5).

125   Centro di Studi Economici Avanzati, 'Information', undated typescript, probably December 1982 or January 1983 (7/7). No details are given of the Advisory Board for Section B. The less contentious Section C, coordinated by Parrinello, was to deal with 'Development and Technical Progress. Economics of International Trade and Natural Resources. Mathematical Economics with a Critical Perspective'.

126   Parrinello to Weintraub, 13 January 1983 (7/7).

127   Centro di Studi Economici Avanzati, '3rd International Summer School of Economics, Marina di Aurisina (Trieste) from 21 to 31 August 1983', six-page undated typescript, probably enclosed with the letter cited in note 106.

128   Personal communications from Fred Lee (29 March 2005), Peter Kriesler (22 September 2005) and Geoff Harcourt (10 May 2005).

129   Weintraub to Bronfenbrenner, 23 January 1978 (4/3). Original emphasis.

130   Weintraub to Earl J. Hamilton, 25 October 1951 (1/3). The reference is to Weintraub (1950).

131   Weintraub to Lerner, 2 January 1960 (1/11).

132   Weintraub to John A. Flynn, 29 March 1959 (1/10). The reference is to Weintraub (1959).

133   John Maynard Keynes to George Bernard Shaw, 1 January 1935 (Keynes, 1973: 492–3); this letter is also cited in Harrod's biography of Keynes (Harrod 1951, p. 462).

134   Weintraub to John Gurley, 1 July 1964 (1/15). See Cain (1964), reviewing Weintraub (1963).

135   Weintraub to Rendigs Fels, 6 January 1967; Fels to Weintraub, 23 January 1967; Weintraub to Fels, 28 January 1967; Fels to Weintraub, 7 February 1967 (all 1/18).

136   Sidney Weintraub to E. Roy Weintraub, undated but probably 1975, according to the handwritten date assigned to it by Roy Weintraub (personal communication, 15 September 2005). This letter, cleanly typed and not obviously written under the influence of alcohol, is one of several added to the

Correspondence files of Weintraub archive and not assigned a box or folder number.

137   Sidney Weintraub to Roy Weintraub, 13 May 1981 (see note 131).

138   Davidson to Weintraub, 29 March 1978 (9/1). Davidson's account is confirmed by Robert Dixon of the University of Melbourne, whose article 'A model of distribution' (Dixon, 1981) was accepted for publication only after he had agreed to insert a number of references to Weintraub's many articles on the subject (personal communication).

139   Davidson to Weintraub, 29 March 1978 (9/1). There is no record of Weintraub's reply.

140   Weintraub to E. Ray Canterbery, 4 September 1981. Pastures new were located in Tallahassee, Florida (see note 106 above).

141   Pierangelo Garegnani to Weintraub, 15 April 1981 (7/5). The paper referred to is Garegnani (1976).

8
The Cambridge Keynesians: Kahn, J. Robinson and Kaldor

A Perspective from The Archives

Maria Cristina Marcuzzo and Annalisa Rosselli

Introduction[1]

Richard Kahn, Joan Robinson and Nicholas Kaldor were economists who played an essential role in disseminating and winning approval for the ideas of Keynes. They all had special relations with him and were in constant touch with his ideas. From the post-war period until the end of the 1970s all three, in their own ways, had fundamental roles in shaping the Cambridge that attracted students and scholars in great number from all over the world. They epitomized what is generally understood as the Keynesians, at least as far as Cambridge, UK, was concerned.

R.F. Kahn was Keynes's 'favourite pupil',[2] his main support in the making of the *General Theory*, collaborator in King's College administration and literary executor.

J.V. Robinson was regarded by some as the icon of the legitimate Keynesians against the bastard progeny of Keynes, populariser and proselytiser, contender in the capital controversy and champion of eclecticism in her reliance on Marx, Kalecki and Sraffa in opposing the neoclassical theory, originating an approach which is known as post-Keynesian.

N. Kaldor, a latecomer in Keynes' circle as a convert from the Austrian school and the London School of Economics, was an original thinker in many pure and applied fields; he is best known for his growth and distribution models, the policy counselling he provided to Labour governments at home and in developing countries and his fierce opposition to Monetarism and Margaret Thatcher's economic policies.

This chapter deals with the archives of their papers, which are examined here from three standpoints. First, we use the headings of their catalogues to give some biographical and bibliographical information about each author, in order to place those headings in the context of personal, professional and academic life. Generally speaking, archives are an important source for reconstructing intellectual biographies, perhaps less fascinating but certainly more reliable than personal recollections.

Secondly, we review the unpublished writings, signalling those that are, in our view, most interesting.

Finally, we examine the correspondence, taking into consideration a sample which we find particularly noteworthy.

Here we do not dwell extensively on the letters between Kaldor, Robinson and Kahn that are extant in their archives, and which we have examined elsewhere (Marcuzzo and Rosselli, 2005).[3] These economists were not only heavily, emotionally dependent on Keynes' approval, support and friendship, but also aquiver among themselves with tensions and powerful interpersonal dynamics, love, esteem, hatred and jealousy playing their part.[4]

After examining each author's papers separately (sections 1, 2 and 3), we raise some methodological issues related to archives as a source for the history of economic thought and, as conclusions, we offer a few remarks prompted by the present authors' experience of work on these archives (section 4).

1. Papers and correspondence of R.F. Kahn

1.1 The catalogue

Kahn's papers are preserved in the Modern Archives of King's College, Cambridge;[5] the headings of the catalogue are given in Table 8.1.

Kahn, albeit highly influential in all major theoretical events in Cambridge economics, did not publish much, but his contributions are landmarks in the economics of the twentieth century. To name but a few, we have the articles on the Multiplier (Kahn, 1931), Duopoly (Kahn, 1937) and Liquidity Preference (Kahn, 1954), the *Evidence to the Radcliffe Committee* (Kahn 1958), *Exercises in the Analysis of Growth* (Kahn, 1959) and the article on the rate of interest (Kahn, 1971b). The complete bibliography can be found in Marcuzzo (1989) and, on the basis of comparison, we identify the unpublished writings, which will be examined in the next section.

Kahn's involvement with King's College dates back to the late 1920s when, as a student, he spent three years preparing for the Natural Science Tripos and one year for the Economics Tripos. After his election to a Fellowship (1930), he served as Second Bursar (since 1935), acting Bursar during Keynes' illness in 1937–8, then First Bursar (1946–51) and, after Keynes' death in 1946, Keynes' Trustee.

Table 8.1   Kahn's Papers

1. Published Writings
2. Unpublished Writings
3. King's College: Student, Fellow, Bursar, Keynes' Trustee
4. Cambridge University, Faculty of Economics and Politics: Chairman, Appointments Committee Member, Examiner, Supervisor of Research Students, Lecturer
5. National Institute of Economic and Social Research
6. Ministry of Supply
7. Board of Trade
8. Organization for European Economic Cooperation
9. United Nations Food and Agriculture Organization
10. Department of Economic Affairs
11. House of Lords
12. RFK's Subject Files
13. Correspondence
14. Drafts, Off-Prints and Books by Others
15. Finances
16. Joan Robinson
17. Rachel Rostas
18. Diaries and Address Books
19. Holidays
20. Health
21. Religion, Israel
22. Clubs
23. Photographs
24. Family Papers

Kahn was also active and influential in the Faculty of Economics, where he started as lecturer in 1933, finally becoming Professor in 1951. He chaired many committees and masterminded academic activities and appointments. He was involved in the establishment of the Cambridge Research scheme, funded by the National Institute of Economic and Social Research, originally set up in 1938 also in order to provide Kalecki with a job in Cambridge.

At the outbreak of the war, Kahn found a post at the Board of Trade, where he was involved in the point-rationing scheme to curb consumption and free resources for the war effort; he then acted as Deputy Director of the Middle East Supply Centre in Cairo, where he was given many administrative duties. Subsequently he moved to the Ministry of Supply, where he started working on the Buffer Stocks of raw materials scheme and issues related to post-war organization of the economic institutions.

As from the late 1940s he worked for a number of international organizations (OEEC, UNCTAD and FAO) and the British Labour governments, for which he designed wage and income policy schemes at the Department of Economic Affairs. He received a life peerage in 1965. In the House of Lords he intervened on economic matters and, when the Tories came back to power, he was strenuous in his indictment of monetarism and Mrs Thatcher's government.

Since the early 1930s he had invested in shares, bonds and commodities with alternating fortunes. He was in charge of the finances of friends and relatives and devoted a considerable part of his time to the management of their savings. Unlike Keynes and Piero Sraffa, with whom he frequently discussed financial matters, he made only modest gains and did not die rich.

He was an enthusiastic mountaineer and even late in life would still spend most summers in the Alps. He was a careful planner in all matters, holidays included. He never married and always remained very close to his family, particularly his sisters, supporting them financially and emotionally.

An important aspect of his life was his strong Jewish identity, even when he gave up religious practice, as testified by the fact that he wanted to be buried in the Jewish part of the Cambridge cemetery.[6]

1.2   Unpublished writings

The unpublished writings are to be found not only in the relevant section of the catalogue, but are scattered among many other files.

Kahn never published a book, excluding the fellowship dissertation which appeared in Italian in 1983 (Kahn, 1983) and in English in 1989 (Kahn, 1989). However, at least twice he did plan to write a book, one at the beginning of his career, on the basis of his Dissertation and bearing the same name, *The Economics of the Short Period*. One draft is extant, with annotations and related material, amounting to roughly 300 pages. Of the planned eleven chapters, according to the index, chapters 1,3 and 4 remained unwritten, while 7, 9 and 10 are seemingly unfinished. The draft was most certainly written in the last quarter of 1932 (Marcuzzo, 1996: 20).[7] Part of chapter 7 merged into 'The Marginal Principle' which was an article Kahn submitted to F.W. Taussig in 1933 for publication in the *Quarterly Journal of Economics* and which, having been rejected, still remains unpublished in English.[8]

The second projected book goes back to the 1950s, when Kahn started a monograph on buffer stocks which was to consist of 11 chapters according to an index which might have been drafted in the early 1950s. In this work Kahn advocated the establishment of an international buffer stock agency to prevent price fluctuations of primary commodities. The agency was to be managed by experts so that price determination of raw materials, unlike under the quota system, would be 'not a matter of bargaining strength, but of judgement based on scientific enquiry and expert experience' (chapter IV in RFK/2/12.3).[9]

In fact, in 1952 he began writing a series of letters to friends and colleagues in order to collect bibliographical material and statistics on buffer stocks. Six chapters were probably written between 1953 and 1954, and four of them are preserved in a file labelled by Kahn himself as the 'Long version.' A shorter, but complete version of the book was put together with the help of Joan Robinson, most likely in 1956–7. She drew on material prepared by Kahn, but made several additions and excisions. In the early summer of 1957 this shorter version may have been sent to Gerda Blau, who was an officer at FAO in Rome and a close friend of Kahn and Robinson and had been closely following Kahn's progress with his book.[10] Kahn kept up his work on the book, discussed it in correspondence with James Meade in 1958, and in 1959 still believed he could finish it by the end of the summer of that year (RFK/2/14). Unfortunately this was not to be so, but two papers on buffer stocks of tin and sugar, the former written for FAO and the latter for the International Sugar Council, are extant (Kahn, 1988: 47).

The result of all this delay is that Kahn's only published book is in fact a collection of his essays (Kahn, 1971a). He planned to bring out a second one and drafted various tables of contents, which are extant.

Moreover, among Kahn's unpublished writings, there are a few memoranda, papers and comments, mainly related to his activities as policy advisor and economic expert for various organizations and governments. On the academic side, there is a paper on Sraffa written in 1980, which is a – not particularly successful – attempt to build a steady state growth model based on *Production of Commodities by Means of Commodities* (RFK/2/20).

Of more historical interest are various sets of lecture notes dating to the early 1930s, together with conference papers extending well into the 1980s. Finally, there is the text of a long interview on his life and work, which was given to one of the authors of this paper, published in a small book in Italian (Kahn, 1988), but still unpublished in English.

1.3   Correspondence

Of Kahn's major correspondents, Keynes and Joan Robinson certainly had the lion's share, correspondence with the former amounting to 602 letters and with the latter to over 1300. The women he was personally involved with come second, followed by relatives, colleagues and a few acquaintances. As far as the economists are concerned, the earlier correspondents include: V. Edelberg[11], R.F. Harrod, H. Johnson, N. Kaldor, N. Laski, J. Meade, A.C. Pigou, D.H. Robertson, E.A.G. Robinson and G.S. Shove. Of the later period, correspondents include P. Garegnani, B. Ohlin, L. Pasinetti, R. Skidelsky and R. Solow.

The distribution of the extant correspondence, as expected, is heavily skewed towards recent years, the bulk of it dating to the late 1970s and, above all, the 1980s, with the exception of the colleagues mentioned above, family and lovers.

It is impossible to provide here a detailed account of the correspondence preserved in Kahn's archive, its interest ranging from the biographical to the scientific; we must perforce limit ourselves to a sample. We chose a group of 37 letters that Kahn wrote to Joan Robinson during his visit to the United States between late 1932 and April 1933,[12] selecting them from the hundreds kept in Kahn's archive as offering a good example of the wealth of information that might be drawn from perusal of his correspondence. First, these letters give us a picture of academic life in the USA in the early 1930s as seen through the eyes of a Cambridge don. They point up the lack of communication that still existed in those years between the academic worlds on the two sides of the Atlantic and reveal the gulf in styles and approaches to research and teaching. Secondly, they show how economic theory, as developed in the USA at the time, was perceived by a born and bred Keynesian economist like Kahn. Thirdly, they give us insight into the personalities of the two correspondents and their closest interlocutors.

Kahn's letters are a series of long accounts dispatched from Chicago, where he spent a few weeks; from Harvard, where he was guest of Taussig and Schumpeter; and from New York, where he spent the last month of his visit. His first impression of the United States was not favourable, and changed little during his stay. Of the academic life he endorsed neither the research organization nor the teaching methods. He felt that too much money went on providing professors with secretaries and research assistants (engaged in what he considered a futile pursuit of data) and too little on creating an environment that would in both spirit and substance favour the exchange of ideas and a serene quest for knowledge.

Above all it was the didactic methods that failed to convince him, the students having no opportunity for discussion with their professors apart from the seminar Schumpeter held with his pupils at Harvard. As he wrote to Joan Robinson at the end of his visit to Chicago: 'But what annoys me is the isolation in which most of these young men do their economics. Several of them have complained to me of the difficulty of working under such asocial conditions' (24 January 1933, RFK/13/90/1/75).

There was no forum for debate like the Keynes Club or the Marshall Society in Cambridge, and everyone seemed utterly to ignore his neighbour:

> Take, for instance, the case of Chamberlin's book. He has been working on it for at least six years. And yet I can find nobody who can give me the inkling of an idea of what the book is going to contain. I have no doubt that Chamberlin is well endowed with 'research assistants' (I shall come to that phase of this lunatic asylum later.) But that is the whole point. The pursuit of learning is regarded as a business, to be discussed with underlings at 'conferences', rather than as a social art which pervades one's whole life (17 February 1933, RFK/13/90/1/132-4).

None of the economists encountered made much of an impression on him, particularly in Chicago, where he went no further than a handshake with Irving Fisher. Knight aroused his sympathy: 'Knight is friendly in a forbidding kind of way. He is very disgruntled with economic theory – in fact he is disgruntled about most things but his cynicism is of the pleasanter variety' (15 January 1933, quoted in Rosselli, 2005a: 265).

Viner and Schultz initially impressed Kahn favourably with their intelligence, but appalled him with the attitude they took to Cambridge, UK:

> Both Schultz and Viner try to be extremely contemptuous of Cambridge . . . Viner is also very proud of not having read more than a few passages from the Treatise. And he has never finished the Symposium (but this does not prevent his telling me how surprised they were when it came out. They had been doing that kind of thing for years).
> (15 January 1933, RFK/13/90/1/44-51)

At Harvard Frank Taussig, then 72 years old, made the greatest impression on him, while of the younger generation – practically his own – it was the recently arrived Leontieff who appeared to him as 'very definitely a man to watch' (15 February 1933, quoted in Rosselli, 2005a: 265).

His impressions in New York were far more agreeable: 'Wesley Mitchell had a lunch party for me at Columbia, and he struck me this time as a rather superior type of American professor, genial and moderately human! [Harold] Hotelling is a perfect dear which is just as it should be' (23–4 March 1933, quoted in Rosselli, 2005a: 266).

At the same time, the state of economic science and in particular of monetary theory seemed hopeless to Kahn, fresh from the Circus debates and involved in the work on the future *General Theory* of Keynes. While deflation was reaching its worst, the only remedies proposed were balancing the budget and reducing the gold content of the dollar. After attending a conference, he wrote:

> My God, it was nearly all the most doctrinaire sort of nonsense about how hard it is to inflate the currency and what about reducing the gold value of the dollar (without any suggestion that its rate of exchange was what mattered). If a business man were to deliver the best of those papers to the Marshall Society we should feel we had been sold a pup. These people are living in the Dark Ages. If I were not a coward I should there and then have made up my mind to devote the rest of my life to a crusade against the Quantity Theory. In no other way could I do more to better the lot of mankind.
>
> (8 January 1933, RFK/13/90/1/36-40)

And he bitterly reached the conclusion: 'why is it that the only people in the world with whom conversation on so-called monetary subjects conforms to the most rudimentary canons of common sense all live in Cambridge?' (10 February 1933, RFK/13/90/1/105-7).

Greater satisfaction came from his meetings with business people who he kept interviewing in the hope of finding a solution to the problem of price determination:

> My experience so far has been extremely limited, but I am now absolutely convinced that every business man is at a kink (a pretty kinky kink too) on his demand curve, or thinks he is. This creates a quandary. It is quite true that it does not pay either to raise or lower the price. But what on earth determines the position of the kink? This is going to be my main theoretical problem. (27 February 1933, quoted in Rosselli, 2005a: 266)

As these few passages show, this American correspondence testifies to the seminal role of Kahn at two cornerstones of Cambridge economics: the fight against the Quantity Theory of Money and generalization of the Marshallian method.

2. Papers and correspondence of J.V. Robinson

2.1 The catalogue

Joan Robinson's papers are preserved in the Modern Archives of King's College, Cambridge; the headings of the catalogue are given in Table 8.2.

Table 8.2   Robinson's Papers

1. Books and contributions to books, 1920–79
2. Articles published or intended for publication, 1932–81
3. Oral presentations, 1941–81
4. Papers concerning work in progress, 1936–73
5. Juvenilia, 1914–23
6. Notes from the work of others, 1961–74
7. Correspondence, including unpublished papers written by others, 1922–80
8. Miscellaneous memorandums, 1930–80
9. Address books and loose notes of Addresses, 1945–80
10. Engagement diaries, 1963–83
11. Field notebooks and travel journals, 1945–79
12. Other travel records, 1945–65
13. Photographs, 1930–87
14. Pieces published by others, 1926–78
15. Reviews of Joan Robinson's writings and career, 1932–86
16. Printed copies of Joan Robinson's publications, 1925–82

Unlike Kahn, Joan Robinson was an exceptionally prolific writer – her published writings amounting to over 440 items (Marcuzzo, 2002b) – and left very little unpublished. Unlike the other two economists examined here, she lived an almost entirely academic life, mainly in Cambridge. She held no administrative positions in the University, nor in her colleges, Girton and Newnham, where she became Fellow only in 1965, when she was made Professor, having been appointed Lecturer in 1937 and Reader in 1949.

In the latter part of her life she became a world-wide traveller, making frequent visits to India, China, the former Soviet Union, Cuba and Canada.

The catalogue of her papers reflects these activities, drafts and original typescripts of some of her published works forming the bulk. Of her entire production, however, the extant material amounts to only a small fraction. As far as her first and most famous book, the *Economics of Imperfect Competition* (Robinson, 1933), is concerned, extant is a draft of the Introduction (JVR i/3.3), which was probably kept because it contains Keynes' suggestions and corrections. Nothing is left of her other books (Robinson, 1937; 1942; 1956; 1960; 1962a; 1962b; 1966; 1970; 1971; Robinson and Eatwell, 1973). Of the published articles, it is mostly the material relative to the recent ones (after 1970) that has been preserved. Oral tradition has it that on her retirement, when she was obliged to leave her office in the Cambridge Faculty Building, she destroyed almost all her papers.

2.2   Unpublished writings

Most of the extant material in this section of the catalogue consists of notes for talks and lectures, either academic or for the general public. Noteworthy is the text of a lecture on Jevons, written in 1942 for the 'wartime Circus' (according to Joan Robinson's inscription), delivered most certainly on Pigou's suggestion that all Faculty members were to give a lecture on a selected economist.[13] The lecture draws heavily on Keynes' biographical essay on Jevons (Keynes, 1971–89, vol. X) as far as his life and activities are concerned. However, unlike Keynes, under the influence of her recent reading of Marx Joan Robinson stressed how Jevons broke away from the tradition of British political economy by introducing a radical change in his approach not only to the theory of value, but to economics itself. She wrote:

> Jevons was wrong in supposing that he had found a new answer to the problems of political economy. He had not found a new answer. He had altered the question. For Ricardo the problem of the theory of value was subsidiary to the problem of distribution . . . Jevons is not concerned with this problem, he is interested in what determines relative prices.
>
> (JVR/iii/2/6-7)

Three other manuscripts are worth mentioning. First, there are the notes for a talk to undergraduates on Nazism in Europe, dated 17 November 1941 in Robinson's handwriting (JVR iii/1). The talk, given in one of the worst moments of the war, is a hymn to the ideal of liberalism, interpreted as 'the ideal of human equality, of the rule of law, of government by reason and compromise instead of by force and fear'. Confronted by Hitler's tyranny, she spurs the audience to 'raise the standards of freedom and justice' and free Britain from the 'anonymous, silent, bloodless tyranny of money and privilege [which] denies education to the mass of our own people'. Given the circumstances, the talk is full of passion, but admirably devoid of any hint of jingoism. Robinson invites her audience to learn and understand: 'We must learn to feel, when we hear these tales of horror, not "this is how Germans behave", but this is what human nature can become'.

Secondly, there is a set of lecture notes, entitled *Short Period Model*, probably drafted in the early 1960s. These are written in a sort of shorthand form, to sketch out the content of the lectures. The first part looks at the differences between (a) family economy, (b) planned economy, and (c) capitalist economy as far as the forces beyond accumulation and the pace of growth are concerned. In a capitalist economy the crucial role is played by technical progress. The last part of the lectures deals with the short period, described as a 'snap-shot of [an] economy at a moment of time', and analyses the effects of changes in investment, consumption, prices and money wages on the system (JVR iii/8).

Also extant is a much later set of notes on the Cambridge Tradition, which was the basis for a course she was persuaded to give in Cambridge after her retirement, in the Michaelmas Terms 1976–81. The number of lectures apparently varied from year to year, but the archive yields only the notes for four of these lectures. In JVR/iii/16.1, 16.3, 16.4 there is an analysis of Marshall's thought, deemed 'necessary to understand Keynes'. The Marshallian heritage in Keynes is seen as the 'sense of an actual economy moving through historical time' and the 'short period idea'. She wrote that 'For Marshall [short period is the] time it takes to get back to normal profits after an unforeseen change. For Keynes [it is a] given position with plant, organization of industry, utilization function'. Marshall comes out better in comparison with Walras because Marshall lacks a model with 'transactors with endowments and in which all questions are treated as "maximizing under restraints". Marshall gives a view of the economy [with] family business, workers, banking system, international trade'. The other lectures are on 'The rate of profit' (JVR/iii/2,5) and 'The Classical revival' (JVR/iii/6,7).

2.3   Correspondence

There are about 490 correspondents listed in this section of the catalogue, although most of them are represented by only one extant letter. It is always hard to judge how much of a correspondence has been preserved by chance or as the result of deliberate choice. If the latter was the case with Joan Robinson, the variety of authors whose letters she thought worth keeping would confirm what a younger friend of the latter part of her life once wrote: 'Joan's gift for friendship was perhaps where she found her greatest freedom and pleasure, cutting right across class, culture, age' (Narasimhan, 1983: 217). In her archive we find letters from all over the world, from women friends from school days at St. Pauls' School for Girls in London or student years in Cambridge, who kept in touch long after. The major correspondents, besides friends, family and relatives, include: S. Adler[14]; H.R. Altounyan[15]; D.G. Champernowne; M.H. Dobb; R.F. Harrod; F.A. Hayek; J.R. Hicks; R.F. Kahn; N. Kaldor; M. Kalecki; J.M. Keynes; A. Lerner; A.C. Pigou; K. Raj[16]; P.A. Samuelson; G. Shove; J. Schumpeter; and P. Sraffa.

Here again we chose to focus on a small fraction of the correspondence preserved in her archive: the letters that Gerald Shove wrote to

Joan Robinson in the years 1931–3 of the making of *The Economics of Imperfect Competition*. Their interest derives from the paucity of information we have on the scientific contribution of Gerald Shove, whose role as teacher and researcher in the true Marshallian tradition was acknowledged by many in Cambridge (Kahn, 1987; Austin Robinson, 1977). However, we have scant evidence to assess his role in the Cambridge debates, since Shove wrote much, but published little, as Kahn wrote in his obituary (Kahn, 1947), and all his papers were destroyed after his death, as he had wished.

When Joan Robinson began writing *The Economics of Imperfect Competition* in May 1931, Shove had already spent several years working on a book which was to expand on the Marshallian ideas on value and costs (Rosselli, 2005b). For two years, from 1931 to 1933, the 17 letters that Shove sent to Robinson show him living in fear that her book and the lecture course that Robinson was working on might anticipate his ideas, depriving them of their originality.

The ideas Shove was afraid that might be 'stolen' from him by Robinson are listed in a letter he sent her – the first of those extant – on 24 October 1931:

> Dear Joan, from conversation with Kahn, I gathered that, though the theorems in your book about monopoly are new and original, a good deal of the fundamental apparatus or line of approach (e.g. the treatment of 'costs' and 'rents', heterogeneity of resources, Increasing Returns and Diminishing Returns and so on) is derived, directly or indirectly, from suggestions which I have put forward at various times in teaching, lectures etc.
>
> I am delighted that any of my ideas or methods of exposition should bear fruit in this way, but may I say that I think some acknowledgment should be made of their source?
>
> (24 October 1931, quoted in Rosselli, 2005b: 357)

Since then, any step forward made by Joan Robinson in her career and in the development of her ideas aroused Shove's discontent, anxiety and somewhat aggressive reactions. When Joan Robinson gave her first course of lectures on Monopoly, Shove informed Robinson of the topics he intended to expound in his course in the following term and inquired whether she had already dealt with any of them (2 December 1931, JVR/vii/412/8-9 and 48–50). Shove was particularly anxious that Robinson might invade one of his favourite fields of teaching, diminishing returns, and particularly those that originate from the heterogeneity of factors of production. It seems that Robinson assuaged Shove's anxiety by telling him that her treatment differed in many respects.

In June 1932, Shove heard from Kahn that Robinson was revising the first draft of her book extensively and this, again, made him suspicious. (9 June 1932, JVR/vii/412/20-21). This time Robinson reacted angrily to his insinuations. We do not have her letters (she must have sent three at least) but the tone of Shove's replies (17, 23 and 24 June 1932, JVR/vii/412/22-29) becomes ever humbler and more apologetic. After further reassurances that Robinson had not changed her mind significantly, he concluded that 'so far as I am concerned the incident is dead, buried, bricked-over, forgotten and (if there is anything to forgive) forgiven' (23 June 1932, JVR/vii/412/26-8). However, he was still convinced that Robinson had wronged him when she began 'preparing for publication and lectures a treatment of Diminishing Returns very similar to mine' (17 June 1932, quoted in Rosselli, 2005b: 361), without consulting him. At any rate, he was aware of his own limitations and declined Robinson's offer to wait for the publication of his book: 'It is very kind and generous of you to offer to postpone publication, but please don't. I shall probably never publish and anyhow I should hate to keep you back' (*ibid.*).

Again, when Joan Robinson published her first article (Robinson, 1932) where she first presented the long- and short-run equilibrium conditions for a firm under imperfect competition, Shove interpreted the article as an attack against himself and convinced Keynes to publish a comment that, as usual, he gave to the printer at the very last moment. Robinson was given a few hours and very little space to write a rejoinder; Shove, having put her into such a difficult situation, wrote her a letter immediately afterwards full of sympathy for what she had to go through (16 February 1933, JVR/vii/412/34).

The same schizophrenic attitude, between aggression and admiration, was to be found a few months later when Shove at last brought himself to read *The Economics of Imperfect Competition*. He wrote her a letter of congratulations, but when the review came out it proved not exactly enthusiastic. It was her 'technique' that he did not like, her recourse to heroic assumptions in order to make the problems manageable in mathematical terms: 'an essay in geometrical political economy' (Shove, 1933: 660), as he called the book.

Can we tell from these letters that Shove's grievances had some grounds? He was right in seeing many overlaps between their fields of research, both having an interest in classifying the possible sources of increasing costs and factor productivity, but the similarities end here.

They may have reached the same results, but along completely different routes.

3. Papers and correspondence of N. Kaldor

3.1 The catalogue

Nicholas Kaldor's papers, too, are preserved in the Modern Archives of King's College, Cambridge; the headings of the catalogue are given in Table 8.3.

Unlike the other two economists examined here, Kaldor was not a born and bred Cambridge economist. He was raised in Budapest, got his education in economics at the London School of Economics, and was converted to the Keynesian Revolution after the publication of the *General Theory*. He was consultant to the governments and institutions of various countries, deeply involved in British politics and active in the Labour Party, serving on several parliamentary committees. He joined the economics faculty of Cambridge University in 1949, when he also became Fellow of King's College. Over the post-war years he was economic and taxation adviser to several governments, central banks and the Economic Commission for Latin America. (The 'country files' in his papers cover 26 countries, from 'America' to 'Venezuela', that invited Kaldor over the years or required his services as consultant.) He became Professor in 1966 and received a life peerage in 1974.

Table 8.3 Kaldor's Papers

1. Writings, 1912–89
2. Lectures and conference papers, 1932–86
3. Correspondence, 1926–86
4. Academic career, 1925–79
5. National Institute of Economic and Social Research, 1937–46
6. United States Strategic Bombing Survey, British Bombing Survey Unit, 1939–73
7. United Nations, 1945–71
8. Royal Commission on the Taxation of Profits and Income, 1910–55
9. Economic Advice to foreign governments, 1947–82
10. Economic Advice to Labour governments, 1961–78
11. Labour Party, Fabian Society, Trade Union Congress, 1959–86
12. Press cuttings, 1960–86
13. Diaries, 1963–76
14. Personal, family and financial papers, 1940–86

Kaldor's papers were sorted by his literary executor, who organized the material and used it to write his biography (Thirlwall, 1987). The first heading comprises writings both by Kaldor and by various other authors, in chronological order, dating from his early work for the Hungarian press in the 1920s. When extant, the correspondence concerning each individual work is included in its folder. Texts of his speeches to the House of Lords are kept in this section.

Kaldor's main contributions in the field of pure economic theory are his models of economic growth (Kaldor, 1957, 1961; Kaldor and Mirlees, 1962) and his theory of income distribution, which followed up the thread of a Keynesian idea, namely that profit earners have a higher propensity to save than wage earners (Kaldor, 1956).[17] In his most famous book (Kaldor, 1955), which developed out of his work on the Royal Commission on the Taxation of Profits and Income, Kaldor proposed to tax people not on the basis of their income, but rather on that of their expenditure, since by taxing income savers are taxed twice, both on present income and accumulated savings.

Kaldor was a prolific writer both in his academic output – there are nine volumes of his collected economic papers (Kaldor, 1960–89) – and in his contributions to the political debates on economic issues, advising governments and the general public alike.

He was blessed with a large family and many friends. In her speech at his memorial service in King's College chapel, the eldest of his four daughters, Frances Stewart, who also was an economist, traced a vivid picture of how Kaldor came across and what he stood for:

> He was completely and explicitly on the side of the underdog, the have-nots, the underprivileged in society, and this was a fundamental motivating force in all his work, both in economic theory and as adviser and commentator on economic policy. He believed that much of conventional economics – neo-classical theory and monetarism – was a huge cover-up, an elaborate and well concealed structure for preserving privilege and downgrading the underprivileged. A consistent theme in his own economics, right from the 1930s, was to show up the logical fallacies and empirical falsities of orthodox economics, and to develop alternative theories which would be in the interests of a fairer system. Examples abound: his work on the Beveridge Report, on taxation, on an international commodity-backed reserve currency, on monetarism and so on. Where perhaps he was a bit naive – in the light of experience – was in believing that it only needed logic to convince the privileged to give up their privileges. But logic is a first step, and

there he has left us a rich heritage, not only in ideas but also in shared commitment among colleagues and students (not to mention family) to detect the phoney, to uncover true motives, and to develop alternatives.

(Stewart, 1987: 2–3)

3.2 Unpublished writings

Since a complete bibliography including articles for newspapers and magazines is not available,[18] it is hard to sort out the unpublished papers from those preserved in the archives. The sheer quantity of manuscripts, memos, reports and lecture notes is truly formidable, and we cannot do justice to it in the present chapter. Here again we will take a sample – mainly lecture notes – hoping to entice others to delve further into the material.

Luckily, the lecture notes for his courses at the LSE and in Cambridge have been preserved as from 1932–3, when Kaldor joined the staff of the former, starting from the courses on 'The Theory of Costs', later renamed 'The Theory of Production', on 'Advanced Economic Theory (Statics and Dynamics)' and on 'Capital and Interest', as well as – when the LSE moved to Cambridge – the courses on 'Theory of Employment', 'Value and Distribution', 'Economic Dynamics' and 'Growth.' These provide interesting material to place the development of Kaldor's ideas in their context. Here we shall take a look at three different sets of lectures.

The first that we consider here were given in Harvard in 1935. They are on imperfect competition (NK 2/32/2-10) and determinateness of equilibrium (NK 1/8/60-9), and show how little of Keynesian thinking he had taken with him to America. The lectures deal with the issues examined in his articles (Kaldor, 1934, 1935), such as the difference between market and individual 'imagined' demand curves and the assumptions necessary for a state of equilibrium to be attained. They show Kaldor already at some distance from the Hayekian influence, but still embedded in the general equilibrium approach and yet to become acquainted with the new developments in Keynesian macroeconomics.

Secondly, we take the notes for the lecture on Ricardo (NK/2/23/1-28) which Kaldor agreed to give in substitution of Sraffa who withdrew from the task at the last minute, incurring Pigou's disapproval. According to Kaldor, Sraffa gave him enough material 'for an entire course on Ricardo, not for one single lecture' (Kaldor, 1986: 50, *our translation*). The influence exerted by Sraffa can be detected in at least two areas. The first is the importance attached to the labour theory of value, interpreted as an instrument to determine relative prices and therefore liable to be considered as 'a necessary preliminary to the main problem: the problem of distribution'. Secondly, Ricardo is described as a 'practical man', concerned with real issues – such as inflation, depreciation of the exchange and the high price of corn – unlike the traditional picture of Ricardo the abstract thinker. The lecture has a distinctly Kaldorian flavour in the emphasis given to the importance of modelling in economics – in which Ricardo is said to excel – and to the role given to the rate of profit in determining the pace of accumulation.

Thirdly, a manuscript entitled 'The General Theory and the open economy', for a lecture scheduled for 14 November 1986, which Kaldor could not deliver since he died on 30 September 1986. Here we find an interesting formulation of the principle of effective demand in terms of the capital account and income account of a balance sheet, and the distinction between decisions 'arising out of the contemplation of a capital account, and those arising from his [the individual's] preferences and decisions on income accounts.' Keynes' principle of effective demand is seen as implying a two-stage process: 'autonomous decisions to increase expenditure on currently produced goods on capital account, and second, consequential changes in incomes and hence on expenditures on income account' (NK/2/170/1-14).

3.3   Correspondence

Thirty-five boxes of correspondence are extant; files 1–121 are catalogued individually and in alphabetical sequence, while files 122–46 are linked to countries. The catalogue substantially preserves the filing system followed by Kaldor himself. One file labelled 'economics, important letters' contains the correspondence with L. Robbins, F. von Hayek, J. Hicks, F. W. Taussig, M. Allen, F. Machlup and P. Rosenstein-Rodan and goes back to the 1930s. Some of these correspondents also appear later, above all J. Hicks, with whom exchange was continuous over the years, while with Robbins and Hayek relations deteriorated dramatically in the late 1930s. The Cambridge economists figure prominently among the correspondents (Pigou, Robertson, Joan Robinson, Kahn). Of the other British economists, some (Ralph Hawtrey, James Meade, Roy Harrod) merit files of their own, while others are included in the numerous files having to do with the academic and political activities of Kaldor.

Our choice is once again constrained, and by no means easy. We focus here on the issue which saw Kaldor – in the span of just a few years, 1934–6 – opposing Hayek and drawing closer to the Cambridge stance against *laissez-faire* and the perfect competition assumption.

In 1935 Hayek and Kaldor exchanged two typescript notes in a controversy on imperfect competition, prompted by Kaldor's article in *Economica* in 1935 , in which Kaldor argued that strategic interactions between firms in an environment of free entry, market imperfection and increasing returns might lead to 'technical wastage', since the productivity of factors 'will be less than it would be if each producer produced a smaller number of products and a large proportion of total output of each' (Kaldor, 1935: 49).

Not unsurprisingly, Hayek contested Kaldor's approach; in a letter of February 1935 he wrote:

> Mr. Kaldor's argument and indeed the argument of all planners, is however, that competition left to itself will not secure the degree of standardisation which in some sense can be regarded as desirable, and that in consequence compulsory standardisation might increase economic welfare in general.
>
> (Quoted in Ingrao and Ranchetti, 2005: 400)

Hayek criticizes Kaldor's contention, maintaining that it is based on two arguments, the first of which is fallacious, while the second is based on particular assumptions which do not seem likely to occur frequently in practice. The fallacy would lie in neglecting consumers' preferences and the taste of the public for variety. The mere fact that, because of the advantages of large-scale production, more could be produced of each product if their variety were less, does not imply that the increased production is equivalent to increased welfare.

Since information is in any case incomplete, there can be no presumption that the public authorities have an advantage over private agents, and so there is no guarantee that they will do better by intervening in an attempt to reduce the social cost of excess capacity.

In his answer to Hayek's criticism, Kaldor argues that 'A case against "laissez faire" is not necessarily a case in favour of "planning" ' (NK/2/3/81-6), and reiterates the argument that 'reducing the number of produced "varieties" does not imply a substantial standardisation and loss of variety . . . since brands or varieties do not necessarily bring about true product differentiation' (quoted in Ingrao and Ranchetti, 2005: 401). He casts doubt on the degree of foresightedness required by entrepreneurs to produce the output most profitable in the long run, so that freedom of entry into any trade does not lead to the beneficial results for the consumers usually assumed.

Kaldor, like Hicks[19] later on, following Chamberlin's thread, saw in the imperfect competition 'revolution' the need to think in terms of general equilibrium and strategic behaviour among firms. In this respect, from the very outset Kaldor was not attuned to Joan Robinson's Mashallian method of partial equilibrium, and this was the focus of their first exchange.

Robinson had praised Kaldor's article on the equilibrium of the firm (29 March 1934, NK/3/5/45-7), a conception that she regarded as crucial to both the Paretian and the Marshallian method. In his reply of 10 April 1934, Kaldor pointed out that the introduction of demand curves for the individual firms in imperfect competition makes the concept of a supply curve of a single industry untenable since 'it will not be possible to formulate any functional relationship between price and the amount produced, since a whole series of output can be associated with any particular price' (quoted in Rosselli and Besomi, 2005: 314). He reiterates the same critique – which obviously stems from his general equilibrium approach – in his review of Robinson's book in the same year.

However, a few years later, when his shift from the LSE to the Cambridge camp had been accomplished, mainly through his conversion to Keynesian economics, he stood by Robinson against Chamberlin and his article on the differences between his monopolistic and Robinson's imperfect competition.

He wrote to Robinson on 7 October 1937: ' I would take the liberty to defend you and Kahn and Pigou as well' (quoted in Rosselli and Besomi, 2005: 315). They seem to have shared the view that Chamberlin was 'alarmed at finding out the anti *laissez-faire* implications of his own analysis' (quoted in Rosselli and Besomi, 2005: 315). Their alliance in the anti-*laissez-faire* battles, which they fought throughout their lives, was definitely sealed.

4.   Working in archives

The widespread interest in working and researching archives that we have seen blossoming among historians of economics and also economists in recent years has already yielded a rich crop of literature, as these Palgrave volumes witness. Perhaps the time is now ripe to assess this activity and measure the value-added it holds for the profession; we offer a small contribution in this direction.

We can start by asking what the main motivations are behind research on the papers of Great Economists of the more or less recent past (disregarding here the no less valuable research on the papers of the less famous). To answer this question we need to ascertain whether or not those papers have *already* been used for scholarly investigation. *Prima facie*, it would seem that if indeed they have, then precious little would be left for further research. On the other hand, we are faced with the striking fact that not even the publication of 30 volumes of the *Collected Works of Keynes* and three biographies of the man have as yet slowed down the flow of visitors to King's College Modern Archives to peruse his papers. Its former archivist has given a vivid account of the stream of people working on Keynes' papers, their queries and curiosities:

> So, installed in the archives, how do these new converts to the delights of documentary research conduct themselves? They make their notes by hand or laptop, which are, depending on the strength or otherwise of their English, succinct précis or laborious transcripts. Their document selection is either methodical or serendipitous; sidetracking diversions may uncover gems. They are reverential, excited (one academic who shall be nameless always speaks of 'fondling the files'), or indifferent to the mystique of the original document that bears Keynes's own autograph.
>
> (Cox, 1995: 173)

The other case is when research on an author is still in progress and his/her papers are an 'unploughed field'. Sraffa's papers – to confine ourselves to the Cambridge tradition – are a case in point (Smith, 1998). Scholars are lured by the mystery of his life and the scantiness of his publications; his papers promise to make Sraffa more accessible and understandable than he was in person or through his few published writings.

Joan Robinson is a similar case, although she published a lot and left little unpublished. A full-size biography of her still remains to be written, leaving a void in an area of great interest to many of her followers, admirers and critics.

So far we have stressed the role of archives in filling the gaps in our knowledge of the personal and intellectual lives of Great Economists. Undoubtedly no significant biography can be written without spending long hours on documentary research, but what is their value in increasing our grasp of the *theories* of the authors concerned? How are we to answer the critics who view these activities as a sort of antique collecting?

There are, we would suggest, two legitimate answers. First, theories should always be referred to their context. By context we mean the set of questions which framed them, the intellectual interlocutors to whom they were addressed and 'the state of the art' at the time of their conception. Papers and correspondence afford insight into the motivations behind the choices of a particular set of questions, assumptions or tools. These are not always explicitly stated in the published version where the solutions discarded and definitions abandoned are left out. Archives allow us to travel the road towards a theory rather than, as it were, visit the final destination.

In Sraffa's words: 'In economic theory the conclusions are sometimes less interesting than the route by which they are reached'.[20]

On the other hand, we believe that it should not be encouraged to search archives in the spirit of a 'treasure hunt', or in other words in the hope that unpublished papers or unknown letters might unveil the true meaning of a concept or 'prove' one interpretation rather than another. These are very rare occurrences and it is, rather, the patient, persistent, sometimes unrewarding search for clues and facts which fits our discoveries into the pre-existing knowledge, as in a jigsaw.

Finally there is some educational value in working on archives for an economist, at least once in his/her professional life, to become aware that the road from error to 'truth' is a winding one, with many detours and obstructions. Acquaintance with the historical method of investigation is a challenge to faith in the purely scientific nature of economic investigation; history, unlike mathematics, fosters doubts in the search for universal truths in economics.

As far as the three archives which have been presented here are concerned, we may conclude by saying, on the basis of our experience and knowledge of them, which are the promising and still little explored sections.

The correspondence between Kahn and Joan Robinson, and between Kahn and Keynes (almost two thousand letters) appears to us an inexhaustible mine of information on many aspects of Cambridge life and economics, also in relation to the outside world. Moreover, there are the travel notes by Joan Robinson which give us a first-hand account of many countries at the time she visited them. Similarly, it may be well worth researching the 'country files' of Kaldor for the material he assembled and produced in his capacity as economic adviser to those countries. To these we would add his memos and preparatory notes written on several occasions during the many years of his political activities.

In conclusion, the inheritance of these three great Cambridge economists is treasured in their archives, over and above the material they published.

References

Cox, J. (1995) 'Keynes: An Archivist View', in A.F. Cottrell and M.L. Lawlor (eds), *New Perspectives on Keynes*, History of Political Economy Annual Supplement: 163–75.

Harcourt, C.G. (1991) 'R.F. Kahn: A Tribute', *Banca Nazionale del Lavoro Quarterly Review*, 45: 15–30.

Hicks, J. (1935) 'Annual Survey of Economic Theory: The Theory of Monopoly', *Econometrica*, 3: 1–20.

Ingrao, B., and F. Ranchetti, (2005) 'Hayek and Cambridge: Dialogue and Contention', in Marcuzzo and Rosselli (eds): 392–413.

Kahn, R.F. (1931) 'The Relation of Home Investment to Unemployment', *Economic Journal*, 41: 173–98.

Kahn, R.F. (1937) 'The Problem of Duopoly', *Economic Journal*, 47: 1–20.

Kahn, R.F (1947) *Obituary of G.F. Shove*, King's College Annual report (unsigned but attributed to RFK).

Kahn, R.F. (1954) 'Some Notes on Liquidity Preference', *Manchester School of Economics and Social Studies*, 24: 229–57.

Kahn, R.F. (1958) 'Evidence' Submitted to the Radcliffe Committee, Q.10938–11024 in Radcliffe Committee on the Working of the Monetary System, *Minutes of Evidence*, London: HMSO.

Kahn, R.F. (1959) 'Exercises in the Analysis of Growth', *Oxford Economic Papers*, 11: 146–63.

Kahn, R.F. (1971a) *Selected Essays on Employment and Growth*, Cambridge University Press.

Kahn, R.F. (1971b) 'Notes on the Rate of Interest and the Growth of Firms', in Kahn (1971a).

Kahn, R.F. (1983) *L'economia del breve periodo*, Torino: Boringhieri.

Kahn, R.F. (1984) *The Making of Keynes's General Theory*, Cambridge University Press.

Kahn, R.F (1987) 'Shove, Gerald Frank', in J. Eatwell, M. Milgate and P. Newman (eds), *The New Palgrave*, London: Macmillan.

Kahn, R.F (1988) *Un discepolo di Keynes*, edited by M.C. Marcuzzo, Milano: Garzanti.

Kahn, R.F. (1989) *The Economics of the Short Period*, London: Macmillan.

Kahn, R.F. (1999) *Concorrenza, occupazione e moneta*, Bologna: Il Mulino.

Kaldor, N. (1934) 'A Classificatory Note on the Determinateness of Equlibrium', *Review of Economic Studies*, 1: 122–36.

Kaldor, N. (1935) 'Market Imperfection and Excess Capacity', *Economica*, 2: 33–50.

Kaldor, N. (1955) *An Expenditure Tax*, London: Allen and Unwin.

Kaldor, N. (1956) 'Alternative Theories of Distribution', *Review of Economic Studies*, 22: 83–100.

Kaldor, N. (1957) 'A Model of Economic Growth', *Economic Journal*, 67: 591–624.

Kaldor, N. (1961) 'Capital Accumulation and Economic Growth', in D.C. Hague and F. Futz (eds), *The Theory of Capital*, London: Macmillan.

Kaldor, N. (1960–89) *Collected Papers*, London: Duckworth.

Kaldor, N. (1986) *Ricordi di un economista*, edited by M.C. Marcuzzo, Milano: Garzanti.

Kaldor, N., and J.A. Mirlees (1962) 'A New Model of Economic Growth', *Review of Economic Studies*, 29: 174–92.

Keynes, J.M. (1971–89) *Essays in Biography*, in *The Collected Writings*, edited by D. Moggridge, vol. X, London: Macmillan.

King, J.E. (1998) ' "Your Position Is Thoroughly Orthodox and Entirely Wrong": Nicholas Kaldor and Joan Robinson, 1933–1983', *Journal of the History of Economic Thought*, 20: 411–32.

Marcuzzo, M.C. (1989) 'Bibliography. Articles and Books by R.F. Kahn,' in Kahn (1989), pp. 182–90.

Marcuzzo, M.C. (1996) 'Short Period Economics in Retrospect', in P. Arestis, G. Palma and M. Sawyer (eds), *Capital Controversy, Post Keynesian Economics and the History of Economic Theory: Essays in Honour of Geoff Harcourt*, vol. 1, London: Routledge.

Marcuzzo, M.C. (2002a) 'The Collaboration between J.M. Keynes and R. Kahn from the *Treatise* to the *General Theory*', *History of Political Economy* 34: 421–47.

Marcuzzo, M.C. (2002b) 'The Writings of Joan Robinson', in Palgrave Archive edition of *Joan Robinson, Writings On Economics*, vol. 1, London: Macmillan.

Marcuzzo, M.C., and A. Rosselli (eds) (2005) *Economists in Cambridge. A Study Through Their Correspondence, 1905–1946*, Abingdon and New York: Routledge.

Marcuzzo, M.C., and E. Sanfilippo (2007) 'Dear John and Dear Ursula, Cambridge and LSE, 1935: 88 letters unearthed', in R. Scazzieri, A.K. Sen and S. Zamagni (eds), *Markets, Money and Capital: Hicksian Economics for the 21st Century*, Cambridge University Press.

Narasimhan, S. (1983) 'Joan Robinson: In the Radical Vein. A Laywoman's Homage', *Cambridge Journal of Economics*, 7: 213–19.

Palma, G. (1994) 'Kahn on Buffer Stocks', *Cambridge Journal of Economics*, 18: 117–27.

Pasinetti, L. (1979) 'Nicholas Kaldor', in *International Encyclopedia of the Social Sciences, Biographical Supplement*, London: Macmillan.

Pasinetti, L. (1991) Richard Ferdinand Kahn: 1905–1989, *Proceedings of the British Academy*, 76: 423–43.

Robinson, E.A.G. (1977) 'Keynes and His Cambridge Colleagues', in D. Patinkin and J.C. Leith (eds), *Keynes, Cambridge and the General Theory*, London: Macmillan.

Robinson, J. (1932) 'Imperfect Competition and Falling Supply Price', *Economic Journal*, 42: 544–54.

Robinson, J. (1933) *The Economics of Imperfect Competition*, London: Macmillan.

Robinson, J. (1937) *Introduction to the Theory of Employment*, London: Macmillan.

Robinson, J. (1942) *An Essay on Marxian Economics*, London: Macmillan.

Robinson, J. (1956) *The Accumulation of Capital*, London: Macmillan.

Robinson, J. (1960) *Exercises in Economic Analysis*, London: Macmillan.

Robinson, J. (1962a) *Economic Philosophy*, London: Watts and Co.

Robinson, J. (1962b) *Economics: An Awkward Corner*, London: George Allen and Unwin.

Robinson, J. (1970) *Freedom and Necessities: An Introduction to the Study of Society*, London: George Allen and Unwin.

Robinson, J. (1971) *Economic Heresies: Some Old-fashioned Questions in Economic Theory*, New York: Basic Books and London: Macmillan.

Robinson, J., and J. Eatwell (1973) *Introduction to Modern Economics*, Maidenhead: MacGraw Hill.

Rosselli, A. (2005a) 'The Enduring Partnership', in Marcuzzo and Rosselli (2005): 259–91.

Rosselli, A. (2005b) 'The Defender of the Marshallian Tradition', in Marcuzzo and Rosselli (2005): 350–70.

Rosselli, A., and D. Besomi (2005) 'The Unlooked-For Proselitizer', in Marcuzzo and Rosselli (2005): 309–27.

Shove, G.F. (1933) 'The Economics of Imperfect Competition' by Joan Robinson, Review, *Economic Journal*, 43: 657–61.

Smith, J. (1998) 'An Archivist's Apology: The Papers of Piero Sraffa at Trinity College, Cambridge', *Il pensiero economico italiano*, 6: 39–54.

Stewart, F. (1987) 'Nicholas Kaldor', mimeo.

Targetti, F. (1992) *Nicholas Kaldor. The Economics and Politics of Capitalism as a Dynamic System*, Oxford: Clarendon Press.

Thirlwall, A. (1987) *Nicholas Kaldor*, Brighton: Wheatsheaf Books.

Notes

1 We are grateful for copyright permission granted by Professor D. Papineau (Kahn papers), the Provost and the Fellows of King's College, Cambridge (Joan Robinson papers) and A. Thirlwall (Kaldor papers). We are also grateful to F. Stewart, Kaldor's daughter, for granting permission to quote from her speech at her father's memorial.
2 As Keynes himself described him in a letter to his wife Lydia in 1928 (see Marcuzzo, 2002a: 422).
3 The book presents the results of research on the correspondence between Keynes, Kahn, J. Robinson, Robertson, Harrod, Sraffa, Pigou, Kaldor, Shove and Hayek from 1907 to 1946, with detailed tables of the extant letters. This chapter draws heavily on it.
4 These issues are examined, as far as Kaldor and Robinson are concerned, in King (1998) and, in relation to Robinson and Kahn, in Rosselli (2005a).
5 A very few items from his personal papers, together with most of his library and collection of off-prints, are at present conserved at the Asahikawa University, Hokkaido, Japan.
6 Biographical information about Kahn's life and work can be found in Kahn (1984), Harcourt (1991), Pasinetti (1991).
7 Joan Robinson wrote to Kahn on 24 January 1933: 'I have read your book thus currently. It's certainly a very impressive work. I hope you are going to let me help you with polishing it up' (RFK/13/90/1/75).
8 The Italian version is in Kahn (1999).
9 The papers of the three authors examined in the text are held in the Modern Archives of King's College, Cambridge and referred to as the RFK, JVR, NK papers. The numbers given are those of the corresponding classmark of the file or the document.
10 Contrary to the sequence presented in Palma (1994), the shorter version is not the older one. We know from the correspondence between R.F. Kahn and Gerda Blau, preserved in the FAO Archives in Rome, that chapters III, IV, V and VI were ready by October 1953 and that chapters I and VIII were added subsequently. The excessive length of the projected book led Gerda Blau to ask Kahn for a shorter version, which is probably the one prepared with the help of Joan Robinson and preserved in RFK/2/12.3.
11 Victor G. Edelberg, economist, studied at the LSE under Robbins' supervision. In the 1930s he wrote on the Ricardian theory of profit and on capital theory.
12 For unknown reasons these letters are kept in Kahn's rather than in Joan Robinson's archive.
13 Kaldor recollects that after the outbreak of the war 'Pigou, as Chairman of the Economics Faculty, arranged for a special series of lectures to be given by Cambridge economists entitled "The Great Economists", each of which was assigned to a different economist who would be considered as a "specialist" on that person or subject . . . Joan Robinson was asked to lecture on Jevons, a less happy choice; . . . and it was the obvious choice to ask Piero [Sraffa] (as editor of Ricardo's Collected Writings) to speak on Ricardo' (NK 3/138). These recollections are contained in an interview that Kaldor gave to one of the authors of this chapter and which was published in Italian (Kaldor, 1986).

14 Salomon Adler, economist, expert on China, translated into English some of Mao's writings.
15 Ernest H. Riddal Altounyan, poet and doctor who practised in Syria; his most famous poem was dedicated to Lawrence of Arabia.
16 Kakkadan Nandanath Raj, economist, set up the Delhi School of Economics and the Centre for Development Studies in Trivandrum. He published on the Indian and other Asian economies.
17 On Kaldor's life and activities, see also Pasinetti (1979) and Targetti (1992).
18 Targetti's bibliography, which builds upon Thirlwall (1987), by admission of the author does not include Kaldor's 'numerous letters to *The Times* (which over the thirty years between 1932 and 1986 numbered around 260)' and his articles for many newspapers, excluding those re-published in his collections of essays (Targetti, 1992: 363).
19 'I think the problem of imperfect competition is harder, and less important than you do', wrote John Hicks to Joan Robinson three months after the publication of *The Economics of Imperfect Competition* (15 June 1933, JVR vii/200/1). And he maintained the same point later, when reviewing the matter for his Monopoly article (Hicks, 1935): 'I think the real difference between us' – he wrote to her – 'is that you are more optimistic than I am about the application of the theory of imperfect competition, just because you think that theory is simpler than I do' (letter 28 February 1935, JVR vii/200/25). See Marcuzzo-Sanfilippo (2007).
20 Letter from Sraffa to Charles P. Blitch, 6 October 1975, in possession of the recipient. We are grateful to Nerio Naldi who kindly gave us a photocopy of this letter.

Index